Military Legacies

Landmines, cluster bombs, chemical pollutants, and other remnants of war continue to cause death to humans and damage to the environment long after the guns have fallen silent. From the jungles of Vietnam to the arctic tundra of Russia, no region has escaped the legacy of warfare.

To understand the legacy of modern militarism, this book presents an overview of post-conflict societies, with an emphasis on the human toll exacted by modern warfare.

James A. Tyner (Ph.D., University of Southern California) is Professor of Geography at Kent State University. His research interests include population geography, political geography, and Southeast Asia. He is the author of ten books, including *The Philippines: Mobilities, Identities, Globalization* (Routledge).

D1564860

Global Realities: **A Routledge Series**
Edited by **Charles C. Lemert**, *Wesleyan University*

The Series **Global Realities** offers concise accounts of how the nations and regions of the world are experiencing the effects of globalization. Richly descriptive yet theoretically informed, each volume shows how individual places are navigating the tension between age-old traditions and the new forces generated by globalization.

Books in the Series

Available
Australia by Anthony Moran
Global Ireland by Tom Inglis
Global Hong Kong by Cindy Wong and Gary McDonogh
The Koreas by Charles K. Armstrong
The Netherlands by Frank J. Lechner
The Globalization of Israel by Uri Ram
Morocco by Shana Cohen and Larabi Jaidi
On Argentina and the Southern Cone by Alejandro Grimson and Gabriel Kessler
The Philippines: Mobilities, Identities, Globalization by James A. Tyner
China and Globalization, Second Edition, by Doug Guthrie
Iberian Worlds by Gary McDonogh
City Life from Jakarta to Dakar: Movements at the Crossroads by AbdouMaliq Simone

Also of Interest from Routledge

Common Ground: Readings and Reflections on Public Space edited by Anthony Orum and Zachary Neal
The Gentrification Debates edited by Japonica Brown-Saracino
Disrupted Cities: When Infrastructure Fails edited by Stephen Graham
The Making of the American Landscape, Second Edition, edited by Michael Conzen
Contesting Development: Critical Struggles for Social Change edited by Phillip McMichael
Global Gender Research: Transnational Perspectives edited by Christine Bose and Minjeong Kim
Making Transnational Feminism: Rural Women, NGO Activists, and Northern Donors in Brazil by Millie Thayer
Poverty Capital: Microfinance and the Making of Development by Ananya Roy

Military Legacies

A World Made by War

JAMES A. TYNER

Kent State University

Routledge
Taylor & Francis Group

NEW YORK AND LONDON

First published 2010
by Routledge
270 Madison Avenue, New York, NY 10016

Simultaneously published in the UK
by Routledge
2 Park Square, Milton Park, Abingdon, Oxon
OX14 4RN

Routledge is an imprint of the Taylor & Francis Group, an informa business

Typeset in 11/14pt Joanna by RefineCatch Limited, Bungay, Suffolk
Printed and bound in the United States of America on acid-free paper by Edwards Brothers, Inc.

Library of Congress Cataloging-in-Publication Data
Tyner, James A., 1966-
Military legacies : a world made by war / James A. Tyner.
p. cm. – (Global realities)
Includes bibliographical references.
1. War–Environmental aspects.   2. War–Psychological aspects.   3. Postwar reconstruction–
Environmental aspects.   4. Postwar reconstruction–Psychological aspects.   5. Unexploded ordnance–
Environmental aspects.   6. Unexploded ordnance–Psychological aspects.   7. Land mines–
Environmental aspects.   8. Land mines–Social aspects.   9. War and society.   I. Title.
QH545.W26T96 2010
363.34′98–dc22

2009028014

ISBN10: 0–415–99593–0 (hbk)
ISBN10: 0–415–99594–9 (pbk)
ISBN10: 0–203–86145–0 (ebk)

ISBN13: 978–0–415–99593–1 (hbk)
ISBN13: 978–0–415–99594–8 (pbk)
ISBN13: 978–0–203–86145–5 (ebk)

Contents

For Jessica and Anica Lyn

Acknowledgments

As a geographer, I am particularly interested in landscapes. Whether the deep green rice fields of central Cambodia or the serrated mountain ridges of northern Laos, I admire and respect the diverse environments of our world. As a global citizen, though, I am frustrated by the continued militarism and acquiescence of warfare that threatens these environments. I am frustrated also by the ignorance and naivety of a society that too often sees war not only as natural and normal, but also as a self-contained event. But war has no end-points. The First World War neither *began* on July 28, 1914, nor did it *end* on November 11, 1918. And the same holds true for all other wars. The causes are multiple and are found in the days (if not years) leading up to the time when actual fighting begins. And wars do not end when the fighting ceases. In *Military Legacies* I hope to provide some understanding of the consequences of war, and the deadly legacies that continue well into the future.

Writers, even academic ones, are not confined to ivory towers. Rather, they read and talk and interact with innumerable other people who in various ways contribute to the final manuscript. Their influence may be direct or indirect, but it is ever-present. And both tradition and appreciation require an acknowledgment of that influence. At Routledge, thanks are extended to my editor, Stephen Rutter. Apart from being an outstanding editor, he is a great guy; I am fortunate to have worked with him on this, our second book. Thanks also are extended to Leah Babb-Rosenfeld, who skillfully guided my book through the production process.

There are numerous people who through personal conversation and their writings have challenged me to think critically on the intersection of population, politics, and war. These include Carl Dahlman, Michael Dear, Colin Flint, Derek Gregory, Curt Roseman, Gerard Toal, Shannon O'Lear, and Steve Oluic.

Many thanks are extended to former and current graduate students, including Steve Butcher, Sutapa Chaddopaya, Donna Houston, Josh Inwood, Rob Kruse, Olaf Kuhlke, Steve Oluic (again), Gabe Popescue, David Stasiuk, Rob Schwartz, Andrew Shears, and Stacey Wicker. Special mention must be made of Dave and Andy, for their thoughtful comments, critiques, and suggestions on earlier drafts of this book. Special thanks are also extended to Gabe and the two Steves for our lengthy discussions on all things political.

At Kent State University, I acknowledge Robert Frank (Provost), John West (Vice President of Research), and Tim Moerland (Dean, College of Arts and Sciences). Combined, these individuals have provided crucial support over the years, support that has allowed me the opportunity to pursue my research and writing.

I am grateful to Youk Chhang (Documentation Center of Cambodia), Shannon O'Lear (University of Kansas), Steve Oluic (US Military Academy), Dr. Scott Sheridan (Kent State University), and Dr. Gerald Tyner (retired, California State University Northridge) for permission to use some of their photographs.

Closer to home, thanks are extended to Bond (my now eight-year-old puppy) and Jamaica (my sweet, yet sometimes snotty, cat). Thanks also to David, my brother, and Karen, my aunt. Special thanks are given to Dr. Gerald E. Tyner and Judith A. Tyner. Apart from being supportive and inspirational parents, Mom and Dad (both retired geographers) also prepared the maps for this book.

My deepest appreciation lies with Belinda; I am her husband and she is my best friend. Were it not for Belinda, I doubt that I could function. Indeed, during the course of my writing this book, Belinda replaced the plumbing and insulation in our laundry room, stained our deck, and paid the bills (I do mow the lawn, however, and I try to do the laundry). Belinda: *Mahal kita. Maraming salamat.*

And lastly, a special thank you, and the dedication of this book, goes to Jessica (now aged seven) and Anica Lyn (now eight). As always, I write for my daughters. I write so that they may gain some understanding of the world in which we live, and to cultivate the courage to transform the world for social justice. As they inspire me with the exuberance of youth, so too would I like to inspire them with the wisdom of experience.

Series Editor's Foreword

Carl Von Clausewitz's *On War* is widely considered the classic work on war in modern times. It was published, posthumously, in 1832 and is obviously based on General Clausewitz's study of the military theories and practices of Napoleon Bonaparte. *On War* begins with a line that dates the theory: "War is nothing but a duel on an extensive scale." Hence came the famous idea that war is, in the long and short run, politics by another means. Clausewitz's definition of war as "nothing but a duel" is true to ancient military theories but false to the theories of war and military practice that came to dominate in the twentieth century. Of all the differences, the most fundamental is hinted at in the definitional allusion to the duel, a gentleman's mannered way of settling differences of personal politics. The rules of the duel were well defined, reasoned, scrupulously judged for fairness by seconds, and, above all, according to the moral assurances of a civil social class; likewise war, up through the Napoleonic era and well into the nineteenth century.

If you read *On War* side-by-side with Napoleon's *Maxims* of military theory, you will see one common principle—that war could be politics by another means because the army, at its best, is a well-defined, rule organized machine for observing, controlling, and ultimately dominating the field of battle. The opposing forces were meant to be seen, and thus reveal themselves in open field. The battle was fair so long as the victory went to the side with overwhelming forces, speed, and above all a well-disciplined corps deployed on the chivalric principle of courage, hence bravery. The army was, thus, a machine that was formed on the basis of moral discipline.

In the twentieth century, beginning with the Great War of 1914, all this changed. As that most appallingly violent of all modern centuries unraveled toward its premature end somewhere around 1991, the twentieth century was one of continuous conflicts of an extreme nature that defied the nineteenth century's norm of a civil duel. The legacy of war and conflict after 1914 is, of course, the decline of the army as a moral corps and the rise of the state as a killing machine. Holocausts and gulags, killing fields and camps, chemicals and smart-bombs—and all the rest—revealed as much about the modern era as it did of the military.

James A. Tyner's Military Legacies is the field guide to this sad—worse than sad—history. Though a short book, Military Legacies is long on wisdom, painful accounts of what war has become in our time, and more lessons than one would wish to learn about what has become of our world. From Tyner's first chapter, "A World Made by War," with its gut-wrenching stories of the merciless consequences of postmodern violence in every corner of the world, to its concluding theme of the "wasteful legacy" of the military state without borders or moral limits of any kind, James A. Tyner forces readers to see what they have long known but not wanted to come to grasp. The military legacy of the twentieth century has been to weaken, undermine, and corrupt the moral and human stand-ards that, in the nineteenth century, applied even to warfare and the military. Tyner makes us think, all at once, of lands laid waste, of bodies crushed and crippled, of the rusting machinery of impersonal destruction, of children ravaged and abandoned—and of all the rest that ought to have, but has not, come to disturb the frontal lobes of what remains of our moral conscience. Tyner's last question haunts: "Will we hear the echoes in their children's voices?" Only the echoes remain of humanity lost to this global violence.

Charles C. Lemert
Wesleyan University
Series Editor, *Global Realities*

Preface

Beginning during the First World War, and continuing to the present day, societies around the world have witnessed a deepening of the military-industrial complex and a concomitant rise of private corporations, business entrepreneurs, and academics. While these developments are captured in the globalization of the international arms industry, they are experienced by men, women, and children as they go about their daily activities.

The rise of an industrial militarism dramatically altered the conduct of warfare. The end result has been a greater mortality among civilians both during and after war. Long after the fighting has stopped and treaties have been signed, people continue to be killed or injured. They are casualties of both the trauma of conflict as well as the material manifestation of war: landmines and cluster bombs, chemical and nuclear weapons. No continent has been spared the legacy of twentieth-century warfare; no body of water is immune from actual or potential contaminants of warfare. These remnants are the product of a militarized globalization: the presence of this military legacy.

The industrialized character of modern warfare, as exhibited by the use of landmines and cluster bombs, chemical weapons and depleted uranium, is more lethal and more indiscriminate. The lasting effect of post-conflict violence is thus related to the ways that wars are increasingly fought—and justified.

To understand the legacy of modern militarism within a globalizing world, this book presents an overview of post-conflict societies, with an emphasis on the human toll exacted by modern warfare. I first consider the psychological trauma of the millions of people who survive war and how for these men, women, and children, violence remains part of their daily reality. Next, I address the material legacies of warfare—the military detritus that continues to pose risks to both people and the environment years after the fighting has ceased. Chapter Three presents the hidden legacies of land-mines and unexploded ordnance, while Chapter Four details the remnants of chemical weapons. In Chapter Five I present the legacy of nuclear weapons, and the dangers resultant from the testing and stockpiling of these weapons; I conclude the chapter with a discussion of the lasting dangers of depleted uranium. Lastly, I explore how the globalization of the inter-national arms industry poses an unrealized danger to future generations. Throughout, I hope to convey the understanding that the global proliferation of weapons, and the willingness to use more lethal and more indiscriminate armaments, is intimately personal; that globalization is not only *lived*, but it is also *died*.

One

> To ravage, to slaughter, to usurp under false titles,
> They call empire;
> And where they make a desert,
> They call it peace.
>
> Tacitus, *Agricola*

One of the world's most spectacular archaeological sites is found in the highlands of northern Laos.[1] Set within Xieng Khouang Province lies the Plain of Jars. Massive jar-shaped stones, carved of sandstone, dot the windswept landscape. The origin of these megaliths remains a mystery and indeed their enigmatic history is part of our continued fascination.[2]

There is, however, another more tragic geography to the region, for the Plain of Jars is pockmarked with deep depressions—bomb craters from a war long since passed. Now, red-and-white signs are posted throughout the archaeological site, warning visitors to stay within cleared paths. The threat comes in the form of unexploded ordnance (UXO).

Between 1965 and 1975, as part of the larger Second Indochina War, Laos was the most heavily bombed country in the history of warfare. According to Nay Htun, between 1964 and 1973, the United States dropped more than two million tons of bombs on the country; the Plain of Jars alone was subjected to between 74,000 and 150,000 tons of bombs

Figure 1.1
Located in northern Laos, the Plain of Jars remains an archaeological
mystery. Kind permission of the author.

between 1964 and 1969.[3] Indeed, the province of Xieng
Khouang was bombed approximately every eight minutes for
nine years. Stated in more bodily terms, two tons of explosives
were expended across the landscape for every man, woman,
and child.

The immediate effects of the bombing campaign were
horrific. In northeastern Laos, for example, American officials
estimated that 15 percent of the 250,000 to 300,000 people
living in the region were killed between 1968 and 1971.[4] One
observer of the bombing campaign wrote that "after a
recorded history of seven hundred years, the Plain of Jars
disappeared."[5]

And still, decades after the bombings ceased, one person is
killed or injured as a result of unexploded ordnance every
other day in Laos.[6] Overall, an estimated 10,000 people have

Figure 1.2
Decades after the Vietnam War, bomb craters are clearly visible across the Plain of Jars. Kind permission of the author.

been killed or injured since the cessation of aerial bombing in 1973. And therein lies one of the more tragic global realities of the twentieth and twenty-first centuries: Men, women, and children, long after military conflicts have ended, are being killed and injured as a result of the legacy of war. From the plains of Laos to the farmlands of Belgium, from the rice paddies of Cambodia to the savannas and woodlands of Angola, the detritus of past military conflicts endangers the lives and livelihoods of millions of people.

The industrial battlefields of the twentieth and twenty-first centuries are decidedly more deadly than the battlefields of, say, the fourteenth century. Were one to walk the fields of Flodden in the County of Northumberland in northern England, one would be standing on the site of the largest battle between the Scottish and English nations.[7] Remnants, if found,

Figure 1.3
Warning signs of the dangers of unexploded ordnance are ever-present at the Plain of Jars. Kind permission of the author.

would include swords, pikes, and polearms—deadly when used, but hardly lethal otherwise. The battlefields of today, however, are often riddled with discarded weapons and munitions that, in many cases, remain just as deadly years afterwards as when first used. In part, this shift in post-conflict effects is related to the increased precision and "craftsmanship" of modern weapons. Chris McNab and Hunter Keeter, for example, relate the experience of a young officer who served in the Rhodesian African Rifles during the Bush War in the late 1970s and early 1980s. The officer in question, while crossing a stretch of the Zambezi River, came across a partially submerged AK-47 sticking out of the sand. Members of his unit were able to fire all 30 rounds of the weapon's magazine with no problem.[8] Even more deadly, and indiscriminate in their lethality, are the millions of uncleared landmines and

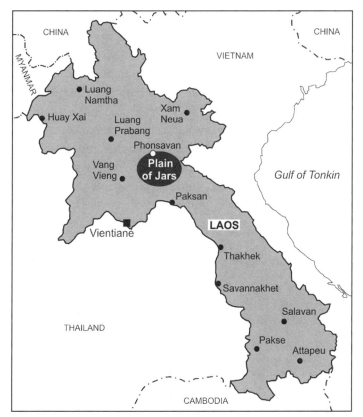

Figure 1.4
Map of Laos.

unexploded ordinance that remain on battlefields. Indeed, unlike a visit to Flodden, most people would think twice about setting across a battlefield if it were known that landmines remained.

For many people, such as the farmers of Angola, Cambodia, or Laos, survival depends on the use of the land. The remnants of war, such as UXO or radioactive dust from depleted uranium shells, either take agricultural lands out of production (for fear of death or injury), or the men, women, and children of those affected areas must "accept" the risk and farm the fields. It is because of this legacy of twentieth-century militarism and warfare that I embarked on this project. Thus, in line with the work of Donovan Webster, Philip Winslow, and Carolyn Nordstrom, among others, my purpose is to study the post-conflict landscapes of twentieth-century militarism and the emergence of modern, industrialized, warfare. Indeed, to paraphrase Webster, the weapons we have warred with, and their effects on the world's landscape, have become our century's most prevalent history.[9] Simply put, the military legacies of the twentieth century remain a global reality for the twenty-first century. And the cost of these legacies—measured in psychological trauma, physical injury and death, economic loss, and environmental degradation—are paid largely by the innocent, by men, women, and children who in most cases were not yet born when conflict enveloped their homelands.

MILITARISM: A MODERN REALITY

Twentieth-century militarism is inseparable from contemporary processes and practices of globalization; militarism has, in fact, become a global reality. To fully comprehend the implications of this statement, however, it is necessary to distinguish between "military" and "militarism." Following Chalmers Johnson, "military" refers to all those activities, qualities, and institutions required by a state[10] to fight a war in its defense.[11] As such, there is an immediate *territorial imperative* assigned to military institutions. Consequently, the right of all states to control and defend their territory is recognized by the international community; this recognition is known as sovereignty.[12] By definition, all political boundaries are artificial. They have been constructed at particular times, for particular purposes. Indeed, the period of Western imperialism since the

1500s has been one of formation, consolidation, and maintenance of geographically specified territories; this has not been a question of a struggle between fully formed states, but rather of the historical and geographical struggles to impose state sovereignty.[13]

Regardless of their origin or formation, states perform specific functions. That is, states—and their corresponding apparatuses—operate to maintain order and to compete with other actual or potential states (including non-state actors). These functions include, among other tasks, political socialization, political communication, interest articulation, policy-making, policy implementation, and policy adjudication.[14] In more general terms, however, these functions may be subsumed under three overarching goals: security, stability, and prosperity. Security, or the defense of the state, is generally given the highest priority. A second cluster of goals includes those of stability. States attempt to ensure order and stability within their borders through the prevention of individual and group violation of social norms. Not surprisingly, the promotion of stability is exceptionally contested. On the one hand, the state itself is not a monolithic entity, but rather a composite of many disparate apparatuses. As such, different components of the state may forward one agenda at the expense of another. On the other hand, different interest (or lobbying) groups also attempt to forward their own agendas, thereby coming into competition with various state apparatuses. Consequently, states may censure or repress individual or group goals that depart from the "interests" of the state.[15] Police and security forces, as well as the military, are often used to maintain social order.

Lastly, states seek to prosper, i.e., to achieve economic growth. However, the promotion of economic growth entails potential trade-offs. On the one hand, economic prosperity may include (1) an increase in the scale, complexity, and specialization of the production system; and (2) the capacity to obtain, manage, and transform resources. On the other hand, welfare distribution may be pursued in the name of prosperity. Reflecting a normative dimension, welfare distribution refers to the public or private allocation of adequate and increasing levels of valued goods to enhance the quality of life of the citizenry.[16] Similar to the promotion of stability, economic growth and development and the management of resources can (and often does) lead to contestations both within and between states. Moreover, an important question is "prosperity" for whom? Rare is the situation wherein the citizenry of any given state has equal—or equitable—access to the prosperity promoted by the state. Instead, it is more likely that state policies are enacted that benefit only a select few individuals or institutions.

To the extent that the military is called upon to promote economic gain (e.g., through colonial practices) or to ensure social control within a state's boundaries, then we have evidence of an increasing militarism. Rachel Woodward defines "militarism" as "the shaping of civilian space and social relations by military objectives, rationales and structures, either as part of the deliberate extension of military influence into civilian spheres of life and the prioritizing of military institutions, or as a byproduct of those processes."[17] This conforms with Johnson, who argues that one sign "of the advent of militarism is the assumption by a nation's armed forces of numerous tasks that should be reserved for civilians."[18]

For many states, regardless of religious or political affiliation, militarism itself has become a daily reality. This is seen in China, Turkey, and Pakistan, just as it is seen in Israel and the United States. Many countries, as Barry Levy and Victor

Sidel note, in fact spend large amounts of money per capita for military purposes. In 2005, for example, the United States' military expenditure was US$478 billion; this amount comprised nearly half (48 percent) of the world's share of military spending. As Levy and Sidel explain, war and the preparation for war divert huge amounts of resources from health and human services and other productive societal endeavors.[19]

Many societies throughout history have exhibited some form of militarism. However, a fundamental shift occurred between the late eighteenth and early twentieth centuries. In particular, this period witnessed an expanding role of civilian participation and input into military preparation. Indeed, what is distinctive about the advent of militarism during this era is the changing character of military-industrial relations, namely the "military-industrial complex." Although a term most commonly associated with former U.S. President Dwight D. Eisenhower's (1961) injunction against "an immense military establishment and a huge arms industry," the fear of a military-business arrangement actually has a longer history. The first president of the United States, George Washington, for example, recognized that a large peace-time military establishment was dangerous to the liberties of a country. James Madison, in 1795, concluded that "war is perhaps the most to be dreaded, because it comprises and develops the germ of every other. War is the parent of armies. From these proceed debts and taxes. And armies, debts and taxes are the known instruments for bringing the many under the domination of the few . . . No nation could preserve its freedom in the midst of continual warfare."[20] In short, since the inception of the United States most politicians and military commanders fostered an anti-militarist tradition.

As Ismael Hossein-Zadeh explains, what these earlier U.S. leaders opposed was the military establishment as an end in itself. Therefore, while supportive of the use of the military in pursuit of economic and/or territorial gains, military leaders and politicians were wary of the possible power and influence of a large military establishment.[21] Consequently, at the end of each conflict U.S. leaders would scale back the expanded wartime military force to its pre-war level out of concerns that "standing armies in time of peace are inconsistent with the principles of republican governments, dangerous to the liberties of a free people, and generally converted into destructive engines for establishing despotism."[22]

What sets apart the militarization of modern Western societies was the development of industrial capitalism as the dominant mode of economic production. As explained by Paul Knox and colleagues, the earlier transition during the eighteenth and nineteenth centuries from merchant capitalism to industrial capitalism was part of a wider economic, social and political transition.[23] Briefly, the late mercantile period[24] saw the ascension of industry organized on capitalist lines by entrepreneurs employing wage labor and producing commodities for sale in regional, national, and (later) international markets. Furthermore, this transition witnessed a number of innovative economic and technological changes, including the pursuit of new ways of exploiting internal and external economies of scale; the exploitation of new, cheaper sources of labor and/or raw materials and energy; the penetration of new foreign markets (especially throughout Africa, Asia, and the Middle East); and the development of new products.[25] Crucially, business entrepreneurs recognized that military activities held a tremendous potential for capital gain, namely through the production and distribution of military armaments and munitions.

The industrial revolution, as John Horne writes, rapidly affected the way war was waged. He maintains that a sweeping economic mobilization was required to apply modern technology to war, transforming the range of violence that could be effected against civilian populations.[26] Hossein-Zadeh, however, makes an additional important point in that the arms industries of past empires were not subject to capitalist market imperatives. Those "industries" that produced military weaponry (i.e., swords, spears, rifles) up to the eighteenth and nineteenth centuries were, for the most part, owned and operated by imperial governments; in other words, armaments and munitions were not produced by market-driven corporations. As such, arms production was largely dictated by immediate war requirements.[27] However, under industrial capitalism—and especially during the First World War—the nature of arms production (and consequently war itself) underwent a profound transformation.

The development of the modern machine gun effectively captures the growing symbiosis between industrial production and the military. Although the concept of a "machine"-powered gun that could rapidly fire rounds was present in the fourteenth century, it was not until the 1860s that the first practical machine guns began to appear. Most notable was the invention of the Gatling gun, named after its designer, Richard Gatling. Although sympathetic to the Confederacy during the American Civil War, Gatling was not opposed to selling his six-barrel, crank-operated weapon to the federal government. However, the Union Ordnance Department showed little interest (until after the war, in 1866) and so Gatling was compelled to market his weapons to Britain, Russia, Spain, Japan, and other countries.[28]

In the wake of Gatling's development, other inventions followed, including a gun built by Hiram Maxim. Max Boot explains that as a young American inventor Maxim had already received a patent for a hair-curling iron, but in the 1880s he began to develop a gun that would use the force of the recoil from the first shot to operate its ejection, loading, and firing mechanisms until an entire ammunition belt (another of his inventions) had been expended. In 1888 Maxim joined with a Swedish company, Nordenfelt, to form the Maxim-Nordenfelt Guns and Ammunition Company. Maxim's company, similar to the other major armaments companies (e.g., Krupp, Winchester, Schneider, and Armstrong), maintained close relationships with their home governments but also marketed their products abroad. Boot writes that "capitalist competition among these large corporations combined with political competition among various states to drive weapons development at a feverish pace." In short, the activity of these entrepreneurs facilitated Europe's development of "its military technology very rapidly through a combination of private enterprise and public spending: what would later become known as a military-industrial complex."[29]

The First World War was an important catalyst in the ongoing militarist transformation of industrial capitalism. Far from being the short-and-decisive war envisioned by the belligerent states (i.e., Germany, France, Russia, and the United Kingdom), the "war to end all wars" was a long, horrific slaughter wrought by the advent of more efficient and deadly weapons, produced, distributed, and used on a scale far greater than in previous wars. As the First World War bogged down into trench warfare, new or recent innovations were used to break the stalemate: machine guns, chemical weapons, armored vehicles, howitzers.

Ironically, while many of these weapons had been developed in the late nineteenth century, their use met (initial) reluctance on the part of military leaders, many of whom believed that these were not "sporting" or "fair" in the conduct of war.[30] Indeed, a theme emerged that would recur throughout the twentieth century: new and improved weapons of mass killing were (and are) often supported more by civilians than by those in the military. Max Boot explains that, prior to the First World War, "most generals were intensely suspicious of these industrial death machines that upset traditional military doctrines and seemed to leave little room for individual feats of valor. Sales did not take off until the start of the Great War."[31] Military officers, by and large, would continue to abhor the immorality of the new weapons—machine guns, chemical and biological agents—but that did not mean that they would not use them. Indeed, "by the time modern warfare exploded onto Europe in 1914, the [European] Powers were exposed to an unfortunate reality: their promotion of conflict during the previous century had not done anything but create a mentality conducive to war but ignorant of what it really meant."[32]

The First World War also heralded an increased role for academics in the military-industrial complex. As the war dragged on, many advances in armaments resulted from battlefield improvisations. However, on the whole, this was an inefficient and haphazard method of weapons development. Consequently, "Governments turned to civilian scientists and engineers to provide technological assistance to military action."[33] As early as 1915 the belligerent governments of Europe began to look for ways and means to find technological innovations in the craft of war. In France, for example, the Ministry of Inventions, headed by Paul Painlevé, was established in 1915. An outgrowth of the earlier Commission of Inventions for the Army and Navy, this newly created agency sought the advice of leading French scientists and mathematicians. Painlevé in particular sought out chemists, physicists, electrical engineers, and medical research scientists; these civilian employees were subsequently tasked to work on ballistics, armaments, electricity and wireless telegraphy, medicine, chemical warfare, aviation, and naval technology.[34]

Unlike its European counterparts, for the United States, the First World War was a profoundly profitable and largely positive event. As Michael Adas explains, the transcontinental technological systems the United States had been building for a half-century provided a powerful matrix for the projection of American technical and material assistance overseas. In particular, by 1917, when America entered the war, its trade with Britain and France had increased by 184 percent; the U.S. dominated markets in Latin America and Asia that the British, French, and Germans had been forced to relinquish on account of the war. Overall, the U.S. went from being the world's greatest debtor to its largest creditor, and by 1918 New York displaced London as the center of the global financial network.[35]

Nevertheless, the United States did experience significant growing pains in its mobilization for war, lessons that would be continually expanded upon throughout the interwar years (1919 to 1941) and the subsequent Cold War. In particular, and indicative of an increased militarism, key industries were developed to ensure an adequate system of weaponry development, production, and distribution. To give but one example, in 1924 the U.S. War Department established the Army Industrial College. As Terrence Gough writes, inadequate preparation for the mass, mechanized conflict of the First World War had produced a near-chaotic and largely ineffective industrial mobilization. Consequently, the Army Industrial College was developed to "make sure that the [Army] possessed the knowledge and skill necessary to carry out the effective industrial mobilization that a future large-scale war would demand."[36] Although the Army Industrial College no longer exists, approximately 150 other military-industrial-academic institutions are in operation, including the National War College, the Industrial College of the Armed Forces, the Defense Acquisition University, the Joint Military Intelligence College, the Naval Postgraduate School, the Naval War College, the Air Force Institute of Technology, and the Uniformed Services University of the Health Sciences.[37]

In short, the tightening bonds between capital and the military changed the nature of warfare in the twentieth century. Beginning (arguably) during the First World War, and certainly by the Second World War, Western societies witnessed a broadening of wartime civilian power. As Alfred Vagts explains, wartime civilian militarism refers to "the interference and intervention of civilian leaders in fields left to the [military] professionals by habit and tradition." This transformation, according to Vagts, "led to an intensification of the horrors of warfare." In particular, by the 1940s politicians and scientists "not only had anticipated war more eagerly than the professionals, but played a principal part in making combat, when it came, more absolute, more terrible than was the current military wont or habit."[38]

The manner in which wars were waged would profoundly impact the landscape and lives of non-combatants. As Mark Kurlansky explains, prior to the First World War, Europeans were "so used to the idea of war that at first they did not understand that this one would be different." However, the "difference lay in all the armaments that had been developed in the industrial age—huge destructive artillery pieces, chemical weapons, rapid-fire machine guns, and airplanes."[39] Consequently, in the First World War we see clearly a deepening of the military-industrial complex and the rise of private corporations, business entrepreneurs, and academics affecting the conduct of warfare, leading to the intense militarization of the twentieth century. One immediate consequence of this twentieth-century militarism is that war has become big business. As Hossein-Zadeh explains, private ownership and the market-driven character of the arms industry have drastically changed the conventional relationship between the supply of and demand for arms. He argues that modern wars and the demand for armaments and munitions are nowadays precipitated more by sales and/or profit imperatives than the other way around. In fact, he contends that "peace," imposed or otherwise, would actually mean sales stagnation for the military-industrial complex; peace, likewise, would mean that these beneficiaries of war dividends would find it increasingly difficult to justify their inordinately large share of national resources and tax dollars.[40] War became big business.

THE REALITIES OF MODERN WARFARE

The rise of an industrial militarism within Western societies throughout the late nineteenth and early twentieth centuries dramatically altered the conduct of warfare. The end result has been a greater mortality among civilians both during *and after* war.

Now, in the twenty-first century, war can no longer be defined simply as a major armed conflict between states, because "the diverse forms of armed conflict now include declared and undeclared wars between nations; full-scale civil wars, including many with genocidal motivations; so-called low-intensity conflicts between competing national political groups; and a wide variety of 'dirty wars' of repression mounted by governments against their own citizens."[41] In fact, modern war is directed primarily against civilians.[42] Throughout the twentieth century, civilians in general (and children in particular) have comprised an ever-increasing proportion of the direct—and indirect—casualties of war and other major armed conflicts.[43] During the First World War, for example, civilian casualties comprised between 5 and 19 percent of all war deaths; during the Second World War, this figure had jumped to approximately 50 percent. Throughout the late twentieth century and now into the twenty-first century, however, at least 80 percent of the approximately 20 million killed and 60 million wounded in declared wars, civil wars, and other major conflicts have been civilians; of these, three of every five have been children.[44] Hugo Slim concludes that "It is obvious from the massive violence against civilian populations around the world today and throughout history that most warring parties do not see civilians as humanitarian agencies might like them to. Either they do not find civilians particularly innocent or they decide that, innocent or not, killing them is useful, necessary, or inevitable in their wars."[45]

And the moral exclusion of humanity is deepening. Writing of the 2003 Iraq War, Derek Gregory explains that the callous attitude toward civilian death is the product "not only of a culture of military violence but also of a political culture of denial and dismissal, which treats its civilian victims not even as 'collateral damage'—objects and obstacles who got in the way—but as irrelevancies. No regret, nor remorse. . . . They simply didn't matter."[46]

On the one hand, the increased proportion of civilian casualties is a function of the weapons designed (i.e., the types of munitions developed) and, on the other hand, the way in which these weapons are used in combat (i.e., area- or carpet-bombing). To better understand these functions, it is useful to separate out the forms in which these war-related violations take place.[47] First, there is the direct assault on civilians by "conventional" (i.e., artillery shelling, aerial bombardments) means. This includes the massive air campaigns conducted by Allied Forces in the Second World War (e.g., the fire-bombings of Dresden, Hamburg, and Tokyo as well as the Japanese assaults on Chinese cities). And the indiscriminate bombing of cities has continued throughout the twentieth century. During the 1980s, for example, the war in Yugoslavia was marked by the sustained and systematic shelling of Vukovar, Dubrovnik, Zvornik, Srebenica, Mostar, Bihac, and Sarajevo. Likewise, the 1994 Russian assault on Grozny in Chechnya produced horrific results for the civilian population. At one point, an estimated 4,000 detonations per hour fell on the city; within the first three months of the conflict, an estimated 15,000 civilians were killed.[48]

From Vietnam to Yugoslavia to Afghanistan, the "city" and its civilian inhabitants has been a "legitimate" target for military operations using conventional weapons. However, civilians are also dying as a result of direct assaults through the use of indiscriminate weapons. This second form includes the use of conventionally defined weapons of mass destruction, such as nuclear and chemical weapons. As Geiger explains, these indiscriminate weapons, by their effects and defining characteristics, are almost certain (and are usually intended) to harm both military combatants and civilians.[49] One particularly insidious weapon is the landmine. Current estimates place the number of uncleared landmines around the world at approximately 100 million. These weapons continue to kill and maim—mostly civilians—in many countries on a daily basis.

A third form of war-related killing entails the indirect assault on civilian populations. According to Geiger, "modern military technology, especially the use of high-precision bombs, rockets, and missile warheads, has now made it possible to attack civilian populations in industrialized settings indirectly—but with devastating results—by targeting the facilities on which life depends, while avoiding the stigma of direct attack on the bodies and habitats of noncombatants."[50]

This is seen, for example, in the deliberate targeting of an enemy state's infrastructure, including its electrical, water, and sanitation systems. Denied these key functions that are necessary to promote life and health, many civilians are susceptible to infectious diseases. Furthermore, resultant from the destruction of transportation systems (i.e., highways, bridges, and fuel-refining and distribution centers), these societies are often unable to provide necessary medical care to the sick and injured.[51]

Lastly, there exists the deliberate targeting of civilians as a means unto itself. Described in various terms as genocide or ethnic cleansing, this refers to the planned annihilation of a group of people—often defined based on conceived religious, ethnic, or political differences—in an attempt to "purify" one's own territory. From the Nazis' industrialized slaughter during the Holocaust, to the horrific violence unleashed in Cambodia, Rwanda, and, now, Darfur, these murderous practices of violence often include the torture and murder of men, women, and children; the widespread and systematic use of rape; the destruction, by explosives and arson, of residences, farms, industries, and basic infrastructures that provide water, electric power, food, fuel, sanitation, and other necessities; denial of medical care and other violations of medical neutrality; and siege, blockade, and interference with humanitarian relief.[52]

And yet how, in the twenty-first century, can these atrocities continue? Why is violent death still a global reality for much of the world's population? In part, as Hedges laments, "Modern industrial warfare may well be leading us, with each technological advance, a step closer to our own annihilation."[53] However, an equally important explanation lies in the continued justification—indeed, acquiescence and tolerance—of (especially) civilian deaths. This explanation, furthermore, hinges on the continued promotion of the idea of a "just war" and how the industrial machinations of warfare are promoted as morally legitimate.

Since the dawn of recorded history, certainly within the Western context, there has been an idea of "limited warfare." In the thirteenth century Pope Gregory IX compiled a list of those persons who should be protected in warfare. Reflecting no doubt his religiosity, the Pope identified eight groups, on the principle of non-combatant immunity, to be shielded from war: priests, monks, friars, and other religious persons; pilgrims; travelers; merchants; peasants cultivating the land; those who are "naturally weak;" women, children, widows, orphans; and animals, goods and lands of the peasantry.[54] Pope Gregory IX, of course, was simply adding to much earlier discussions. Indeed, the idea of a "just war" is generally attributed to an Algerian bishop, Augustine of Hippo (St. Augustine, A.D. 354–430). Writing in the fourth and fifth centuries, Augustine declared that the validity of war was a question of inner motive and he conceived of war as an unfortunate, but natural part of a greater divine necessity. Violence, for Augustine, was judgmental and discerning. He argued, for example, that if a pious man believed in a just cause and truly loved his enemies, it was permissible to go to war and to kill the enemies he loved because he was doing it in a high-minded way. Of most significance, from Augustine's point of view, was not whether an individual died in war, or how they died, but rather their relationship with God, and whether their actions in war would facilitate their passage to eternal life or seal their damnation. This idea of "just" killing has continued to permeate discussions of warfare ever since.[55]

Writers in medieval Europe also began to differentiate between *jus ad bellum* (the justice of war) and *jus in bello* (justice in war). As Michael Walzer explains, these grammatical distinctions point to deep issues that underlie our approaches to civilian populations.[56] Jus ad bellum requires us to make judgments about aggression and self-defense, i.e., should a state go to war? Jus in bello, conversely, forces us to consider how warfare is conducted.[57] Walzer explains that during the Middle Ages Catholic casuists invoked the principle of a "double effect," a way of reconciling the absolute prohibition of attacking non-combatants in war (jus in bello) with the legitimate conduct of military activities (jus ad bellum). The killing of non-combatants, it was argued, was permissible if four conditions held: (1) the act was good in itself or at least indifferent, i.e., actions resulting from a legitimate or "just" war; (2) the direct effect was morally acceptable, i.e., the destruction of military supplies and/or the killing of enemy soldiers; (3) the intention of the actor was moral, i.e., the death of non-combatants was unintentional but unavoidable; and (4) the effect of the action was sufficiently good to compensate for the "immoral" act, i.e., the benefits of the action outweigh the downside of killing a non-combatant.[58] This latter condition presaged the idea of proportionality in warfare, the perspective that "collateral damage" is acceptable if it contributes to the overall war effort.

In moral terms, the concept of proportionality is a classic form of consequentialist thinking, in that an action is judged good or bad not based on the action itself, but instead on what that action might achieve. This leads to the relative position that killing civilians through the use of indiscriminate weapons may be right and acceptable in some contexts.[59] By extension, this concept leads to the justification of certain types of armaments and munitions that can continue to kill after the conflict has ended.

The concepts of "just war" and "proportionality" were modified over the centuries. During the seventeenth century John Selden and Thomas Hobbes, both Oxford scholars, furthered the idea of war as natural and, in most instances, acceptable. Selden, for example, concluded that the extension of an empire was a valid reason for going to war, while Hobbes maintained that war and violence were simply part of humanity's natural state.[60] Whereas these individuals contemplated more so the reasons for war, other philosophers or theologians, such as Francisco de Vitoria and Francisco Suárez, contemplated the conduct of war and, especially, the place of civilians in war. Vitoria, for example, concluded that "It is no doubt a big crime to let a city be devastated, especially a Christian city, unless it is absolutely necessary. But if the requirements of war demand such a thing, it is not forbidden, even if it is feared that soldiers commit some of those horrible transgressions that their masters ought to stop, and if possible, prevent."[61]

The French philosopher Jean-Jacques Rousseau, while arguing that warfare was the natural condition for states, also suggested that the enemy was only the enemy while wearing a uniform of that state. In other words, Rousseau argued against the essentialism inherent in many discussions of war and humanity, namely the idea of a permanent separation of "us" versus "them." For Rousseau, enemy soldiers were in fact signifiers of the enemy state; consequently, war should be restrained as much as possible because "private persons are only enemies accidentally."[62]

Coincident with the development of a militarizing industrial capitalism, the late nineteenth century witnessed many modifications of the idea of a "just war" and the protection of certain peoples. However, as Slim explains, more attention was devoted to the conduct of war, and the protection of soldiers in battle and of prisoners-of-war than to the protection of non-combatants. The First Geneva Convention of 1864, for example, concentrated solely on the wounded in war, while the Hague Conferences of 1899 and 1907 were more preoccupied with weapons development—gases, bombing from balloons, expanding bullets, submarine mines—than they were with details of the safety and protection of the civilian population.[63] Indeed, the word "civilian" emerged and was widely used only after the First World War and especially after the horrors of the Second World War. Following the civilian atrocities of the First World War, and the genocide of the Second World War, the Fourth Geneva Convention of 1949 began to consider more so the idea of civilian protection. This trend was continued with the Additional Protocols to the Geneva Conventions of 1977. Now, the "principle of civilian protection has emerged as a strong global ethic which is formally embodied in international legal conventions and the mandates of many international agencies."[64]

And yet, as Slim further argues, despite the rhetoric of "limited wars" and "just-wars," the tragic fact is that these views remain in the minority among the actual practitioners of organized mass violence. Most modern wars have been governed by "more merciless philosophies of war."[65] Those planners, strategists, and theoreticians who espouse "limitless" philosophies of war often have a total disregard for the whole "enemy" population. According to Slim, "the [enemy] civilian population may be seen as sub-human, an operational irrelevance, totally complicit with the enemy, utterly dispensable in the light of higher goals or as a strategic soft spot in which to hit the enemy hard. From any of these perspectives, the civilian population is not reckoned and seen as valuable in itself. It is just a part of war."[66]

Such a perspective conforms readily with larger discussions of morality and justice. Susan Opotow, for example, explains that moral inclusion "in the scope of justice means applying considerations of fairness, allocating resources, and making sacrifices to foster another's well-being." Conversely, *moral exclusion* "rationalizes and excuses harm inflicted on those outside the scope of justice. Excluding others from the scope of justice means viewing them as unworthy of fairness, resources, or sacrifice, and seeing them as expendable, undeserving, exploitable, or irrelevant."[67] When an individual (or a state) accepts civilian losses as merely "collateral damage" or an unfortunate consequence of war, those people suffering death and injury are morally excluded from humanity.

The moral exclusion of civilian populations during warfare did not originate in the twentieth century. Horne's analysis indicates rather that the French Revolution significantly reshaped warfare in accordance with new criteria of mass political participation, creating (through a principle of universal military service) the possibility not only of larger armies, but also of a different type of soldier: the citizen-soldier. Horne explains that as part of the *levée en masses* the French state sought to mobilize not only the military, but all other "resources," including women and children. Consequently, as warring states mobilized their own populations to contribute to the war effort, it was assumed that the enemy state must likewise be mobilizing its own population.[68] These attitudes contributed greatly to a blurring between "combatant" and "non-combatant." It was therefore easier, for the military leaders at least, to justify the death of the enemy's population. Civilian populations were thus transformed into "legitimate" military targets.

Throughout the twentieth century, as Horne writes, warfare "was characterized not only by propaganda campaigns of unprecedented violence but also by the identification of the enemy's political, psychological and moral resource as military targets—even if that meant erasing the distinction between soldiers and civilians."[69]

Militarism therefore helps promote a sense of moral exclusion. This is seen in the ready acceptance not only of civilian deaths as a result of war, but also in the ways in which wars are fought. During the Second World War, for example, both Germany and England chose to wage war on civilian populations through massive aerial campaigns. These were widely recognized as having no direct military advantage, but rather were designed to instill terror in the enemy's civilian population. These means of waging war also would inflict a greater toll on humanity's habitat: the Earth itself. Indeed, the Second World War "laid bare the fact that the existing means and methods of conducting armed combat were already close to causing irreparable damage to the biosphere."[70] As Sergey Tikhomirov finds, the Second World War damaged some 20 million hectares of Europe's forests; one high-caliber shell alone would cause damage over an area of 2,000 square meters.[71] For a number of locations throughout Europe, pre-war agricultural levels would not be reached until many years had elapsed since the end of hostilities.

As discussed in later chapters, both civilian-scientists and military leaders were (and are) confronted with the choice of using or not using weapons (i.e., landmines and nuclear weapons) that may lead to the indiscriminate killing of innocent civilians both during and after the conflict. How these decisions are rendered is part of the military legacy of the twentieth century.

Militarism contributes also to an acceptance of warfare because it often hides the gruesome realities not just of conflict, but of the post-conflict. Hedges explains: "We do not smell rotting flesh, hear the cries of agony, or see before us blood and entrails seeping out of bodies."[72] This is all the more true when the consequences of militarism take place *over there*. The maker of an AK-47 or M-16 does not necessarily see the effects of his labor; neither does the chemist who develops a more efficient delivery system of phosgene see the devastating results of her contributions. And neither do the arms dealers always know where, or in whose hands, their products will end up. Consequently, simply because of the physical distances involved—the geographic separation of militarism and actual conflict—the deadly consequences are ignored. For most people in the United States, for example, the daily reality of U.S. military interventions in Afghanistan and Iraq are not fully appreciated. As Kurlansky concludes, "War is always more popular with those who don't experience it."[73]

And that is where we should look: to the consequences for people and the environment *after the war*. One need only look so far as the U.S. President George W. Bush's (in)famous proclamation of "Mission Accomplished" in May 2003 following the U.S.-led invasion of Iraq. Untold hundreds of thousands of Iraqi civilians (as well as American and other coalition forces) continued to die and be maimed long after the "war" was supposedly won. This is an obvious example. But people are still dying and being injured from the legacy of the wars in Africa and Central America that were fought during the 1980s; people are still dying and being injured from the wars in Indochina (i.e., Cambodia, Laos, and Vietnam) of the 1960s and 1970s; people are still dying and suffering from the nuclear attacks on Hiroshima and Nagasaki in 1945; and people are still dying from the unexploded ordnance left over from the First World War. And with the massive arsenals of nuclear and chemical weapons, along with the stockpiles of "conventional" munitions, there exists the very real possibility that humanity will suffer the effects from the increased militarism of the twentieth and twenty-first centuries for decades (and centuries) to come. Our future generations, five, six, seven times removed from the actual production and/or use of contemporary weapons, will still be at risk.

THE SCOPE OF THE BOOK

My main thesis is straightforward: The industrialized character of modern warfare, produced by militarized societies that seek above all to profit from war, has led to the proliferation of more insidious weapons and munitions that remain more lethal, and more indiscriminate, in their destructive power. The lasting effect of post-conflict violence is thus related to the ways that wars are increasingly being waged throughout the twentieth and twenty-first centuries.

My main concern is not the justification of killing civilians during war or the killing and wounding of people during the heat of battle; rather, my present concern lies in the lasting effects of military intervention and warfare after the fighting has stopped.

Post-conflict landscape does not mean "after" but rather "beyond:" to adopt a penetrating look at the militarized landscapes beyond the immediacy of war and to consider the enduring violence that remains a part of these landscapes. After the armies have departed, and ceasefires or treaties have been negotiated, the indiscriminate violence continues. The presence of uncleared landmines, the lethal residue of chemical and nuclear weapons, the psychological scars of unimaginable (yet real) violence: these constitute an integral part of the day-to-day life of millions of women, men, and children across the earth. These are the landscapes that make up our militarized world.

First, I consider the millions of people who survive the conflict, many of whom are often not considered: the refugees and internally displaced persons (IDPs), the orphans and widows. This "living suffering," which can last for the duration of the war and long afterwards, is often overlooked in popular conceptions of war.[74] Consequently, in Chapter Two I explore the mental legacies of war and militarism, namely Post-Traumatic Stress Disorder (PTSD). The remainder of the book is devoted more so to the material legacies of warfare, including landmines and unexploded ordinance (Chapter Three), chemical weapons (Chapter Four), and nuclear weapons (Chapter Five).

Two

Michael Clodfelter is a Vietnam veteran. He is also a historian and author of many books. In *Mad Minutes and Vietnam Months* Clodfelter describes his reaction to viewing the bodies of two Vietnamese soldiers: "Both wore ironic expressions of contentment on their young faces. Though caking, scarlet pockets of bullet wounds and vacantly staring eyes were the only indications that these men were dead instead of dreaming, they already seemed somehow less human to me." He writes that "Violent death still brought grief when a friend fell, but the death of a Vietnamese, any Vietnamese, not just the enemy, was looked upon with no more pity than a hunter gives his prey . . ." Clodfelter understood the psychological implications of war. He concludes that "War was working insane logic on us. We were learning to deny the enemy's humanity, and because it was so difficult to distinguish the enemy from those who merely hated us, it had become easier to kill both."[1]

Sey is a 65-year-old widow.[2] Born and raised in Cambodia, she came to the United States as a refugee following the Cambodian genocide (1975–1979). Sey is now haunted by nightmares, recollections of the violence she endured over three decades ago. Her story is not uncommon among refugees of war and mass violence. During the genocide Sey was witness to traumatic events on a near-daily basis. One day, for example, while heading to work in the rice fields as part of a forced-labor work brigade, she came upon two Khmer Rouge soldiers who were each holding a small child by the legs; they swung each child in such a way that its head repeatedly hit against a tree stump. Sey turned and saw the bodies of the parents nearby; they were Sey's friends. Now, in her sleep, Sey often sees a black figure approaching her body; she has flashbacks of the killing of the small children; she recalls clearly the children's heads being cracked against the stump. In trying to make sense of the brutal event Sey believes that the approaching black figure is the spirit of one of the dead children—or perhaps of the parents—that has followed her to the United States.

Menachem Rosensaft was born in the Nazi death camp, Bergen-Belsen; his cradle was but a short distance from the mass graves in which Anne Frank and tens of thousands of other European Jews lie buried anonymously. Although Rosensaft's parents survived the horrors of Auschwitz, his grandparents and brother did not. He explains that sometimes, when he is alone, he sees (or imagines that he sees) a fading image of a five-and-a-half-year-old boy named Benjamin. Rosensaft writes:

> Once upon a time, in the spring and early summer of 1943,
> that little boy lived and laughed and played with his parents
> and grandparents in the ghetto of the Polish city of Sosnowiec.
> On August 1, 1943, the Germans began liquidating the various
> ghettos in that part of Poland, and three days later, upon
> arriving at Birkenau, the death camp at Auschwitz, my brother
> was separated from his—our—mother and murdered in a
> gas chamber together with his father and our grandparents. I
> am haunted by his face, his eyes, and I listen to a voice I
> never heard. But do I see him, or is it merely my reflection?
> Are my tears mine, or are they his? I do not know. I shall
> never know.[3]

For much of her early childhood, Liesel Appel lived a "charmed" life. The daughter of loving parents and a large extended family, she lived in a "beautiful, spacious home" where concerts were held regularly. She learned to recite poetry and to play the piano. But then, in the early years after the war, her childhood ended when she learned about her parents' past. Appel explains that, after learning of her father's Nazi past, she turned against her parents, basing her decision on the morality she had been taught by them. She writes: "I became a self-destructive child and woman, unrelenting and unforgiving. I tried to kill myself by swallowing a handful of rat poison. The past made me who I was, bounded in fear, pain, and loneliness with the shadow of guilt hanging over me. I did not believe that I deserved happiness or love."[4]

For readers familiar with war, genocide, and mass violence, the stories of Clodfelter, Sey, Rosensaft, and Appel are remarkably familiar, for they are testimony to the mental legacies associated with traumatic conflict. The soldier who has killed in battle; the civilian who has witnessed death; the children of both civilian and soldier: all remain trapped within their own realities of violence. Fear and anxiety, according to Daniel Flannery, are normal instincts rooted in our biological responses to stress and trauma, particularly as manifest in war and mass violence.[5] Flannery explains further that exposure to violence and mental health are inextricably linked. Among the most commonly noted symptoms are increased depression, anxiety, anger, and dissociation or desensitization to the effects of violence.[6]

In this chapter I consider the mental legacy of warfare, of how violent events continue to harm and hinder people long after the initial traumatic experiences have passed. Long after the fighting has stopped, the treaties have been signed, and the militaries demobilized, the legacies of violence endure: the sights, sounds, smells, and other sensations of conflict remain part of many people's everyday lives. The "post" traumatic events are all too real and continue to affect both the survivors and their relatives for years and even decades. In fact, there is no "post" in trauma, for the mental anguish of violence extends beyond war.

THE TRAUMA OF WAR

> Everywhere we saw traces of death; it was almost as though there wasn't a living soul anywhere in this wasteland. Here, behind a disheveled hedge, lay a group of men, their bodies covered with the fresh soil that the explosion had dropped on them after killing them; there were two runners lying by a crater, from which the acrid fumes of explosives were still bubbling up. In another place, we found many bodies in a small area: either a group of stretcher-bearers or an errant platoon of reservists that had been found by the centre of a ball of fire, and met their end . . . The way was littered with dead, their pale faces staring up out of water-filled craters, or already so covered with mud that their human identity was almost completely masked. [7]

The mental stresses incurred by soldiers in battle have long been recognized. The Greek historian Herodotus, for example, wrote of an Athenian soldier who went blind after witnessing a fellow soldier die in battle. Herodotus also wrote of Leonidas, the Spartan commander who, at the battle of Thermopylae Pass in 480 B.C., dismissed his men from combat because he recognized that they were mentally exhausted from fighting. [8]

Over the centuries, physicians (among others) dutifully observed, wrote, and speculated about the mental condition of soldiers returning from war. In 1678 the Swiss physician Johannes Hofer suggested that soldiers suffered from "nostalgia," an illness characterized by melancholy, an incessant thinking of home, disturbed sleep, insomnia, weakness, anxiety, loss of appetite, cardiac palpitations, and fever. [9] Although the causes of "nostalgia" ran the gamut of explanations, most physicians concurred that physical factors (rather than psychological) were predominant.

Throughout the late nineteenth and early twentieth centuries, psychologists and psychiatrists witnessed and documented increased symptoms of stress among soldiers returning from combat. During the American Civil War, for example, "those soldiers either unwilling or unable to continue [to fight], who seemed lost in the middle of all the bloodshed and slaughter, or those who survived and went home only to remain distant and angry, or who woke up in the middle of the night screaming, were said to be suffering from an 'Irritable Heart.' "[10] Such a diagnosis, Ronald Glasser explains, conformed with the military establishment and the general public as well. The visible signs of trauma-induced distress, for example insomnia, nightmares, anxiety, and depression, were attributed to a *physical* cause: an over-stimulated heart. According to Glasser, "military leaders have always tried to dismiss the anxiety and desperation of the battlefield . . . as something that is physical; something that *happens* to soldiers; something that is real."[11] Glasser concludes that the military's "goal has always been to keep its troops in line and, where necessary, at the tip of the spear. It had always been easier for the military to blame the psychiatric problems of being in battle on the disruptive physical forces at work rather than on the apparent vagueness of fear, mental confusion, and emotional trauma."[12]

During the First World War, as soldiers returned from battle exhibiting signs of psychological trauma, the cause was again thought to be physical. Soldiers were diagnosed as having "Shell Shock;" their mental conditions were the consequences of being in too close of proximity to artillery barrages. Thus, rather than an "irritable heart," it was a physical problem to the brain and central nervous system. Simply put, the symptoms of depression and anxiety, the agitation and confusion, were all viewed as the result of neurological damage caused by both the noise and the commotion of the high-energy explosions.[13] And similar to those soldiers of the Civil War, the diagnosis of "Shell Shock" was both militarily and politically correct. The theory of massive physical trauma to the brain, resultant in psychological disorders, was both understandable and acceptable to the military and the general public.[14]

A search for physical causes continued through the Second World War and the Korean War.[15] Soldiers of the former conflict were said to suffer from "Battle Fatigue," while those of the latter suffered from "Combat Exhaustion." The stresses of war required little more than added "rest and recreation" from which the soldiers could recuperate. Not only did this wash away any concerns that the experience of war itself was traumatic, it ensured that the majority of "exhausted" or "fatigued" soldiers would be redeployed to the battlefield. Indeed, according to Glasser, throughout the Korean War, 100 percent of soldiers with an initial diagnosis of "Combat Exhaustion" went back to their units; furthermore, 90 percent of those diagnosed with "Combat Neurosis," 56 percent of the supposed psychotics, and 85 percent of the psychoneurotics were also sent back to fight.[16]

The Vietnam War changed the medical profession's understanding of war-induced trauma. In the late 1960s and early 1970s, clinical psychologists and psychiatrists began noting an exceptionally large proportion of Vietnam veterans reporting symptoms of depression, aggression, anxiety, and confusion. Moreover, these veterans spoke of difficulties adjusting to their everyday lives, of maintaining stable relationships with their spouses and children. Now, the medical profession began to seriously rethink its earlier diagnoses.

In response to the mounting studies reporting the existence of war-related mental disorders, the American Psychiatric

Association's (APA) Committee on Nomenclature and Statistics in 1952 forwarded a classification of *gross stress reaction* as a psychiatric category. This diagnosis was used in instances where patients were exposed to severe physical demands or extreme stress, such as in combat; it was applied to otherwise "normal" people who experienced intolerable stress. In 1968 this diagnosis was modified when the term *gross stress reaction* was replaced with *transient situational disturbance*. According to the APA, this newly introduced diagnosis referred to transient disorders of any severity that occurred in individuals who previously exhibited no underlying mental disorders, and who were subjected to overwhelming environmental stress.[17]

As the war in Vietnam escalated, so too did the number of returning veterans complaining of problems adjusting to civilian (or post-combat) life.[18] Veterans exhibited signs of depression, anxiety, and aggression; they spoke of difficulties in maintaining relationships with their spouses or partners; they were found to have alcohol and drug problems; interpersonal and cognitive problems, including criminal behavior and emotional numbness, were also identified. In response, Horowitz and Solomon coined the term "delayed stress response syndrome" to describe symptoms of returning veterans.[19]

Subsequent research (and professional deliberation) led to the inclusion of "Post-Traumatic Stress Disorder," or PTSD, in the 1980 edition of the *Diagnostic and Statistical Manual of Mental Disorders*.[20] Based on this new diagnosis, a person is said to be suffering from PTSD if he or she has experienced, witnessed, or been confronted with an event or events that involve actual or threatened death or serious injury, or a threat to the physical integrity of oneself or others; and the person's responses involved intense fear, helplessness, or horror.[21]

Although the existence of PTSD is relatively accepted in the psychological and psychiatric communities, there are a number of critiques.[22] Medical anthropologists, for example, have questioned whether PTSD is a *universal* mental illness, or if it is manifest differently across cultures. To this end, Bracken and his colleagues question the validity of applying a Western-based "trauma model" to non-Western societies. The diagnosis of PTSD in these societies, they suggest, may in fact reflect nothing more than a Western medicalization of responses to trauma. However, despite reservations as to the universality of PTSD, there is wide agreement that war and violence—as human-induced events—are exceptionally traumatic; that in addition to coping with the deaths and physical destruction wrought by such violence, survivors are left with the psychological and social effects of bereavement, torture, rape, starvation, and other forms of trauma.[23] Thus, whether one is diagnosed with PTSD or some other "label," the tragic fact remains that trauma is a significant *possible* and indeed *probable* legacy of warfare.

THE TRAUMA OF "COLLATERAL DAMAGE"

"We have a large photo of him on the wall," said the young widow of a Soviet combatant killed on Afghan soil. "My daughter says to me: 'Take Daddy down. I want to play with him . . .' She surrounds his picture with toys and talks to him . . . I take her to nursery school . . . she cries . . . 'Where is my Daddy?' . . . I am worn out with crying every day . . . If you could only come back for a moment . . . See how your daughter has grown!"[24]

Whether called "Shell Shock," "Battle Fatigue," or some other term, war-induced psychological trauma has always been associated with conflict. On this count, modern warfare differs very little from previous eras. What is different in our contemporary world, however, is the industrialized slaughter of modern warfare and an increasingly blurred line between "combatants" and "non-combatants." Indeed, in many parts of the world, the threat of innocent civilians being killed, maimed, or traumatized by organized mass violence is an everyday reality.

The battlefields of contemporary wars, as exemplified by the chaotic character of the wars in Iraq, Afghanistan, and Georgia, have destroyed the separation between "combatant" and "non-combatant." Carolyn Nordstrom effectively captures the changing "place" of today's battlefields:

> There was a time when people used to study war, up front and close. Journalists, poets, and researchers used to go to the front lines of wars like the American Civil War to document the battles. They set up chairs and sat with paper and pen to record the volleys that were unleashed and the bodies that fell. . . . [I]n these historical periods, battles were circumscribed. . . . But the dynamic of war has changed. . . . War itself now spills across the landscapes and cityscapes of prosaic life. The image of the complete battle, separate from the civilian life around it, is antiquated, unreal.[25]

The battlefields of today's wars are also witness to the most destructive weaponry ever developed. Twentieth- and twenty-first-century weapons are more powerful, more pervasive, and able to kill more people more rapidly than in any other era. Consider, for example, the .50-caliber Browning machine gun, which can fire a round "through 7.87 in (20cm) of reinforced concrete at 1,312 ft (400m), and can smash an engine block at well over 4,921 ft (1,500m)." These guns, moreover, can fire 500 rounds per minute.[26] An American veteran of the Iraq War details the devastating effects of machine-gun fire on non-combatants:

> We were supposed to be in a secure area. Hell, we're a maintenance unit. We set up the roadblock. The sedan didn't

stop. It looked like a lot of people in the back seat. Someone yelled, "Gun." You don't have a lot of time to decide. Fifty-caliber rounds can do an awful lot of damage to a Toyota. When we opened the back door, one of the guys started to throw up. There were three little girls in the back seat. Two were cut in half and the third was missing her head . . .[27]

According to Marc Pilisuk, as the technology of warfare has improved, the cost in civilian lives has increased. He, along with other historians, has targeted the massive aerial bombing campaigns of the Second World War as defining events. The fire-bombing of Dresden, for example, killed 135,000 civilians.[28]

Significantly, a small number of psychiatrists and psychologists began studying the effects of war-induced trauma on children and other civilians during the Second World War. In 1941 Bodman reported on a survey of 8,000 schoolchildren which found that approximately four percent presented some psychological symptoms (e.g., nightmares) that could be attributed to German air raids. Mercer and Despert (1943) and Bradner (1943) likewise found evidence of trauma among French and Finnish children, respectively.[29] There was, however, no real sustained work on war-induced trauma among children and adolescents until the 1980s.[30] Sadly, these early studies also did not dissuade military planners from targeting cities and other civilian-populated areas for destruction.[31] The presence of "collateral damage" has become an everyday reality of modern warfare.

Today's soldiers are also better equipped and better trained in the science of killing. It is not natural for humans to kill other humans. Militaries around the world have long recognized this aversion and, consequently, have developed training exercises to overcome this resistance. However, as Meagher writes, while "the military goes to great lengths to decode the psychology behind our natural aversion to killing, they balk at teaching troops about the moral justifications of combat killing, are not curious about understanding the connection between killing, guilt, and PTSD and are not aggressive enough in treating these side effects once the mission is complete."[32]

The lack of clearly demarcated battlefields coupled with the increased firepower being used in today's wars has two significant consequences. First, a greater number of "civilians" are being killed and wounded. As indicated in Chapter One, approximately 90 percent of all casualties in today's conflicts are civilians, and more children now die in wars than do soldiers.[33] Unfortunately, these numbers often go unannounced, in part because they are not even counted. In Iraq, for example, the number of civilians killed is not officially recorded; the military argues that it is not its role to count civilian dead.[34] What is known, however, is the payments made to the families of killed Iraqi civilians. According to a Government Accountability Office report released in 2007, the Department of Defense issued approximately US$31 million in "condolence" payments between 2003 and 2006 to civilians in Iraq and Afghanistan as a result of U.S. or coalition forces' actions. According to the report, civilians in Iraq are paid up to $2,500 for death, $1,500 for serious injuries, and $200 or more for minor injuries.[35]

Second, the brutality of today's conflict has greatly increased the traumatic experience of warfare for both "combatants" and "non-combatants." Josh Middleton, an Army medic who served in Iraq, describes a "typical" combat action—a raid on the house of a suspected insurgent:

> They put . . . a shape-charge, and the door was blown open. And there was a pregnant woman on the other side. And apparently

it blew . . . the fetus out onto the ground and killed [the mother] instantly. . . . [B]asically, they knocked on the door and then they detonated it. So they kill the first person who answers the door and then go through. And then, the guys are, "Oh," like "this is war. You've got to deal with it."[36]

Although statistics are difficult to come by, Ilona Meagher suggests that, by 2006, one-in-four discharged Iraq and Afghanistan veterans (nearly 150,000) have filed disability claims, over 60,000 of which have been for mental health issues.[37]

The impact of war on civilians continues to affect the lives of survivors long after the end of active hostilities; this constitutes a tragic, and often unseen, legacy of war.[38] As Chris McNab and Hunter Keeter write, "like ripples caused by stones thrown into a pond, every time a weapon strikes a human target grief spreads out into the world through mothers, fathers, children, siblings, and friends."[39] From Nicaragua to Iraq, Kuwait to Lebanon, psychologists and psychiatrists have documented the trauma of war and the lasting effects of violence directed toward civilians. The conflicts in Central America throughout the 1980s, for example, left hundreds of thousands of people (mostly civilians) dead or injured, or scattered throughout the Americas as refugees. In El Salvador alone an estimated 70,000 persons were killed; tens of thousands of people were tortured and physically, mentally, and sexually abused.[40] In Nicaragua, likewise, approximately 60,000 people were murdered, injured, or abducted during the war. An estimated 15,000 children were orphaned and 1,500 maimed or physically disabled.[41] Those who survived continue to endure the trauma of these experiences.

According to Marc Pilisuk, war has "caused more than three times the number of casualties in the last ninety years than in the previous 500. Upwards of 250 major wars have occurred in the post-World War II era, taking over 50 million lives and leaving tens of millions homeless."[42] In the following section I consider but one of these conflicts—the Cambodian genocide—to look more concretely at the trauma endured by non-combatants both during and after the violence.

CAMBODIA'S GRIEF

My family was killed in 1975 and I cried for 4 years. When I stopped crying, I was blind.[43]

In 1975 a Marxist-based revolutionary group, known as the Khmer Rouge, assumed power in Cambodia. Their ascension followed five years of brutal civil war and was marked by a radical and horrific practice of social engineering. Between April 1975 and January 1979 the Khmer Rouge promulgated a wide-reaching genocidal campaign to completely re-structure Cambodia. In the process, approximately two million Cambodians—over a quarter of the country's pre-war population—died from execution, torture, forced labor, disease, or famine. Apart from the physical death and injuries incurred by the Cambodian population, the specific practices enacted by the Khmer Rouge set in place a legacy that would continue to traumatize the survivors for many years after.[44]

War and organized mass violence often damage traditional ways of life and cultural institutions. Indeed, as exemplified by the Cambodian genocide, specific family and communal structures were deliberately targeted. Throughout the genocide, all aspects of daily life were to be regimented and reoriented toward the Khmer Rouge. The Cambodian people, for example, were separated into labor brigades, based on age and sex. Thus, male adults aged 14 and older were placed in mobile work brigades and sent to plow fields, plant and harvest rice, or dig irrigation canals. Elderly women, conversely, were required to raise the children and perform "lighter" work, such as sewing, gardening, or collecting wood. Overall, these age/sex divisions facilitated the severing of traditional familial bonds and relationships. Children were no longer tied to their parents and, in most instances, were not permitted to live with their parents. Indoctrination sessions taught that all children belonged to the revolution and, indeed, that parents were enemies of the new regime. Haing Ngor, a survivor of the Cambodian genocide, describes "life" under the Khmer Rouge:

> . . . the old way of life was gone and everything about it half forgotten, as if it had never really existed in the first place. Buddhist monks, making their tranquil morning rounds, didn't exist anymore. Three-generation families, where the grandparents look after the little children, didn't exist anymore. Shopping for food in the markets and staying to gossip. Inviting friends over to eat and drink and talk in the evening. It was all gone, and without that pattern we had nothing to hold on to.[45]

For those who lived through the genocide, violence, and the fear of violence, became an everyday reality.[46] The trauma of living in constant fear, of witnessing death, of not knowing if one would live from one day to the next. Haing Ngor describes the everyday terror: "What was worse than hunger was the terror, because we couldn't do anything about it. The terror was always there, deep in our hearts. In the late afternoon, wondering whether the soldiers would choose us as their victims. And then feeling guilty when the soldiers took someone else. At night, blowing out our tiny oil lanterns so the soldiers wouldn't notice the light and come investigate, and then lying awake and wondering whether we would see the dawn. Waking up the next day and wondering whether it would be our last."[47]

For many Cambodians, the knock on a door brings back memories of the Khmer Rouge coming to take someone away to kill. Sreytouch Svay-Ryser, for example, describes the terrifying living conditions during the genocide: "[The Khmer Rouge] usually came and took people away during the night. So when it got dark, we couldn't sleep."[48] Rouen Sam, a young woman who was only 14 years old when the Khmer Rouge came to power, relates a similar experience: "When night came I always worried. I stayed up even when they told us to go to sleep. [Guards] walked around with a flashlight at night to see who was asleep and who wasn't. I was afraid that maybe next time it would be me. I would die before I saw the sun rise. I had little rest, and then I heard the whistle and inside I sighed, 'Oh, I'm alive!' I got up and got in line. From one night to the

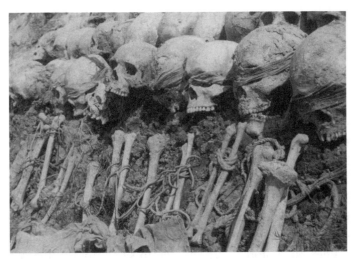

Figure 2.1
For many Cambodians, the genocide remains a painful, haunting legacy. Kind permission of the Documentation Center of Cambodia.

next it was the same."[49] These experiences are re-experienced, often many years after the events.

Throughout the Cambodian genocide, children and adults were routinely subjected to violent, traumatic events—productions, in fact—that were designed to instill fear and to ensure docility among the people. According to Henri Locard, self-criticism and mutual criticism constituted basic mental exercises during the genocide.[50] Children and adults were required to attend nightly meetings—following long days of arduous forced labor—to announce their shortcomings. The purpose was to encourage public denunciations, and the humiliation, of malingerers, in an attempt to expose "enemies" of the revolution. Locard continues: "Accusations, arising almost always from commune leaders, invariably led to arrest, and then to liquidation [execution]. How often in public did people confess their wrongs, errors, flaws, or denounce their neighbors, almost always under threat and in fear for their own safety? People did their best to be invisible, lower their heads, and keep their opinions to themselves."[51]

These nightly events were especially traumatic for children. Consider the experiences of Rouen Sam, introduced earlier. She describes how the Khmer Rouge assembled a group of children and adults at a place called Thunder Hill. The meeting took place at a temple, with the children sitting in front. Two adult prisoners were called before the children. A Khmer Rouge official informed the children that "If someone betrays [the Revolutionary Party], they will be executed. We want everyone to know that these people are bad examples, and we don't want other people to be like this." Sam explains that the Khmer Rouge forced the children to sit in front of the two prisoners; the children were warned, "If anyone cries or shows empathy or compassion for this person, they will be punished by receiving the same treatment." Sam describes what happened next:

> [The official] told someone to get the prisoner on his knees. The prisoner had to confess what he had done wrong. Then the prisoner began to talk but he didn't confess anything. Instead, he screamed, "God, I did not do anything wrong. Why are they doing this to me? I work day and night, never complain, and even though I get sick and I have a hard time getting around, I satisfy you so you won't kill people. . . . This is injustice . . ." Suddenly, one of the [Khmer Rouge guards] hit him from the back, pushed him, and he fell face to the ground. It was raining. We sat in the rain, and then the rain became blood. He was hit with a shovel and then he went unconscious and began to have a seizure. Then [a guard] took out a sharp knife and cut the man from his breastbone all the way down to his stomach. They took out his organs. . . . They tied the organs with wire on the handlebars of a bicycle and biked away, leaving a blood trail.[52]

This brutal and traumatic performance was intended to instill fear and ambiguity among the children. They were left bewildered, scared, and confused. Why was the man killed? What did he do wrong? Afterwards, Sam explains: "I was now a prisoner in my mind and my body. My mind says, Don't remember, because this could be me. The air smelled like blood. Clear rain drops coming from the sky became blood. . . . Then [the soldiers] told us to get in line, and we all headed back to the place we lived."[53]

Many survivors continue to "live in the past;" they remain guilty about abandoning their homelands as refugees; they experience guilt for not fulfilling obligations to the dead; they feel guilty for simply being alive.[54] Moreover, it is not uncommon for these mental stresses to manifest in physical symptoms, such as sleep paralysis or psychosomatic blindness. In a sleep paralysis, the person, either upon falling asleep or awakening, suddenly cannot move his or her arms, legs, or head; he or she may also be unable to speak. Additionally, the person may see a "being" approach, typically in shadow form. Other symptoms include a tightening of the chest, and shortness of breath. These episodes may last from a few seconds to several minutes.[55]

Consider Buth, a 58-year-old Cambodian refugee living in Lowell, Massachusetts. Prior to the Khmer Rouge coming to power, Buth was a soldier in the former Lon Nol government. During the genocide Buth, along with three friends, was arrested on suspicion of being a Lon Nol soldier. The Khmer Rouge promised that anyone who admitted to being a soldier would be spared; those who lied, and were discovered to be lying, would be killed. Buth remained quiet, but his three friends admitted their former military positions. Subsequently, the three friends were executed. Buth was still under suspicion and was sent away for interrogation. During his imprisonment Buth was repeatedly tortured; often his head was submerged under water, to the point of losing consciousness. Having survived the genocide, Buth now suffers from frequent flashback nightmares and irritability. About once a month he relives the interrogations and tortures; frequently, in his nightmares, Buth sees a man-shaped shadow approaching his bed. During the "visitation" Buth feels short of breath and fears dying. In trying to make sense of the nightmares, Buth believes that the shadow is a ghost sent by a sorcerer to kill him.[56]

Choup, a 52-year-old Cambodian refugee, suffers from similar nightmares and sleep paralysis. Approximately once a week Choup relives traumatic events that happened over 20 years earlier. One event in particular stands out in Choup's nightmares. During the genocide Choup, along with the other villagers, was forced to view the bodies of two people who were executed after being captured while trying to escape. The bodies, Choup recalls, were cut into pieces and stacked. In one pile, the Khmer Rouge placed the arms; in another, the legs. Choup also relates that the two bodies had been eviscerated, with skin flaps opening like two small doors on to the partially emptied abdominal cavity; the two livers were stacked one atop the other. Three months later Choup was forced to watch the execution of his two brothers; they were similarly eviscerated. In his sleep paralysis, Choup sees two black shadows moving toward him; he assumes that the shadows are the spirits of the two dead people. Other times, when falling asleep, Choup sees an *ap*[57] floating toward him: a head on a trunk, arms emerging from the trunk, with a liver and intestines hanging down. The *ap* places its hands around Choup's neck, causing him a shortness of breath. Often, the *ap* materializes as his younger brother. Choup believes that because his brother died a "bad death," his soul continues to roam the earth.[58]

In Khmer culture, as in many societies, the context of death is significant. Also crucial is the role religion plays in coping with death. In Cambodia a syncretic form of Buddhism is widely practiced. Indigenous folk beliefs, including a host of ghostly or demon-like spirits, have been incorporated into more traditional Buddhist practices, such as reincarnation. Furthermore, in Khmer society, Buddhist rituals are required at all events that symbolize significant life transitions, such as birth and death. Key aspects include the practice of attempting to assure a superior rebirth by proper religious devotion prior to death, as well as the calling of Buddhist monks to recite prayers when death is imminent. After death, the corpse is bathed and dressed in white clothing; the body is then cremated.[59]

During the Cambodian genocide the Khmer Rouge outlawed all religious practice. Indeed, most Buddhist monks and nuns were executed, while the temples were either destroyed or converted into storehouses for rice or grains. As a result, as people were murdered or died from other causes during the genocide, funerary rites were forbidden. Even to show grief following a relative's death might result in torture or execution. Now, survivors of the genocide suffer the mental trauma not only of seeing their relatives or friends die horrible deaths, but also the guilt of not being able to ensure a proper funeral and thus a good rebirth. James Boehnlein, for example, describes the experiences of a 45-year-old widow who suffers from anorexia, depression, nightmares, and intrusive memories of the war and genocide. One event stands out more than any other. In her presence, while a young woman, her father had committed suicide with an overdose of medicines. He had been living in constant fear of being discovered by the Khmer Rouge to have formerly held a position as a military officer in the Lon Nol regime. This discovery would have meant the immediate torture and/or execution of his family. The young woman struggled with her father in a desperate attempt to prevent him from committing suicide. However, in her weakened condition, as a result of starvation and malnutrition, she was unable to stop him. She wanted to cry over his death, to mourn his loss, but could not, for fear of being seen by the Khmer Rouge. Now, she remembers her failure and helplessness at not being able to prevent his suicide. She regrets also that her father's body was not cremated but, instead, was buried in a mass grave. In trying to come to terms with her father's death, she remains worried that the manner of his death and the lack of cremation may have eternally affected his reincarnation.[60]

For Cambodians, it is difficult to reconcile the especially violent deaths of relatives and friends because it is impossible for a person to have a good reincarnation if his or her mind was filled with evil thoughts as a result of violent death. Consequently, spirits are believed to endlessly roam the earth. Many of the spirits that continue to haunt the dreams of survivors, therefore, are believed to be the spirits of dead persons, especially those who have committed suicide or who have been murdered.[61] Chea, for example, is a 48-year-old survivor of the Cambodian genocide. On one occasion during the Khmer Rouge regime, she witnessed three blindfolded persons, arms tied behind their backs, being escorted by soldiers. As the prisoners were taken to a clump of trees, Chea recognized them as friends from her village. She heard the sound of a skull being cracked with a club, followed by a desperate cry. The sounds were repeated twice more. Chea began shaking uncontrollably and was unable to return to work. The Khmer Rouge accused her of feigning illness and threatened to kill her. Even more terrified, Chea fell ill and, over the next few days, her hair began to fall out. Years later, Chea has recurring nightmares of the event. In her dreams, three demons approach her. One comes near her head, while the other two hold down Chea's arms and legs. During these experiences, which last for about half an hour, Chea tries to yell, but no sounds are forthcoming. She believes that the demons are in fact her three friends who were executed; they return to haunt her in her sleep to ensure she will not forget them.[62]

The lives of Buth, Choup, Chea, and many other survivors of war and genocide are reminders of the lasting mental legacy of mass violence. As Boehnlein writes, individuals who suffer a series of traumatic experiences are faced with the task of explaining to themselves or to others why the seemingly meaningless events occurred.[63]

The trauma of violence would continue after the genocide. Afterwards, living as refugees in Thailand or the Philippines, or in settlement countries such as the United States and Australia, survivors faced a new set of difficult and traumatic conditions. While fleeing as refugees, or staying in camps, survivors continued to experience or witness brutal murders, tortures, and rapes. Many more endured starvation and malnutrition. In many of these camps, diseases, including malaria, respiratory infections, and dysentery, were rampant. There was the added trauma for many Cambodians of being physically displaced from their homes, their country, and their relatives and friends.[64]

J. David Kinzie and James Boehnlein, two psychiatrists working in Oregon, summarize a number of Cambodian refugees whom they evaluated at a mental health clinic. They relate the case of a 39-year-old married woman who was evaluated for weight loss, poor concentration, profound sadness, and suicidal thoughts. As a child, this woman was raised in an orphanage following the death of her parents. Later, as an adult throughout the Khmer Rouge regime, she was separated from her husband and child. She endured long years of forced labor and starvation, and was subjected to repeated threats of execution. Having escaped to Thailand in 1980, she gave birth to a mentally retarded child, resultant from her malnourished condition. Once in the United States, she was increasingly unable to provide parenting for her children and often behaved violently toward them. She began to experience auditory hallucinations, nightmares, avoidance behavior, and startle reactions.[65] Another Cambodian refugee evaluated by Kinzie and Boehnlein was a 32-year-old married woman who complained of feeling frightened, irritable, easily startled, and fatigued. During the genocide, she had been separated from her husband and witnessed her mother dying of starvation and a sister being executed. Her three children also died of starvation during the time of the genocide. Having moved to the United States as a refugee, she became increasingly depressed and began to speak of suicide.[66]

Kinzie and Boehnlein conclude that when one listens to those who experienced the Cambodian genocide, one realizes that "the trauma actually did not end in 1979. . . . It continued for [them] during their attempts to survive the massive postinvasion chaos which included desperate attempts to find family members and make their way to refugee camps." And once in the camps, "life continued to be insecure for several years with food shortages, threats of being sent back to Cambodia, and uncertainty about being accepted into another country. Once in the United States, the refugees confronted other problems: a new language and culture, lack of employment, and chronic despair about the future of their families and their country."[67]

War, for those who experience it, does not end when the fighting stops. However, if the legacies of war and mass violence continue within survivors for many years afterwards, what of the children and grandchildren of these survivors? It is to this legacy I turn next.

THE HOLOCAUST AND TRANSGENERATIONAL TRAUMA

Perhaps no other episode of mass violence has received as much attention as the Holocaust.[68] And the raw numbers provide one indication of why this is so: Nearly one-third of the world's 19 million Jews—approximately six million people—perished in the Holocaust. Geographically, the figures are numbing, as numerous European countries lost at least 70 percent of their Jewish population. In Poland, for example, approximately 2.7 million Jews died, constituting 90 percent of the pre-war population; the death of 65,000 Jews in Yugoslavia, likewise, represented 90 percent of the pre-war total.[69]

Beyond the nearly incomprehensible magnitude of the killings lies an even more insidious facet of the Holocaust: the organized process of industrial killing. Although many hundreds of thousands of "ordinary" Germans took part in the Holocaust, the systematic slaughter was the result of a small group of decision-makers, including Adolf Hitler, Heinrich Himmler, Reinhard Heydrich, Joseph Goebbels, and Adolf Eichmann. These men, combined with an army of scientists and other academics, crafted a policy and constructed a physical infrastructure designed to efficiently exterminate an entire population.

Drawing on a bizarre mix of anti-Semitism and pseudo-scientific theories of eugenics, an attempt was made to rid Germany (in particular), but all of Europe (in general), of Jews and other "undesirable" populations (e.g., the Roma, homosexuals, and the mentally ill). Initial attempts to resolve the so-called "Jewish question" included massive deportations. Lucille Eichengreen, for example, grew up in a Jewish family in Hamburg, Germany, during the 1930s. She remembers, as a 17-year-old girl, the circumstances under which the German Jews were forced to live:

> Until 1933 it was a very nice comfortable life. . . . But once Hitler came to power the children that lived in the same buiding no longer spoke to us—they threw stones at us and called us names. And we couldn't understand what we had done to deserve this. So the question was always—why? And when we asked at home the answer was pretty much, "It's a passing phase—it'll normalize."[70]

But it did not normalize; it worsened, rapidly. Jews were forcibly removed from their homes, families were separated, jobs were lost. Entire communities were uprooted and sent to labor camps and factories. Between 1939 and 1941, in particular, the Nazi state set in motion a vast program of social engineering, whereupon hundreds of thousands of Jews were to be resettled throughout Europe.

Aside from deportation programs, German officials utilized sterilization campaigns and other medical "practices" to prevent "unwanted" peoples from reproducing and "infecting" later generations. And then, sometime in 1941, a decision was reached whereupon the Nazi leaders settled on the "Final Solution:" the wholesale annihilation through murder of the Jews. As Christopher Browning explains, this policy entailed "a program of systematic and total mass murder, to begin and be completed as soon as feasibly possible."[71]

A series of camps was established, interconnected by railway, to transport millions of people to gas chambers for mass execution. A cadre of chemical scientists, engineers, and other academics converged to develop the most "efficient" means to kill people and to dispose of their bodies. Dr. Albert Widmann, a Nazi member from the Technical Institute of the Criminal Police, for example, experimented with a range of techniques to kill large numbers of people. One of the first methods Widmann devised was simply to blow people up. To test this method, he corralled several mentally ill patients into a bunker, along with several packets of explosives. One witness to the experiment described what happened:

> The sight was atrocious. The explosion hadn't been powerful enough. Some wounded came out of the dugout crawling and crying. . . . The bunker had totally collapsed. . . . Body parts were scattered on the ground and hanging in the trees. On the next day, we collected the body parts and threw them into the bunker. Those parts that were too high in the trees were left there.[72]

Realizing that explosives were an impractical solution to the problem of mass killings, Widmann turned to the use of gas. In this area, Widmann was in fact able to draw on his medical "training." Previously, Widmann had used bottled carbon monoxide as part of an adult euthanasia program. This technique proved impractical, however, and so other methods were sought. Ultimately, Karl Fritzsch, a deputy leader at Auschwitz, came upon the idea of using crystallized prussic acid—cyanide—to kill people.[73]

The camps operated on assembly-line procedures with large gas chambers that required limited manpower and would kill in relative secrecy. Jews and other peoples were rounded up throughout Europe and transported to the various camps that had been built. McKale provides a glimpse into the scale and scope of the infrastructure that served to facilitate the massive population movements: "Between the fall of 1941 and spring of 1945, more than 260 deportation trains hauled German, Austrian, and Protectorate Jews to the ghettos and extermination camps in Poland and Russia. Other trains took victims to Theresienstadt, the ghetto-transit camp near Prague for many elderly German Jews and decorated Jewish war veterans. Further, approximately 450 trains ran from Western and Southern Europe to the death camps: a minimum of 147 trains from Hungary, 87 from Holland, 76 from France, 63 from Slovakia, 27 from Belgium, 23 from Greece, 11 from Italy, 7 from Bulgaria, and 6 from Croatia."[74]

The Holocaust involved not only the intentional and planned slaughter of an entire people; it also included a psychological component. Apart from the intentional murder of millions of Jews and other selected populations, people were also subjected to inhumane practices that were designed to destroy the individual's personality and identity.[75] Zofia Szałek

Figure 2.2
A young girl stands in front of the crematoriums at the Dachau death camp. Kind permission of Dr. Scott Sheridan.

was an 11-year-old girl who worked in Chełmno, a death camp located near Łódź, Poland:

> They [the Jews] were terribly beaten. It was winter when they came, they wore wooden clogs. . . . Here they used to undress. There was an enormous pile of those clothes. . . . Those who were already undressed were herded into the lorries. What screaming was going on! How terribly they were screaming—it was impossible to bear it! Once they brought children and the

Figure 2.3
The Memorial to Murdered Jews, Berlin, Germany. Kind permission of
Dr. Scott Sheridan.

children shouted. My mother heard it. She said the children were
calling, "Mummy, save me!"[76]

Tragically, people like Zofia are not the only victims to suffer
from the traumatic legacy of mass violence. People born years
or even decades after the traumatic event may exhibit symptoms of post-traumatic stress. Simply put, psychiatrists and
psychologists have identified a "transgenerational" effect of
trauma, suggesting that the psychological effects of experiencing war and genocide may be transferred to the second *as
well as* the third generations.[77] Studies, for example, indicate
the existence of "secondary traumatization;" of those not
exposed, but exhibiting symptoms of post-traumatic stress.[78]
The spouses and partners of combat veterans, for example,
have reported living in an atmosphere of fear, social isolation,

and self-doubt; they experience feelings of loneliness and separation in the face of reduced communication, emotional withdrawal, and the psychological numbing of the veteran. Moreover, it was not uncommon for partners or children to feel anxious or confused, to suffer from low self-esteem and a loss of identity. Spouses especially may suffer feelings of guilt and helplessness for not being able to "heal" their partner.[79]

Numerous studies of both the children and grandchildren of Holocaust survivors indicated heightened awareness of their parents'/grandparents' survivor status. These relatives also exhibit an "overidentification" with their relatives' experiences, and a general fear and mistrust of people.[80] In her qualitative study of the intergenerational transmission of trauma, Rachel Lev-Wiesel finds that trauma was perpetuated across three generations: both the children and grandchildren of people who had undergone significant life traumas appeared to be affected. Indeed, later generations of Holocaust survivors reported having nightmares of themselves being chased by Nazis, or of being haunted by the physical separation from loved ones.[81]

The writings of Eva Hoffman, among others, are particular salient.[82] The daughter of Holocaust survivors, Hoffman poignantly writes of the grief and anxiety of growing up as part of the "post"-Holocaust generation. She writes:

I spent much of my childhood waiting for the war. Waiting for it to manifest itself again, to emerge from where it lurked with its violent, ravaging claws. Waiting for danger and destruction, which were the fundamental human condition, to trample the fragile coverlet of peace. I kept anticipating, with a fearful anxiety I took as normal, the death of my parents. After all, every one of the adults who had once formed our family group, and to whom my parents so often referred, was dead.[83]

For Hoffman, the war and genocide were ever-present; they were simply part of her life growing up. And the violence that was her parents' reality so many years earlier became her own reality—a reality that greatly informed her own world-view. She explains:

> Life itself, for children born into families like mine, could seem a tenuous condition, a buffeted island in the infinite ocean of death. The Holocaust was not yet distinguished from "war" in anyone's mind; but the intimations of mortality that followed from it were part of my earliest perceptions of the world as I transformed the felt traces of a historical event into a kind of story about the basic elements and shape of the world . . .[84]

The writings of Hoffman indicate the struggles involved in reconciling a traumatic event that impacted one's life indirectly, long after the event had unfolded. And yet, such reconciliation is based on imperfect knowledge. Hoffman writes:

> A consciousness of war, in its most extreme and cruel manifestations, seemed to come with the first stirrings of consciousness itself. And yet I had no direct experience of extremity or collective violence. . . . The paradoxes of indirect knowledge haunt many of us who came after. The formative events of the twentieth century have crucially informed our biographies and psyches, threatening sometimes to overshadow and overwhelm our lives. But we did not see them, suffer through them, experience their impact directly. Our relationship to them has been defined by our very "post-ness," and by the powerful but mediated forms of knowledge that have followed from it.[85]

Carolyn Nordstrom explains that "violence is set in motion with physical carnage, but that it also doesn't stop there.

Violence reconfigures its victims and the social milieu that hosts them. It isn't a passing phenomenon that momentarily challenges a stable system, leaving a scar but no lasting effects. Rather, violence becomes a determining fact in shaping reality as people will know it, in the future."[86] In the minds of both "combatants" and "non-combatants" who endure war, but also in the minds of later generations, conflict never really ends. For many survivors, it is re-fought every night in their dreams, it is re-experienced with the sounds of a knock on a door, it is re-lived in frightening clarity. As Helene Berman concludes, when one considers "the large number of people affected by war over the last century, military trauma must be recognized as a common part of human experience."[87] For many, it is a global reality, and a daily reality, and it continues as a legacy of warfare.

But the war goes on; and we will have to bind up for years to come the many, sometimes ineffaceable, wounds that the . . . onslaught has inflicted . . .[1]

On June 2, 1990 Chisola Jorgeta Pezo[2] and her friend, Zhinga, set off down a well-trod path to dig cassava roots near the Kavungo River, from which her village takes its name. Food was scarce; Angola was in the midst of a long-running civil war and, although it was dangerous to move about, the villagers of Kavungo were forced to take risks. The path from Kavungo to the cassava field was not known to have been mined. But then again, with landmines one is never quite certain. And so it was that Chisola's life intersected with the remnants of a globalized arms industry that continues to sow death and destruction throughout much of the "lesser developed" world.

Having only walked about six-tenths of a mile out of the village, Chisola stepped on a landmine. As with most survivors of blast explosions, Chisola neither saw the flash, heard the explosion, nor remembers the event. It is left to Philip Winslow to reconstruct what happened:

> The weight of her foot depressed the pressure plate onto the steel spring. As the spring compressed, it stretched the rubber band holding two plastic collars against the striker pin. When the collars popped out of the way, the spring let the pin hit the top of

the detonator, which exploded and ignited the block of explosive in the mine body. . . . The main explosion shattered the Bakelite mine case and created a high-pressure wave that roared upward and blasted her right foot off just above the ankle. The blast wave, moving faster than the speed of sound, continued its upward rush between the layers of tissue and through the bones and compartments of muscle in the lower leg. The wave took with it carbonized fragments of the mine casing, bone chips, stones and dirt, and bits of leather sandal, hurtling the fragments and whatever bacteria lived on them deep into the wound. The blast wave moved with such force that it stripped soft tissue from the bone and damaged muscle far up the leg. The dead muscles provided the bacteria that had been propelled into the wound with a convenient supply of food. Infection set in rapidly as the bacteria began to multiply. The blast also tore pieces of flesh and muscle off five places on the inside of her left leg and the inside of her left wrist. If you look at the pattern and shape of the scars today, you nearly have a photograph of how her body was positioned at the instant the mine exploded.[3]

Nearly two decades after Chisola was injured, landmines continue to kill and injure women, men, and children in Angola as they go about their daily lives. Indeed, Angola is the most mine-affected country in sub-Saharan Africa and one of the most heavily mined countries in the world. According to a survey completed in May 2007, approximately 2.4 million people in Angola are affected by landmines; no province is free from the threat of these weapons.[4]

Beyond the borders of Angola, an estimated 60 to 70 million landmines lie in wait in over 90 countries and territories. In Afghanistan, for example, there are an estimated eight million landmines; four to six million landmines remain in Cambodia. In Colombia and Rwanda, Afghanistan and

Mozambique, the Sudan and Myanmar, landmines lie silently waiting.

The world over, every year, between 15,000 and 20,000 people are victims of landmines—approximately one person killed or injured every 30 minutes.[5] Indeed, landmines and other explosive remnants of war have killed and injured more people over the past 100 years than nuclear, chemical, and biological weapons combined.[6]

In 2006 civilians accounted for approximately 75 percent of all recorded casualties, with children accounting for over one-third of all civilian casualties. Such sweeping statistics, however, mask even more disturbing country-specific findings. In Afghanistan and Nepal, for example, children under 15 years of age comprise 59 and 53 percent of casualties, respectively.[7] One positive trend identified by the International Campaign to Ban Landmines (ICBL), however, is that the total number of casualties, at the global level, has been declining. In 2007, for example, there were a total of 5,751 casualties from landmines and other explosive remnants of war recorded in 68 countries. This total included 1,367 deaths and 4,296 injuries, with the status of the remaining 88 victims unknown. These numbers constitute a 16 percent decrease from 2005, when 6,873 casualties were recorded in 78 countries.[8] This decline is the result of many factors, including both ongoing demining operations and pro-active mine-awareness campaigns. Sadly, however, military operations underway at the time of this writing may signal an upward turn in years ahead.

The landmine crisis, however, cannot be defined solely by the number of mines laid, nor even of the bodies maimed or killed. Instead, the crisis must be viewed from the standpoint of people's everyday lives: entire families devastated, lands rendered inaccessible or unusable, and economies weakened. Jody Williams and Shawn Roberts write that "the post-conflict

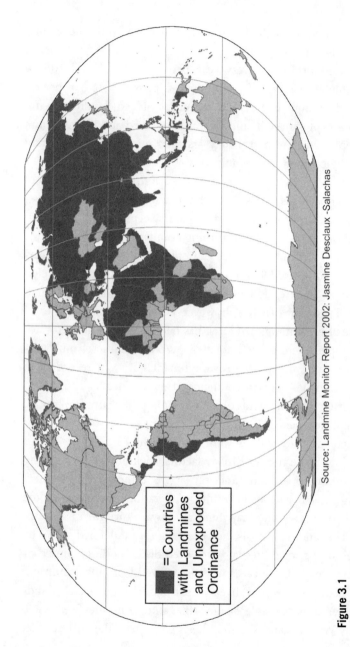

Source: Landmine Monitor Report 2002: Jasmine Desclaux -Salachas

Figure 3.1
Map of World Landmine Problem.

(Legend within image:)
■ = Countries with Landmines and Unexploded Ordinance

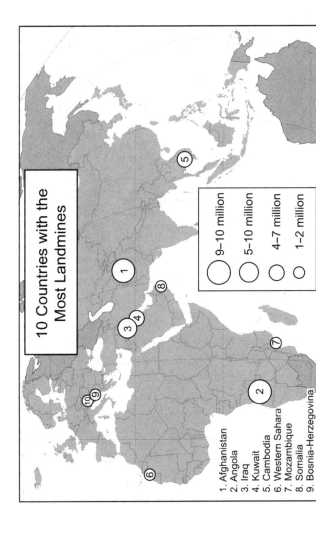

10 Countries with the Most Landmines

- 9–10 million
- 5–10 million
- 4–7 million
- 1–2 million

1. Afghanistan
2. Angola
3. Iraq
4. Kuwait
5. Cambodia
6. Western Sahara
7. Mozambique
8. Somalia
9. Bosnia-Herzegovina
10. Croatia

Source: www.cnn.com/WORLD/9710/10/land.mines/#1

Figure 3.2
Map of 10 Most Affected Landmine Countries.

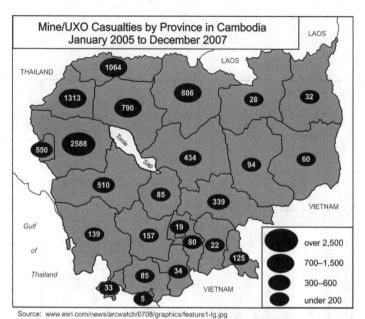

Source: www.esri.com/news/arcwatch/0708/graphics/feature1-lg.jpg

Figure 3.3
Map of Landmine Casualties in Cambodia.

humanitarian cost of continued landmine use [and other munitions] is not a 'potential concern' but a social and economic disaster for the millions of people affected by their use around the world." They state that "because the consequences of landmine use are not conflict-limited, societies are affected by landmines for generations. Landmines are not simply a momentary crisis for a country in conflict—they are a long-term impediment to complete peace and post-conflict redevelopment. People now living with landmines are significantly affected by their use. But so are their children. And their children's children."[9]

In this chapter I consider the legacy of landmines and other explosive remnants of war (ERW) in post-conflict societies.

My principal concern lies in the bodily, social, and environmental impacts of landmines and other explosive ordnances. My attention is directed to both the short-term horrors and long-term consequences. Most germane to this chapter is the understanding that these weapons constitute the most significant legacy of modern warfare. With an average lifespan of 50 to 100 years, landmines and other ERW continue to kill and maim civilians long after the armies have been demobilized, peace treaties signed, and monuments to the war dead erected.

THE REALITY OF LANDMINES

Although historians have traced the use of landmine-type weapons to both ancient China and Rome, it was not until the twentieth century that the "age of land mine warfare" arrived in full force.[10] Indeed, apart from Mikhail Kalashnikov's AK-47, perhaps no other weapon epitomizes late twentieth- and early twenty-first-century warfare as does the landmine.[11]

Since the Second World War, upwards of half a billion landmines have been laid. Although initially considered cowardly weapons by the military establishment, landmines have become an accepted—and bitterly defended—component of many of the world's armies.[12] Established military doctrine, as espoused now by the United States and other industrialized countries, upholds landmines as a crucial factor in the shaping of the battlefield.[13] Landmines, defined as "areal denial weapons," are justified on the grounds that they serve a primarily defensive purpose. The presence of a minefield is intended to prevent, restrict, or inhibit enemy access to particular locations. Minefields also force enemy troops to either slow down (thus providing the mine-laying forces time to retreat or regroup) or to redirect their movement into "killing zones" or sites of ambush.

The military use of landmines, however, has rapidly devolved from a purported defensive function to that of an offensive capability. As the nature of warfare changes, so too does the use of landmines. Throughout the 1960s and continuing to the present, wars have increasingly been characterized as irregular. Unlike the wars of earlier generations, which generally pitted two opposing armies against one another, today's conflicts are less organized, though no less violent. Earl Conteh-Morgan explains that in irregular conflicts, combatants "are characterized by a lack of formal military training. . . . Child soldiers form a substantial segment of the combatants in irregular warfare." Furthermore, where irregular warfare occurs, "members of the armed forces exhibit a degree of lawlessness, indiscipline, and professional incompetence that makes them indistinguishable from the irregular forces they fight against. Embodied in the conduct of irregular warfare is the presence of an extraordinary level of disorganized violence directed by the combatants toward each other and particularly toward the civilian population."[14] This has significant implications in the doctrine of landmine warfare. Whereas "in conventional war, rules, regulations and treaties may hold," this is certainly not the case in guerrilla and most "civil" wars.[15]

In the horrific conflagrations that have engulfed many states of Central Africa, for example, landmines have been utilized specifically to terrorize civilian populations. Over the past 60 years, nearly every country of sub-Saharan Africa has been touched by war. In the wars of Africa and elsewhere, landmines have become routine. Lightweight and easily portable, these weapons have been employed by both government and rebel groups haphazardly. Mines have been laid in and around schools and markets, bridges and roads, rivers and streams, forests and fields. It is estimated that 20 percent of the region's population now lives in countries which are formally at war; low-intensity conflict remains endemic in many other "non-warring" states.[16] And these decades of conventional warfare, genocide, and guerrilla fighting have taken a heavy toll on the population. In what some authors describe as Africa's "World War," the price paid by children has been tragic.[17] An estimated two million children have been killed, with an additional six million disabled, 12 million homeless, one million orphaned or separated from their families, and ten million suffering from psychological trauma as a result of their exposure to armed conflict.[18]

There is a technological explanation for the proliferation of landmines: they are cheap and easy to manufacture.[19] Depending on the model—and between 340 and 360 types of mines have been designed—manufactured landmines may cost as little as US$3 to produce; other, more sophisticated models might approach US$30. And newer models are being developed every year. Not counting home-made or "improvised explosive devices" (IEDs), landmines are manufactured in nearly 50 countries, with the majority of mines designed, produced, and exported by just a handful of states: the United States, Russia, and China.[20]

At the most basic level, a landmine consists of a plastic or metal casing, which houses a detonator (or firing mechanism), booster charge, and main explosive charge. Beyond that, there are two basic types of landmines, based on the primary *intended* target: anti-personnel landmines (APMs) and anti-vehicle landmines (AVMs).[21] Anti-personnel landmines are designed to kill or injure soldiers.[22] However, anti-personnel landmines are often designed to inflict severe injuries as opposed to killing their victims outright. The military rationale is that other, non-injured soldiers are diverted to provide treatment to and evacuation of the victim. In contrast to APMs, anti-vehicle mines are designed to destroy or incapacitate vehicles such as armored trucks or tanks. This does not mean, however, that people are unable to detonate AVMs. Indeed, the pressure plates of many AVMs can be detonated with pressures of less than 330 pounds per square inch. Humans can easily generate this amount of pressure when running or jumping from a vehicle.[23]

Three principal types of APMs are recognized: blast mines, bounding mines, and directional mines. Blast mines operate through explosive forces; these are not necessarily designed to kill victims, but rather to inflict serious injury, resultant from traumatic amputations (i.e., the blowing apart of limbs from torsos). Injuries from blast mines are particularly severe when the victim places his or her heel directly on the mine, thereby causing the force of the detonation to travel upward, shattering ankle and leg bones.[24]

Bounding mines, conversely, explode various fragments into the air upon detonation, usually to a height of about one meter. When detonated, the blast diffuses outward and upward in an arc, with lethal fragmentations striking the victim's (or victims') head and torso. Unlike blast mines, bounding mines are designed primarily to kill people as opposed to injuring them. Moreover, these mines are also designed to take out multiple victims through a single explosion. Bounding mines are frequently equipped with time-delay fuses, thereby ensuring a wider "killing range."[25]

Directional mines are designed to fire a concentrated spread of fragments in a pre-determined direction and pattern. One of the most widely known directional mines is the U.S.-produced M-18, or "Claymore" mine. The Claymore consists of a plastic, convex-shaped pack containing explosive and 700 steel balls, each weighing about 0.03 ounces (0.75 grams). Claymores are planted into the ground via two sets of metal prongs. When detonated, either by tripwire or command, the Claymore blasts out the metal balls in a 60-degree arc upward to a height of 6½ feet (2 meters), and a horizontal arc spanning 165 feet (50 meters) at a range of 165 feet. Directional mines are used to cover routes, and as ambush devices, with a clear intent to kill or wound large numbers of people through a single explosion.[26]

CLUSTER BOMBS AND OTHER EXPLOSIVE REMNANTS OF WAR

Aside from conventional landmines, other explosive devices, known as "explosive remnants of war" (or ERW), function as de facto landmines. Defined by the International Campaign to Ban Landmines (ICBL) as "unexploded and/or abandoned ordnance left behind after a conflict," ERW include unexploded artillery shells, grenades, mortars, rockets, air-dropped bombs, and cluster munitions.[27] Heuristically, ERW are often classified into two main types: unexploded ordnance (UXO) and abandoned explosive ordnance (AXO). UXO refers to unstable explosives (e.g., cluster bombs) that failed to detonate as intended. Consequently, these bombs remain behind and become de facto landmines. Conversely, AXO includes explosive ordnance left behind after the conflict and is no longer under the control of the departing militaries. These munitions may or may not have been primed, fused, or otherwise readied for use. Regardless, AXO remain dangerous to civilian populations.[28]

The ICBL is blunt in its assessment of the global reality of these weapons: ERWs are very much products of modern warfare and have proliferated in part because of the increased tolerance and acceptance of civilian casualties, and, indeed, the deliberate targeting of civilians, either for direct killing and wounding, or through fear-inducement.[29] Cluster submunitions in particular epitomize the various forms of indiscriminate weaponry.[30]

Cluster bombs belong to a family of munitions called "fragmentation" bombs. As the name suggests, fragmentation bombs are those explosives that disperse fragments (shrapnel) outward upon detonation. When an explosive inside a metal case is detonated, the explosive is rapidly converted into a gas. The subsequent outward pressure of the gas causes the casing to rupture, propelling the fragments of the case at a high velocity. The fragments, in effect, become deadly shards of hot metal, knifing through flesh and bone.

Fragmentation bombs were initially developed during the Second World War and later modified during the Korean War. Early munitions were unsophisticated, however, in that the "natural" fragmentation of the metallic casing was sporadic and inefficient. The explosion of a Second World War artillery shell, for example, produced a range of fragments, some large but others so small as to be ineffective in wounding or killing enemy combatants. Consequently, scientists working at the Development Center at China Lake, California, and at Eglin Air Force Base, Florida, made progress in terms of controlled fragmentation.[31] Controlled fragmentation bombs attempt to reduce the random factor in the dispersal of casing fragments. Researchers discovered that by scoring or grooving the case, they were able to predictably control the dispersal of fragments. Depending on the dispensing system, as well as the height of detonation, bombs could be designed to disperse fragments in various patterns (i.e., oval, linear, or figure-eight). A more lethal discovery, however, came when scientists realized that they could insert other bombs within larger bomb casings. Thus was born the cluster bomb.

Cluster bombs consist of metal cases (the Cluster Bomb Unit, or CBU) containing, on average, approximately 650 bomblets, known as bomb live units (BLUs). Each BLU, roughly the size of a tennis ball and weighing about one pound, contains about 300 metal fragments. Dropped from a fighter or bomber aircraft, the outer dispenser splits apart, releasing its contents. The small bomblets are grooved in such a way as to fragment before, during, or after impact, depending on the fuse employed. The casing of the BLU, moreover, is designed to fragment into smaller, lethal pieces. And the impact can be truly devastating. If all of the bomblets detonate from a single CBU, some 200,000 metallic fragments are propelled outward, killing or wounding people over a wide area. For example, some cluster bombs are designed to disperse their fragments so as to kill or wound people at an effective range of 300 meters by 1,000 meters.[32]

Equally troubling is that many bomblets, such as the bright yellow CBU-87 CEM (combined effects munition) that has been widely used in Afghanistan, look like toys or even some humanitarian aid packages. Oleg Bilukha and his co-researchers, for example, found that of the 1,636 individuals injured by landmines and unexploded ordnance in Afghanistan between March 2001 and June 2002, 46 percent were younger than 16 years; the highest cohort was among those aged 7 to 15 years. Furthermore, among injuries to children and adolescents younger than 16 years for whom activity was known, playing and tending animals were the most common activities.[33]

Cluster bombs, similar to landmines, are considered "indiscriminate" killers. The widespread "killing range" of cluster bombs almost guarantees that people other than soldiers will be hurt. Of more concern is that cluster bombs frequently have high "dud" rates, meaning that not all bomblets actually detonate upon impact. Consequently, these live bombs litter the landscape and remain as landmines. And in many regions, these explosive remnants pose more of a risk than landmines. In both Laos and Vietnam, for example, national and local surveys find that over 90 percent—and quite possibly as high as 97 percent—of remaining ordnance in the ground consists of cluster bombs, grenades, aircraft bombs, shells, rockets, and other UXO.[34] Laos, in particular, has been described as the most heavily bombed country in the world.[35] Official U.S. records indicate that over 80 million bomblets were dropped over Laos between 1964 and 1973. Of these bomblets, an estimated 30 percent are believed to have failed to detonate, thus leaving a monumental legacy that continues to kill and maim civilians long after the war has ended. Indeed, surveys indicate that 87,213 square kilometers of land, out of a country-wide total of 236,800 square kilometers, are at risk from UXO contamination.[36]

The dangers posed by these indiscriminate weapons are not simply the result of wars long gone. Indeed, cluster bombs are still widely used in conflicts around the world, including Afghanistan, Iraq, Tajikistan, Georgia, and Lebanon. During the summer of 2006, for example, fighting between Israeli forces and the Hezbollah militia in southern Lebanon resulted in 1,500 (mostly civilian) deaths and the displacement of approximately 900,000 Lebanese and 300,000 Israeli civilians. However, throughout the month-long conflict, an estimated 1,800 cluster bombs—containing over 1.2 million bomblets— were fired into Lebanon. While these explosives immediately damaged the local infrastructure (i.e., hospitals, schools, bridges, roads, factories, airports, residential houses, and seaports), the legacy of their use will continue to plague the rebuilding of Lebanon for years, if not decades, to come. According to the United Nations, an estimated 40 percent of all munitions dropped on Lebanon remain on the ground as unexploded submunitions. By October 2006, two months after the cessation of hostilities, a total of 770 cluster-bomb strike locations had been identified in southern Lebanon.

Within these communities, 20 fatalities and 120 injuries had already been reported. Children accounted for one-third of all casualties.[37] Rob Nixon describes one such casualty. Marwa al-Miri was a ten-year-old girl who lived in southern Lebanon. After the war she was playing in her village with her friends and relatives. On one day, no different from any other, Marwa spotted a shiny can and playfully tossed it to her friend. However, the can—which was, in fact, a cluster bomb—exploded, ripping through her friend's stomach and also blasting shrapnel into Marwa's legs and her cousin's chest.[38]

THE DAILY REALITY OF A GLOBAL PROBLEM

Imagine that whenever you leave the house you have to be careful where you tread. Imagine that every time you dig the garden to plant flowers and vegetables, it may prove fatal. Imagine, as a parent, no matter how many times you have warned the children, you worry that every time they go off to play they might be maimed or killed. And imagine having no choice but to live in constant fear.[39]

And what could I say to that little girl I saw . . . who lost the fingers of her right hand while playing?[40]

As Ian Brown explains, for many people around the world, there is no need to imagine these scenarios. They remain part of everyday life. In fact, in many post-conflict societies, co-existing with mines and other explosive remnants of war is becoming the norm rather than the dreaded, horrible way of life of a few.[41]

Anti-personnel landmines and cluster bombs are designed to either kill or injure people. And to this end, these devices are extremely efficient. Unfortunately, too many discussions on the efficacy of landmines and other indiscriminate weapons fail to convey their bodily effects. Consequently, I begin with a simple question: What exactly happens when a person encounters one of these weapons?

To begin, injuries differ significantly depending on the type of landmine or other explosive device encountered.[42] Blast mines, for example, generally result in multiple injuries and traumatic amputations. Ronald Glasser describes the death of Maria Martinez, who died in 2005 in an ambush while serving in Iraq. Martinez was riding in an unarmored Humvee with an open back. Layers of sandbags had been placed on the floorboard for added protection, although it was widely recognized that these vehicles were especially vulnerable to blast mines and other IEDs. On the day of the ambush, a remote-controlled roadside bomb was detonated as Martinez's Humvee was slowing down to make a right-hand turn. The bomb, which had been placed inside

Figure 3.4
Within Cambodia, landmines are an all-too-real legacy of a war long since over. Kind permission of the author.

a concrete curb, exploded with such force that the Humvee was lifted into the air. Martinez survived the initial blast, only to die of her injuries hours later. According to the pathological diagnosis, Martinez's body exhibited significant damage resultant from the blast. Her corpse revealed external head trauma with a dislocated jaw, enucleated left eye, and evulsed left maxillary sinus. There were numerous fragmentation wounds on the face and neck. Her right leg and left foot were completely severed; fingers from both hands were also traumatically amputated. The cause of death was multiple organ failure.[43]

Unlike blast mines, bounding fragmentation mines or flechette-filled cluster bombs most often produce multiple penetrating injuries to the torso.[44] When a high-velocity projectile, such as a steel pellet from a bomblet, passes through the body, it pushes aside the soft tissues in its immediate path. These tissues, in turn, impart velocity to tissues further away. A "temporary" cavity, several times the size of the wound track, is formed. This rapid expansion of the bodily cavity crushes other organs and tissues, fractures bones, and damages nerves. Within a fraction of a second the fragmentation literally explodes within the body.[45]

From the initial explosion, the social and economic costs— not to mention the psychological and emotional costs—of the mine or other explosive increase rapidly. As Paul Davies explains:

From the moment a man, woman or child stands on a mine three or four others will be involved in the immediate evacuation and in the application of first aid. Many others will be involved in the transfer to the hospital, the operation, the post-operative and rehabilitative care, the provision of prostheses, the provision of benefits and pensions, etc. The financial costs of all these resources, and the long-term opportunity costs of the injury, are all parts of the landmine equation.[46]

Initial medical treatment of mine victims is often inadequate, provided only by friends, family members or neighbors. Coupled with the fact that many mine-affected regions suffer from poor transportation networks, it is often difficult to transport the injured to medical facilities. Indeed, it is not uncommon for survivors to be transported by cart, or on horse- or camel-back, over rudimentary roads or footpaths. In many countries, landmine victims may wait hours before receiving any formal medical care. In Angola, it is estimated that only 28 percent of casualties arrive at hospital within six hours of the explosion.[47] Consequently, pre-hospital fatality rates are quite high for mine-affected countries. It is not uncommon, for example, to find that well over half of all landmine victims die before they are able to receive medical care. Indeed, one study of victims in Mozambique found that 75 percent of all deaths caused by landmines occurred before the victim reached the hospital.[48]

Having arrived at a medical site, the prospect for survival and recovery does not always increase substantially. Again, given that these societies are often economically impoverished and physically devastated by conflict, medical facilities are generally inadequate. Hospitals may lack key resources, including blood supplies, surgical instruments, x-ray film, anesthesia, and antibiotics. In addition, there may be a lack of qualified medical personnel who are trained to deal with the traumatic injuries resultant from landmines and other explosive devices. As Roberts and Williams identify, "modern anti-personnel mines inflict much more severe injuries than wounds made by other conventional weapons. Because this is only recently understood, most medical personnel have not been trained in the surgical techniques necessary to adequately treat landmine injuries."[49]

Victims of landmines (especially) but also of other explosive devices exert a tremendous toll on medical facility resources. Injuries resulting from mines often require substantially more units of blood; multiple surgeries are also necessary. Fiona King explains:

> Aside from tissue/organ repair surgical procedure with mine injury is based on the principle of eliminating the dead tissue around the wound as well as any infected material within it. This process is called debridement, and aims to prevent infection occurring. An important feature of fragment wounds is their degree of contamination by foreign bodies. This is especially so with mine injuries where soil and other fragments are blasted into tissue, in particular the leg standing on a mine. An important determination of infection is the delay between the injury and access to antibiotic treatment (hospital/first aid). An upper limit of 6 hours' delay before antibiotic prophylaxis appears to be "the safety net."[50]

For those victims who survive the crucial first hours, extended hospital stays are necessary; hence families are forced to pay disproportionately high medical bills because of the protracted nature of their injuries. Indeed, surveys often find that households may spend an amount equivalent of up to two-and-one-half times their annual income on immediate costs related to the mine injuries.[51] As a result, it is not uncommon for mine victims to prematurely discharge themselves. And even if families are able to pay for extended treatment, they often must make hard choices, such as paying for either pain control medicines and antibiotics or food.[52]

After being discharged from hospital care, regardless of

length of stay, survivors of landmines and other remnants of war require long-term, if not lifetime, care. Depending on the nature of the injury (e.g., limb loss, blindness, deafness), survivors often suffer from chronic pain, infections, and even the stigmatization of being "disabled." Indeed, it is a tragic and sobering observation that a person surviving a landmine or UXO accident may actually increase the burden on his or her household and society. By design, landmines and many types of cluster bombs are meant to injure rather than kill. Consequently, the ongoing impact of these munitions and weapons on civilian populations after the conflict can be significant.

The vast majority of casualties to landmines and UXO are not soldiers. The victims are most often "ordinary" people who are simply engaged in everyday activities of economic necessity: farming, tending animals; collecting food, water, and wood. Study after study finds the same results: casualties are disproportionately skewed toward young adult men and women. This results from the simple fact of the activities (i.e., farming, gathering of water and wood, and clearing of forests) in which these individuals engage: the places where these activities are carried out are the most heavily mined areas. In Mozambique, for example, there were 2,376 deaths and 2,112 amputations recorded between 1980 and 1993. Most victims were under 45 years of age, and were survived by spouses. They also had, on average, three children. The story is repeated throughout the world, wherever landmines and other ERW are found. In Chechnya, 3,021 individuals were injured or killed by landmines and unexploded ordnance between 1994 and 2005. Of these casualties, 26 percent were among children under 18 years of age.[53]

Often, these victims are the primary wage-earners for their households. Even if these men and women survive the blast, their potential for income-generation is significantly reduced.

Their ability to earn a livelihood is irrevocably altered.[54] Given their injuries—both physical and psychological—mine survivors are often unable to return to their daily activities. Moreover, following months (if not longer) of rehabilitation, many mine victims find that even if they are physically able to work, they cannot return to their pre-accident employment because their jobs have been given to someone else. A consistent finding among surveys of landmine survivors is that the income level of affected families is frequently worse when compared to pre-accident levels.[55] In short, therefore, the human cost is thus decidedly higher than a "simple" count of casualties might suggest. Those who do survive represent not only an immediate loss of income-potential, but also constitute a chronic burden in terms of long-term health costs for the household and society.[56]

It bears repeating that societies impacted by the legacy of landmines and ERW are often recovering from years, if not decades, of war. The violence of military conflict has already exerted a tremendous toll on these societies, including the destruction of existing infrastructure, i.e., education, transportation, and health care systems.[57] Moreover, medical supplies and facilities are often scarce or unavailable, and key medical personnel may have been killed, injured or exiled.[58] To these fragile societies, weakened by years of warfare, the reality and burden of landmines and other remnants of war is added.

There are an estimated 473,000 landmine survivors in the world, for example, many of whom require lifelong medical care and assistance.[59] This demand creates a huge economic burden on both households and societies, many of which are ill-prepared and ill-equipped to rebuild after war. The provision of assistance to mine survivors—no matter how minimal—drains societies' resource potential, thus making subsistence and sustainable development difficult, and perpetuating existing levels of underdevelopment.[60]

When a large proportion of people are disabled within a country, the ability of that country to recover from the legacy of war is hindered.[61] Although it is difficult to place a value on human suffering, it is instructive to consider the economic costs born by society. In Bosnia and Herzegovina, for example, Shannon Mitchell calculates that each year landmine accidents cause serious injuries that result in an extra US$177,877 worth of medical expenses. This money, she notes, would be able to pay for the annual salaries of about 60 general practice physicians for one year. Furthermore, she finds, overall, that the mine-related deaths of and injuries to children and adults in Bosnia and Herzegovina amounts to nearly US$1,577,954 *each year* in the form of lost human capital.[62]

Many medical establishments throughout landmine-contaminated regions are ill-equipped, understaffed, and simply overwhelmed. Landmine-injury victims require nearly three times as many units of blood; these transfusions, conducted in over-burdened health clinics, often contribute to the spread of diseases, such as syphilis, hepatitis, malaria, and HIV/AIDS.[63] Landmine patients also require considerably more surgical procedures than other patients. In general, amputations require at least two operations: the initial amputation and then a second operation, several days later, consisting of a "delayed primary closure," when the wound is finally closed. This delay allows the swelling to go down and ensures that the final stump heals properly, leaving good skin and muscle cover of the bone.[64] Mine victims also typically require longer hospital stays—an added cost often shouldered by the household.

Given that mine injuries frequently consume a disproportionate quantity of hospital resources, compared with other injuries, these costs represent diverted funds. Were it not for the legacy of landmines and ERW, these funds could alternatively be spent on, for example, vaccinations, nutrition programs, and sanitation systems.

There are also more wide-ranging economic costs associated with the presence of landmines. As indicated earlier, a fundamental purpose of landmines is to deny the enemy access to certain areas. During conflicts, vital infrastructure installations, such as bridges, electrical towers, water and sewage treatment plants, hospitals, and even schools, are frequently mined. Until cleared, these areas remain off-limits. When people are denied safe access to areas for farming, grazing, schooling, and other socioeconomic activities, the ability of that society to begin the processes of rehabilitation, reconstruction, and development are significantly reduced.[65] It is estimated, for example, that landmines have restricted

Figure 3.5
Landmines in the process of being cleared, Battambang Province, Cambodia. Kind permission of the author.

agricultural production on a land area equivalent to six percent of the 1,474 million hectares of land cultivated globally.[66] In terms of economic loss, studies suggest that, were it not for landmines, agricultural productivity could have increased by 88 to 200 percent in Afghanistan, by 135 percent in Cambodia, 11 percent in Bosnia, and 3.6 percent in Mozambique, compared to pre-war levels.[67]

When landmines or other ERW restrict access to arable or pastoral lands, the people who depend on those lands are forced to use (or abuse) marginal lands. In Angola, despite abundant fertile lands and adequate precipitation, famine is killing thousands of people in part because of the presence of landmines.[68]

Decreases in the overall availability of land have also been found to increase the need to practice more intensive agriculture, or perhaps to rely on expensive applications of chemical or biological supplements. At a most basic level, these practices may endanger the health of the soil (i.e., rapid exhaustion of the soil's fertility) and, in addition, the excessive use of chemical and other applicants may contribute to accumulation within ecosystems and long-term health impacts on human societies.[69]

Landmines and other ERW contribute to land degradation in a multitude of ways: soil degradation, deforestation, pollution; biodiversity and ecosystem loss.[70] Certainly upon detonation, there is the immediate destruction of vegetation and the compaction and/or disruption of the soil. These contribute to an overall decline in the productivity of the soils and may prevent agricultural or pasture lands from returning to pre-explosion levels of productivity. Studies also indicate that landmines, including those remaining unexploded in the ground, may contribute to the persistence and bioaccumulation of toxic substances.[71]

Figure 3.6
The detritus of war. Kind permission of the author.

It may seem that the adverse affects on an area's soil are a minor concern when set against the horrific impacts on human bodies. However, this speaks to the cumulative effects of landmines and ERWs. Consider a farmer who is injured. His or her family must still till the land and try to make a living. And yet, the deterioration of the soil structure due to the explosion, and the possibility of chemical contamination (see below), may have significant and sustained impacts on the erodibility and productivity of the field. A.A. Berhe explains that when "a 250g antipersonnel landmine detonates, it can create a crater with a diameter of approximately 30cm. The explosion has the ability to facilitate removal and displacement of topsoil while forming a raised circumference around the crater and compaction of soil into the side of the crater." The cumulative negative impacts on the soil and thus on the field are augmented depending on the type of the soil as well as the slope of the land. The adverse effects are greater, for example, in dry, loosely compacted and exposed desert soils but are generally less severe in humid soils. Flooding and soil erosion are also more pronounced in areas with steep slopes.[72]

Depending on the density of minefields, the type and composition of landmines (and ERW), and the length, amount and degree of exposure, landmines and ERW may pose serious pollution threats. It is known, for example, that explosive materials may leach into soils, enter ground waters, and accumulate in plant roots and edible portions of crop plants as well as animals.[73] Depending on the specific contaminants, people living in these areas may be more susceptible to certain types of cancers, congenital birth defects, skin irritations, and so forth.[74]

Of course, chemical contamination occurs not only through the degradation of landmines, but also of other forms of munitions. And, in fact, studies indicate that the threat of pollutants continues for many decades. The region around Ypres in Belgium, for example, exhibits elevated levels of copper concentration, resultant from the intense fighting that occurred there during the First World War. Between 1914 and 1918 an estimated 1.45 billion shells were fired by German, French, and British militaries; around 95 percent of these shells were conventional explosive shells, while the remainder were filled with toxic gases. Each shell, both conventional and toxic, contained sizeable amounts of copper. Decades later, this copper continues to contaminate the soil.[75] Likewise, many of the soils throughout western Slovenia exhibit higher levels of copper, mercury, lead, antimony, and zinc resultant from artillery bombardments of the First World War.[76]

Our understanding of the chemical legacy of landmines and ERW, however, is far from complete. Explosives are typically degraded very slowly and few studies have been able to directly measure the effects of contaminants in post-war ecosystems.[77] Furthermore, it is unclear how stable landmines and ERW remain when exposed to environmental factors over many years. Steel-cased landmines, upon rusting, for example, may lose their structural integrity and thus become non-functioning. Other types of mines, conversely, may become more unstable and thus subject to spontaneous detonation.[78] In all cases, however, these munitions remain as possible threats to the overall health of both the environment and those people living in the area. As Judith Pennington and James Brannon conclude, "Assessing the potential for explosives contamination and the potential for exposure of environmental and human receptors resulting from various military activities will be necessary."[79]

The Gulf War of 1990 to 1991 provides a clear picture of the adverse environmental effects of landmine use. Beginning in August 1990 Iraqi forces, while occupying Kuwait, immediately set up an intricate minefield as a defensive measure. The desert environment of southern Kuwait was devoid of natural features, such as cliffs or ridges, and was thus considered to be particularly vulnerable to enemy forces. By war's end, the total length of mine belts was approximately 504 kilometers, containing close to two million APMs and AVMs. Compounding the damage, the U.S.-led Allied Forces heavily bombed the minefields to open up corridors for its ground forces during the war. Widely used were fuel-air explosive bombs. Over a decade after the war, southern Kuwait continues to suffer considerable environmental damage. Surveys indicate that the fragile desert ecosystem has been weakened through disruption of the desert crust, which has resulted in the depletion of the biological potential of soils. Furthermore, many areas exhibit significant compaction of soils, leading to reductions in water infiltration and higher levels of soil erosion. The vegetation cover of these areas was likewise seriously damaged, with several plant species destroyed.[80]

Landmines may also result in species loss of animal populations. Indeed, this is one of the least studied impacts of landmines and ERW. Elephants and large mammals easily set off AVMs, and smaller, domesticated animals likewise are able to detonate APMs. There is some evidence suggesting that brown bears in Croatia, snow leopards and Bengal tigers in India, gazelles in Libya, and silver-backed mountain gorillas in Rwanda have been pushed to the brink of extinction in part because of remnants of war.[81] Overall, though, very little is known about the impact of landmines and ERW on the status of wild animals; most studies have focused on the heavy toll experienced by domesticated animals. One study, for example, examined 206 communities in Afghanistan, Bosnia, Cambodia, and Mozambique. The authors concluded that more than 57,000 domesticated animals (mostly sheep, cattle, and goats) in these countries were killed due to landmines; the estimated monetary loss of these livestock was equivalent to US$6 million.[82]

There is yet another legacy of landmines that is adversely affecting the world's ecosystems. In parts of Africa and Asia, for example, landmines are being used by poachers to acquire material for the global trade in animal parts. Hence, cases of landmine-based poaching of highly endangered species such as tigers have been reported in Myanmar and in southern Angola, and there are reports of villagers placing anti-tank mines along traditional elephant migration paths. Indeed, entire herds have been slaughtered using this technique. In some instances, the ivory tusks have subsequently been used to purchase additional weapons, thus contributing to the ongoing cycle of violence.[83]

Certainly, landmines restrict access to vast areas of land. However, studies also indicate that landmines or other ERW do not even need to be present to restrict access and thus to take vital land out of production. Simply the fear that explosives might be present serves to take otherwise productive lands out of the equation. Fear therefore hinders everyday activities necessary for survival: access to rivers and wells for water and fields for livestock rearing and farming. In Angola, for example, an estimated one-third of the country's territory is unusable because of actual or suspected landmine contamination. More locally, in Angola's southeastern Mavinga Valley, wide swathes of fertile lands are frequently left abandoned. The region's inhabitants, partly out of fear and partly as a result of ongoing instability, have been forced into more fragile drought-prone environments and have succumbed to starvation and disease. Similar processes have been occurring throughout Sudan, Somalia, and Mozambique.[84]

Landmines and other ERW also pose significant problems as governments attempt to move beyond war. Since the late 1980s Vietnam's economy has been expanding and its government has made substantial progress in modernizing its post-war infrastructure. Relatedly, Vietnam has embarked on significant development projects, including road construction, with neighboring Laos and Cambodia. However, these projects have resulted in increased casualties from ERW. Several of the highway projects, for example, pass through previously inaccessible or underdeveloped areas along the Vietnamese-Laotian or Vietnamese-Cambodian borders—the site of the heavily bombed "Ho Chi Minh Trail." As Vietnam's development has increased, so too has the threat—as well as the actuality—of additional deaths and injuries to civilian construction workers.[85]

Thanks in part to numerous and generous international

donations, many countries are able to conduct much-needed de-mining operations. However, compared to the monetary cost and time of actually laying mines (or of dropping cluster bombs), the cost of de-mining operations is considerable. In Mozambique, for example, the cost to clear 2,000 kilometers of priority roads was estimated to reach US$30 million. Furthermore, de-mining roads will provide safe access to several communities, but it will not prevent most landmine casualties, which are caused by anti-personnel mines laid on footpaths or in fields.[86] Adding to the costs, minefields are often unmapped and unrecorded. They are also spatially extensive. The K5 barrier along the Cambodian-Thai border, for example, stretches for approximately 600 kilometers (372 miles). Estimates suggest that between two to three million mines are present. The human and financial resources required for these clearing operations are phenomenal; and these are funds that, again, could be used elsewhere. Funds otherwise devoted to demining operations could be redirected toward the rebuilding of infrastructure (i.e., roads and railways); funds could be used for educational and vocational training programs; these funds could also be used for other medical needs, such as the control of diseases such as malaria or HIV/AIDS.

Lastly, we would be remiss if we did not also acknowledge the human costs of de-mining operations. The action of entering a minefield to physically clear these remnants of war is a dangerous undertaking. Despite the intensive training programs developed, and the many safety precautions introduced, de-miners still risk death or injury. Between 1991 and 2000, for example, at least 73 mine-clearers sustained 93 injuries while undertaking tasks directly related to mine-clearance operations. Eleven de-miners were killed.[87]

And well into the twenty-first century, landmines continue to be used. Thus, the global reality of these munitions is not

Figure 3.7
In Phonsavan, Laos, members of the Mine Advisory Group prepare to go into the field. Kind permission of Dr. Gerald E. Tyner.

simply to clean up the past remnants of war, for the ongoing conflicts around the world continue to sow the seeds of future destruction. In 2006, for example, there were reports that Israel laid anti-personnel mines during a brief but violent conflict with Lebanon in July and August; Russia claims that Georgian forces laid new landmines in South Ossetia and in the Kodori Gorge in 2006 and 2007; perhaps both Russia and Georgia used landmines in their conflict in 2008; Myanmar's military continues to use landmines in its ongoing "irregular" war against separatist forces. Russia also has reportedly used these munitions in both Chechnya and Dagestan.[88] Landmines are also widely used by non-state actors. Insurgents in both Iraq and Afghanistan have utilized a number of explosives— often in the form of IEDs. There are reports of widespread use, or possible use, in Colombia, India, Pakistan, Burundi,

Guinea-Bissau, Nepal, Somalia, the Philippines, Sri Lanka, Somalia, Thailand, Turkey, and Yemen.[89]

Landmines "are not able to discriminate between an enemy soldier and a child, a grandfather, a pregnant woman, a relief worker or a priest. Landmines have the potential to outlive the men who planted them; they will remain in place, active, ready to kill or maim, for decades after the wars they symbolize are officially over."[90] As an editorial in the *Lancet* concluded, "Landmines and unexploded cluster bombs left over after a conflict continue to wreak havoc in many countries. Clearance remains dangerous and underfunded, and the immediate treatment of victims and their rehabilitation is hampered by lack of resources. The humanitarian ideal is to ban landmines and cluster bombs. Countries that manufacture, export, and disperse these weapons should cease, and must fund the legacy of clearance and help for survivors."[91]

According to Rob Nixon, for those societies that continue to endure the legacy of past conflicts, where landmines, cluster bombs, and other remnants of war continue to inflict belated maimings and what he calls "afterdeaths," the *post* in post-conflict regions has never truly arrived. Instead, he writes, "whole provinces inhabit a twilight realm in which everyday life remains semimilitarized and in which the earth itself must be treated with permanent suspicion, as armed and dangerous."[92] Such is the global reality of living in the footsteps of modern warfare.

My [ex-husband] was in Chu Lai in 1968. He said the smell of Dioxin was so heavy in the air it made it hard for him to breathe. They had just cleared that area. One year later our daughter was born with horrible birth defects. . . . Her abdominal wall didn't close from the sternum to the pubis. It was just opened with all her internal organs [exposed]. Her rib cage was pulled outward as was her pelvis . . . She didn't have a rectum or vagina. She was so horribly deformed you couldn't tell if she was male or female in the genital area . . . Her surgeon said her internal organs looked like they had been taken out [and] put in a pot, stirred and put back into her abdomen. She has to wear a colostomy bag for her stools and an ileostomy bag for urine. Her bladder was split as was her uterus. They were both removed when she was 6 years old. She has severe emotional, behavioral and psychological problems. She has grown up in hospitals. [1]

My dad served three tours in Vietnam in the Army and remembers being doused with Agent Orange by aircraft . . . My brother was born with a double toe and his daughter has the same defect . . . I was born without my right outer ear and can only hear 33 percent. I also have had severe migraines . . . [2]

My father passed away in 1998 [when] he was only 50 years old. He had type II diabetes. He died of a massive heart attack. I am currently 34. I was born without my right leg below the knee and several of my fingers. I also do not have a big toe on my left leg. I was born two months premature and weighed only 3 lbs 3 oz. My mother had two miscarriages prior to me and one between my brother and me . . . [3]

These three vignettes are but a handful from similar stories told around the world. In Vietnam, Iran, Australia, New Zealand, the United States of America. Legacies of poisoning; exposure to chemical weapons. The most widespread use of chemical weapons occurred during the Vietnam War. But weapons were produced, developed, stored, and tested in many other countries, creating a global network of health problems. Consider Innisfail, a small town located in the northern state of Queensland, Australia. In 1966 Australian military scientists test-sprayed chemical weapons on a patch of rainforest 20 kilometers southwest of Innisfail and 100 meters above the Johnstone River, which supplies water for the town. Forty years later, this section of the rainforest remains bare—a desolate landscape covered only with tough Guinea grass. Researchers and activists claim that cancer deaths in the region are ten times higher than the state average.[4]

The production, stockpiling, testing, and use of chemical weapons has left a deadly legacy across the world. Battlefields are not confined to war zones; instead, the effects of chemical weapons use and development is considerably more extensive. Not only people many years removed from combat use are affected; so too are people who have never set foot on a battlefield. And the impact of chemical weapons on those people affected is deeply troubling. Survivors of chemical weapons exposure suffer both psychological and physical scarring, as manifested in damaged lungs, blindness, skin lesions, or nerve damage. But, as with many modern weapons, the legacy of chemical weapons may still affect people far removed from the immediacy of war and military action. Once introduced into the environment, chemical weapons may remain dangerous for generations to come.

THE NATURE OF CHEMICAL WEAPONS

Chemical weapons[5] are classified according to their specific lethal or non-lethal effects on people.[6] The most well-known non-lethal chemical weapons are tear gases. Widely used in the First World War, tear gases cause irritation of the skin, respiratory discomfort, and watering of the eyes. Headaches, dizziness, nausea, and vomiting may also result. In general, these agents are intended to cause maximum discomfort without necessarily being lethal. For example, some agents, such as 3-Quinuclidinyl benzilate, or BZ, are engineered to cause psychomimetic effects, including long-lasting hallucinations. Other agents, such as diphenylarsinous cyanide, or DC, irritate the mucous membranes of the eyes, nose, and throat. Persons exposed to DC suffer headaches, nausea, and violent vomiting.[7]

Apart from these non-lethal chemical weapons, there are numerous lethal weapons that have been, and continue to be, produced and used across the earth's battlefields. One family of chemical weapons, commonly known as "choking agents," have been engineered to damage a victim's respiratory system and/or to cause debilitating chemical burns to the mucous membranes of lung and bronchial tissues.[8] Phosgene and chlorine, for example, primarily attack the airways and lungs, causing respiratory tract inflammation, bronchospasm, and lung injury.[9] These agents have a long and storied history in the evolution of chemical warfare and were widely used by German, British, and French forces in the First World War.

Asphyxiants are chemical agents that cause choking and respiratory problems and are classified as either simple or chemical. The former includes such agents as nitrogen and carbon dioxide; these gases physically displace oxygen in the air, thereby causing oxygen deficiency and hypoxemia when inhaled. Chemical asphyxiants, conversely, interfere with oxygen transport and/or cellular respiration within the body, thereby causing tissue hypoxia. Some chemical asphyxiants, such as cyanide, may also be absorbed through mucous membranes and the skin.[10]

Vesicants (also called "blister agents") cause extensive and irreversible tissue damage, often within minutes of exposure. Delivered in either liquid or vapor form, vesicants, such as mustard gas and Lewisite, can readily penetrate human skin and can even be absorbed through some protective coverings. Skin, eyes, and the respiratory tract are especially vulnerable and sensitive to vesicants. Eyes are especially vulnerable; damage to the eyes includes conjunctivitis, corneal opacification, ulceration, and rupture. When these agents come into contact with skin tissue, the exposed areas blister. When ingested, some vesicants, such as mustard gas, cause vomiting, diarrhea, and even bone marrow failure.[11] Although risk of fatality is relatively low, exposure to vesicants results in significant and permanent damage. Indeed, lifelong disabilities often result from exposure to vesicants.[12]

The most lethal of all chemical weapons are those classified as nerve agents. Indeed, such compounds are almost 100 percent fatal, and are able to kill in truly minuscule amounts.[13] Nerve agents, such as sarin, tabun, and soman, are easily absorbed through the skin, eyes, and lungs. These agents work by inhibiting the enzyme acetylcholinesterase (AChE). This enzyme is important in that it hydrolyzes the neutrotransmitter acetylcholine (ACch), thereby rendering it inactive.[14] Consequently, exposure to nerve agents results in an excessive stimulation of muscles and glands, a subsequent loss of bodily functions (e.g., urination, diarrhea, gastric distress), and, finally, paralysis and heart failure.

The military efficacy of chemical weapons is predicated on the agents' volatility, persistence, toxicity, and latency.[15] Volatility, for example, refers to the tendency of a liquid to evaporate and form a vapor—to become a gas. Most chemical agents are stored in liquid form. When detonated, however, these agents are dispersed in a suspension of fine liquid droplets. The subsequent changes in temperature and pressure result in the evaporation of these droplets and the formation of a gas. Different chemical agents react differently to these changes, a property known as volatility. Phosgene and the cyanides are the most volatile of chemical warfare agents; mustard gas is the least volatile.[16]

Volatility is inversely related to the persistence of a chemical agent. In other words, the more volatile an agent, the more rapidly it will evaporate and disperse. Consequently, extremely volatile agents are less likely to remain and contaminate the exposed surroundings. Most military agents, and especially mustard gas, are less volatile and thus remain a threat for longer periods of time.[17] During the First World War, for example, mustard gas would freeze during the winter months and remain in the soil; consequently, mustard gas used in the autumn of 1917 poisoned men in the spring of 1918 when the ground thawed.[18]

The potential for a chemical agent to cause injury is termed toxicity. In other words, is the agent designed to inflict lethal or non-lethal injuries? For many chemical agents, mortality or morbidity are related to exposure and concentration of the agent. For some highly toxic agents, such as sarin, even a droplet may cause painful death. Latency, finally, refers to the time delay between exposure and onset of clinical symptoms; this is an important characteristic for first responders and medical personnel in treating exposed victims.

A HISTORY OF CHEMICAL WARFARE

Chemical forms of warfare have a long and inglorious history. In 428 B.C., for example, during the Peloponnesian War, the Spartans burned wood that had been saturated with pitch and sulphur to create choking poisonous fumes. More recently, British troops used noxious sulfur fumes against Russian forces during the Crimean War (1854–1856) and artillery shells containing picric acid during the Boer War in South Africa (1899–1902).[19]

However, the production and use of chemical weapons was generally small-scale and limited in scope. It was not until the nineteenth century that an industry emerged that was devoted to the design, manufacture, and distribution of chemical weapons. And, once again, we see the confluence of industrial technology and capitalist practice manifest in the First World War as a catalyst.

The late nineteenth century witnessed several advances in the discipline of chemistry. Most knowledge was focused on industrial and agricultural uses of chemicals, leading to the emergence of a widespread chemical industry. The development of this industry, though, was also accompanied by numerous (and significant) accidents. The increased knowledge of these toxicological effects, however, led some scientists to consider the possibility of their use in battle.[20] Indeed, as Harris and Paxman acknowledge, the chemical industry would become the foundation of Germany's war machine.[21]

In the early morning of April 22, 1915 German troops opened 6,000 cylinders along a four-mile front of the Ypres Salient. The heavy steel containers were filled with liquid chlorine which, when opened, formed a dense poisonous cloud that soon engulfed the panic-stricken French troops. This attack, which resulted in 13,000 casualties, marked the beginning of the large-scale use of chemical weapons in the war. Thereafter, French, British and German forces continued to introduce new chemical weapons (e.g., phosgene and mustard gas), and to refine more effective delivery systems, such as the development of gas-filled artillery shells. Indeed, a chemicals arms race emerged in Europe between the warring parties. In England, for example, 33 different laboratories were testing 150,000 known organic and inorganic compounds in an attempt to develop ever more poisonous gases. The most extensive of these sites was Porton Down, a 7,000-acre facility on Salisbury Plain that employed over 1,000 scientists.[22] When the war ended, chemical weapons had contributed to 100,000 dead and 1.2 million wounded.[23]

The horrors of chemical warfare led to the adoption of the 1925 Geneva Protocol, a measure that condemned the use of asphyxiating, poisonous, or other gases in the conduct of war. Moreover, the use of chemical weapons was viewed by some military officials as unethical. Admiral William Leahy, for example, considered poison gas to be barbarous, noting that such weapons, if used, "would violate every Christian ethic I have ever heard of and all of the known laws of war."[24]

Such moral considerations, however, did not lead to elimination of these weapons. Indeed, chemical weapons were used repeatedly throughout the interwar years. Between 1923 and 1926, Spanish troops used mustard gas in Morocco; Italian forces likewise used chemical weapons in their Ethiopian campaign of 1935 to 1940. In China, also, both Soviet and Japanese troops made widespread use of chemical weapons in suppressing local rebellions.

During the Second World War, both the Allied and Axis powers produced and stockpiled advanced chemical warfare agents, including nerve agents.[25] The only confirmed use of chemical weapons during the war, however, was the mass killing of Jews and other "unwanted" groups (e.g., the Roma, homosexuals, Marxists, and the physically and mentally disabled) by the Nazi regime.[26]

Drawing upon a decade of research, experimentation, and the deliberate killing of perceived "unwanted" individuals, biomedical scientists played an active, even leading role in the initiation, administration, and execution of Nazi extermination programs.[27] In fact, many of the Nazi leaders who set up the extermination camps and then remained as personnel were veterans of the euthanasia program and thought of themselves as having special skills or expertise.[28]

Between 1942 and 1945 Nazi officials devised new killing methods which would facilitate mass murder on an industrial scale. Whereas early attempts as mass gassing included carbon monoxide derived from vehicle exhausts, Nazi leaders ultimately turned to the use of crystallized prussic acid, or cyanide.[29] By the end of the war, the Holocaust had resulted in the murder of approximately six million Jewish men, women, and children.

The horrors of the Holocaust did not stop the scientific development of chemical or biological weapons. Indeed, throughout the Cold War many governments intensified their efforts and became increasingly tolerant to the use of chemical weapons as a means of warfare. In the 1950s, for example, the British military employed aerially sprayed herbicides in Malaya in an attempt to suppress a communist-based liberation movement. During this campaign, the British used both helicopters and fixed-wing aircraft to eradicate food crops as part of a larger program designed to restrict food supplies which could be used to support insurgents.[30] Such a food-denial strategy, however, also had the effect of starving non-insurgents, i.e., "innocent" civilians. The British ultimately abandoned this strategy—not out of any moral consideration, but rather because they realized that food-denial was counter-productive. The destruction of food crops more often than not drove more people to join the enemy ranks.[31]

Although this specific form of chemical warfare was abandoned by the British, it formed a key component of America's military strategy in Vietnam.[32] As early as April

1961, American military planners and politicians began planning for the use of herbicides as a means of destroying enemy cover and also as a strategy of food-denial to the enemy. By August 1961 the first defoliation test mission over South Vietnam had been conducted; two weeks later additional tests were carried out in Thailand and Cambodia. Based on early results, in November President John F. Kennedy authorized the use of chemical defoliants in Vietnam. Operation Ranch Hand, as the campaign was officially named, lasted from early 1962 through 1971. Throughout these nine years, approximately 18 million gallons of chemicals were sprayed on 20 percent of South Vietnam, with 4,747,587 acres of forest defoliated and 481,897 acres of crop-land destroyed.[33]

Over 20 types of chemical combinations—designated by the color-coded identification band painted on the 208-liter storage barrels—were used by American military forces in Vietnam. Initially, the main herbicide employed by the U.S. military was Agent Purple, a mix of 2,4-dichlorophenoxyacetic acid (2,4-D) and two forms of 2,4,5-trichlorophenoxyacetic acid (2,4,5-T). In 1965, however, the military switched to Agent Orange, a faster-acting defoliant consisting of 2,4-D and a single form of 2,4,5-T. These agents often contained varying levels of another long-lived contaminant, 2,3,7,8-tetrachlorodibenzoparadioxin, or TCDD.[34] According to Richard Stone, "in a rogue's gallery of 75 known forms of dioxin, TCDD is the nastiest." Over the past three decades, studies have revealed that dioxins such as TCDD cause deleterious effects in animals, including birth defects, cancers, and endocrine disorders.[35]

Initially, the use of chemical warfare agents was to be selective and carefully controlled—though not limited in geographic coverage. Some early proposals, for example, envisioned a defoliation campaign that would eradicate

31,250 square miles—approximately half of the entire country of South Vietnam.[36] Moreover, a number of politicians, including President John F. Kennedy, expressed initial reluctance at the use of these agents. This reluctance, however, stemmed not from a concern about the effects such a campaign would have on Vietnam or its people. Rather, concerns were expressed over the public image of America's use of chemical agents.[37] Decades later James Clary, a military scientist who designed spray tanks for Operation Ranch Hand, testified before the U.S. Congress. He explained that "When we initiated the herbicide program in the 1960s, we were aware of the potential for damage due to dioxin contamination in the herbicide. We were even aware that the military formulation had a higher dioxin concentration than the civilian version, due to the lower cost and speed of manufacture. However, because the material was to be used on the enemy, none of us were overly concerned."[38]

As America's involvement in Vietnam escalated, so too did the use of herbicidal agents. Beginning in late 1962 American military strategists began using defoliants not simply to clear jungles, but also as a technique for food denial. In one such operation, codenamed Sherwood Forest, American planners targeted the 18,500-acre Boi Loi Woods. Located approximately 25 miles northwest of Saigon, these woods were believed to be a major base for enemy forces. It was also believed that about 100 acres of land were devoted to food crops for enemy troops. A decision was reached to completely eradicate the forest.

The Boi Loi Woods was home to an estimated 6,000 people. Approximately 4,000 of these residents, living in three hamlets, earned their living as farmers; another 2,000 people earned their livelihood by cutting firewood in the forest. Beginning in January 1965, American forces attempted to coerce the inhabitants of the Boi Loi Woods to leave. Leaflets were dropped and messages broadcast over loudspeakers, urging the people to evacuate the area. This initial effort was followed by two days of areal bombing. Between January 18 and January 20, American fighter pilots conducted 139 sorties and dropped nearly 800 tons of bombs on the forest. Riot gas was then used as a dispersal mechanism. At the conclusion of the initial phase of the operation, an estimated 2,182 refugees had fled. The remaining 4,000 inhabitants were either dead, or remained in hiding. On January 22, the second phase of Operation Sherwood Forest began. For nearly one month (until February 18), over 100 sorties delivered 83,000 gallons of herbicide on the woods. An additional 316 sorties dropped more than 372 bombs and fired 85,000 rounds of ammunition.[39]

As the war progressed, the public relations fears of American advisors were slowly realized. It was widely reported, for example, that poisons (such as TCDD) that were banned in the United States were widely used in Vietnam. In the fall of 1969, as a case in point, it was reported that Agent Orange would no longer be used domestically in the United States, as studies indicated that the agent was teratogenic and that the offspring of laboratory animals fed 2,4,5-T showed 100 percent birth defects. Significantly, spokespersons for the U.S. military immediately stated that the restriction on TCDD use would not apply to its use in Vietnam. However, additional pressure against the United States continued to emerge. Also in 1969, hospitals in Saigon began reporting a sharp rise in birth defects. These were linked to the geographic coverage of defoliation campaigns.

Long after America's involvement in Vietnam, chemical weapons continued to be manufactured, stockpiled, and used. In the Middle East, for example, chemical weapons were widely used during the Iran–Iraq War (1980–1988). The first confirmed use of chemical weapons was by Iraqi forces against Iranian soldiers in August 1983. During the war, Iraqi fighter jets dropped mustard-filled and tabun-filled 250-kilogram bombs and mustard-filled 500-kilogram bombs on Iranian targets. Iraqi military scientists also used chemical agents in rockets, artillery shells, and warheads; other reports indicate that Iraq may have installed spray tanks on helicopters.[40] By their own accounts, Iraq used approximately 19,500 chemical bombs, over 54,000 chemical artillery shells, and 27,000 short-range chemical-filled rockets from 1983 to 1988; these munitions contained about 1,800 tons of mustard gas, 140 tons of tabun, and more than 600 tons of sarin.[41] It is unclear how many Iranian soldiers and civilians succumbed to chemical weapons attacks during the war, although estimates suggest that the number of casualties is in the tens of thousands.[42]

Toward the end of the conflict, Iraq also unleashed chemical weapons within its own borders. Between 1987 and 1988 Southern (Iraqi) Kurdistan was subjected to repeated chemical weapons attacks as the Iraqi government sought to repress Kurdish independence movements. In one infamous attack occurring on the afternoon of March 16, 1988, the town of Halabja was attacked with mustard gas, cyanide, and possibly sarin. An estimated 4,000 to 5,000 people died immediately during the attack; thousands more were injured and/or died in the days that followed.[43] Most recently, chemical weapons have allegedly been used in various conflicts raging across sub-Saharan Africa, most notably during Mozambique's civil war.[44]

THE LEGACY OF CHEMICAL WARFARE

Potentially lethal effects of chemical weapons continue long after their military use. These are seen both in the immediate destruction and, at times, the irreparable transformation of various ecosystems. These effects are most readily evident in Vietnam. Indeed, in many respects, Vietnam has become the poster-child of the horrific legacy of chemical warfare. Decades after the war ended, the Vietnamese people and ecosystems continue to suffer the adverse effects of chemical weapons.[45]

During the Vietnam War the intensive use of chemical weapons destroyed large swathes of tropical forests. Studies conducted in the late 1960s and early 1970s documented the initial damage. The findings of Harvard biologist Matthew S. Meselson were particularly important. Meselson was, at the time, head of the American Association for the Advancement of Science's (AAAS) Herbicide Assessment Commission, tasked with investigating the military use of herbicides in Vietnam. Between August and September 1970 Meselson and other commission members conducted on-site inspections in South Vietnam; to these field surveys were added interviews held with various scientists, military planners, and other officials engaged in the ongoing herbicidal campaign in Vietnam. Based on these studies, Meselson and his colleagues determined that by 1970 "about one-seventh of the land area of South Vietnam—equivalent in size to the state of Massachusetts—had been treated with herbicides."[46] Most chemical applications, it was determined, were delivered via "low-flying C-123 cargo aircraft that made more than 19,000 individual spray flights between 1962 and 1969" and "about 90 percent of the herbicide was dropped on forest land and about 10 percent on crop land."[47]

The systematic destruction of southern and central Vietnam's various ecosystems, including the forests and farmlands, was found to be widespread. Meselson's team, for example, estimated that more than half of the forested area in

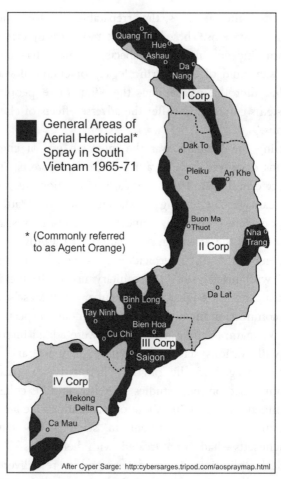

Figure 4.1
Map of Areas in Vietnam Sprayed by Herbicides.

three provinces was very severely damaged. And Arthur Westing, the team's forestry expert, concluded that "about 35 percent of South Vietnam's 14 million acres of dense forest [had] been sprayed one or more times" and that, as a result, "6.2 billion board feet of merchantable timber [had] thus far been killed by herbicides."[48] This amounted to South Vietnam's entire domestic timber needs, based on then-current demand, for the next three decades. The economic implications of the herbicidal campaign would thus be astronomical for South Vietnam—supposedly *America's ally and friend.* Indeed, Westing concluded that the lost timber represented approximately US$500 million in taxes that would have accrued to the South Vietnamese government.[49] Additional studies found that America's herbicidal campaign severely reduced South Vietnam's rubber production.[50]

The immediate impact on Vietnam's people was also disastrous. The AAAS scientists concluded that the destruction of some 2,000 square kilometers of land entailed destruction of enough food (i.e., rice, mango, guava, manioc, and jack fruit) to have fed 600,000 persons for a year.[51] This destruction was especially pronounced in the food-scarce Central Highlands, populated by an indigenous people known as the Montagnards. Related studies indicated that the destruction of food reserves by defoliation chiefly affected the aged and the infirm, pregnant and lactating women, and children under five years of age.[52]

Long after the herbicidal campaign ended in Vietnam, it has taken years for many of those affected regions to rebound. In some areas, however, ecosystems have been permanently altered. Based on studies conducted ten years after the war, Colin Norman found that in many affected areas throughout Vietnam, although agriculture had been established, in most places the soil remained unsuitable for growing crops and the land had become covered with a coarse, deep-rooting grass. Furthermore, the destruction of Vietnam's forests had a major impact on certain animal populations. For example, one survey found that in one heavily sprayed forest, there were only 24 species of birds and five species of mammals, compared to two nearby non-sprayed forests which registered 145 and 170 bird species and 30 and 55 mammal species.[53]

In many contaminated areas of Vietnam, the ecological impacts were irreversible. Many of Vietnam's tropical hardwood forests were being replaced by faster-growing bamboos and other grasses—an environmental transformation that has wide-ranging impacts, including subsequent agricultural practices. When the vegetation of a forest ecosystem is destroyed, its wildlife is often decimated because of loss of their natural habitat.[54] Here, Vietnam's mangrove forests provide an important lesson. Composed of saltwater-tolerant trees, shrubs, and bushes, mangrove forests are found in estuarine environments throughout southern Vietnam. Significantly, mangrove forests were especially vulnerable to herbicides. Early tests revealed that herbicides were 90 to 95 percent effective on mangrove forests, compared to rates of only 60 percent for evergreen and other tropical forests. Consequently, the application of herbicides on Vietnam's mangrove forests was particularly severe.

Ecologically, mangrove forests have been very important for the people of Vietnam. Mangroves provided the Vietnamese with food (as fish, shellfish, and crabs live and flourish within the mangrove environment); these ecosystems also provided firewood and particular types of homeopathic medicines. Defoliation campaigns thus destroyed both food and livelihood. And the effects were far-reaching. The destruction of the mangrove forests led to increased rates of riverbank erosion. The run-off of silt and sediments, in turn, resulted in the rivers becoming more turbid, which subsequently killed many more aquatic plants and fish. By 2004 an estimated US$15 million had been spent by the Vietnamese government to restore its mangrove forests.[55]

Vietnam's coral reefs also have been severely damaged as a

result of dioxin-tainted sediment run-off. As Pavlov and colleagues identify, hundreds of thousands of highly toxic defoliants were sprayed over Vietnam's rivers and tributaries. During the subsequent decades, both soluble and little-soluble toxic components of dioxin-containing chemicals entered into Vietnam's bays via floodwaters and river run-off. Over time, these contaminants have contributed to the deterioration of Vietnam's near-shore coastal reef environments and have exerted a disastrous impact on the ecosystem's productivity and overall level of biological resources.

The human scale and scope of America's herbicidal warfare in Vietnam is equally staggering. Jeanne Stellman and her colleagues, writing in *Nature*, estimate that at least 2.1 million people, but perhaps as many as 4.8 million people, were exposed to some level of herbicidal spraying.[56] And the documented legacy is equally disturbing. In 1999 the Vietnamese Ministry of Health attempted to compile a registry of persons who reported or displayed any possible Agent Orange-associated disease. Over one million people were listed, of which 50,000 were children.[57] In some villages, one in every ten children suffers from serious birth defects, such as spina bifida, cerebral palsy, physical or mental retardation, missing or deformed limbs, or some other congenital malformation.[58]

TCDD is considered to be the most toxic chemical ever manufactured.[59] As an endocrine-disrupting chemical, TCDD has a highly toxic effect on the human reproductive system. Even low concentrations are premised to disrupt the normal reproductive process, leading to diminished fecundity, increased antenatal mortality, and birth defects.[60] Furthermore, in numerous studies, TCDD is associated with increased risks for various cancers, immune deficiencies, reproduction and development abnormalities, diabetes, thyroid disorders, decreased pulmonary functions and bronchitis, eyelid pathology, chloracne, and liver damage. Recently, the National Academy of Sciences determined that "sufficient" evidence also existed to link TCDD with soft-tissue sarcoma, non-Hodgkin's lymphoma, and Hodgkin's disease. Suggestive evidence also exists, linking the dioxin with assorted respiratory cancers, prostate cancer, multiple myeloma, type II diabetes, spina bifida, and acute myelogenous leukemia.[61]

TCDD is extremely persistent. Susan Booker concludes that a quarter of the TCDD released in Vietnam still remains in the environment.[62] Dioxins, furthermore, are highly bio-accumulative. Being fat- and oil-soluble, dioxins bio-accumulate as they move up the food chain. A fish, for example, will have a higher concentration of dioxins than the plants it eats. Humans who eat contaminated fish will have correspondingly higher concentrations.[63] Indeed, according to L. Wayne Dwernychuk and his co-authors, although over three decades have passed since the cessation of spraying in Vietnam, TCDD continues to accumulate in animal tissues used as human food.[64] Dioxins are subsequently passed along to future generations through conception and/or through the breast milk of nursing mothers. As Bea Duffield concludes, in Vietnam "the grandchildren of those who first saw the sweet-smelling yellow powder fall from the sky nearly over 40 years ago are experiencing the effect of it today."[65]

Biological samples collected in southern Vietnam between 1970 and 1973 revealed elevated levels of toxins in fish, food-stuffs, and even human milk samples.[66] And studies continue to report the existence of dioxins in Vietnam's environment and its people. Throughout the 1990s and into the twenty-first century, elevated concentrations of TCDD have been found in fish pond sediments, foods (e.g., fish, shrimp, and duck), as well as samples of human blood and human breast milk.[67] Vietnamese scientists likewise have revealed that the persistence of residual dioxins in the soil is proportional to the areas sprayed.[68]

Decades later, the long-term effects are still unknown.[69] Vietnamese medical authorities claim that continued birth defects in their country are the result of initial parental exposure to chemical agents, as well as the continued exposure to dioxins in Vietnam's soils, waters, and foodwebs. Western scientists, however, have been more circumspect, repeatedly disputing the strength of evidence correlating exposure to dioxin and illnesses in individuals in *Vietnam*.[70] Furthermore, despite small surveys and case studies, as of 2003, no large-scale epidemiological study of herbicides and the health of the Vietnamese population had been conducted.[71]

Curiously, in 1991 the United States Congress passed the Agent Orange Act. As part of this legislation, any *American* veteran who had served, however briefly, in Vietnam, and was allegedly suffering from Agent Orange-associated illnesses, was entitled to healthcare and disability compensation. Subsequent bills were passed to provide a range of benefits to children of Vietnam-era veterans suffering from spina bifida and selected other birth defects. By 2005 approximately 300,000 Vietnam-era veterans in the United States had undergone medical tests; an estimated 2,000 children of these veterans were believed to be suffering from spina bifida.[72]

To date, however, the United States government has refused to compensate victims outside of its borders, claiming (again) that the consequences of dioxins on human health are undetermined and not scientifically substantiated.[73] In other words, the U.S. government has recognized in the case of American veterans that exposure, however minuscule, to dioxins is grounds for compensation, but that the same cannot be "proven" in the case of the Vietnamese. Recently, Cathy

Scott-Clark and Adrian Levy visited Tu Du hospital, located in Ho Chi Minh City, Vietnam. They write:

> The science of chemical warfare fills a silent, white-tiled room at Tu Du hospital. . . . Here, shelves are overburdened with research materials. Behind the locked door is an iridescent wall of the mutated and misshapen, hundreds of bell jars and vacuum-sealed bottles in which human foetuses float in formaldehyde. Some appear to be sleeping, fingers curling their hair, thumbs pressing at their lips, while others with multiple heads and mangled limbs are listless and slumped. Thankfully, none of these dioxin babies ever woke up. One floor below, it is never quiet. Here are those who have survived the misery of their births, ravaged infants whom no one has the ability to understand, babies so traumatized by their own disabilities, luckless children so enraged and depressed at their miserable fate, that they are tied to their beds just to keep them safe from harm.[74]

To the extent that Vietnam's elevated numbers of birth defects and cancers are the result of herbicidal warfare, what are the compounding legacies? As Anh Ngo and his co-authors discuss, babies born with congenital malformations often require extensive surgical and medical care; many such children—if they live—have lifelong disabilities and handicaps. Consequently, these health conditions pose a tremendous burden on families and communities throughout the country. As with victims of landmines and unexploded ordnance, disabled persons require substantial, and expensive, medical care.[75] According to Cathy Scott-Clark and Adrian Levy, "Vietnam's chaotic and underfunded national health service cannot cope with the demands made upon it. The Vietnamese Red Cross has registered an estimated one million people disabled by Agent Orange, but has sufficient funds to help only one fifth of them, paying out an average of US$5 a month."[76] Furthermore, institutional support systems are often necessary to relieve the physical and emotional sufferings of disabled persons and their families.[77]

The environments of Vietnam are not the only ecosystems that bear the scars of chemical weapons. The world's marine environments also continue to bear the legacy of chemical warfare. In large part, the threat to these environments and ecosystems is the result of decades of uninformed practices of disposing of unused chemical warfare agents. Following the Second World War, the Allied Powers dumped tons of stockpiled weapons throughout the world's oceans and coastal waters. Along with unexploded ordnance (e.g., aerial bombs, artillery shells, mines, and grenades), various chemical warfare agents were also dumped. These included mustard gas, phosgene, and assorted nerve agents. In total, an estimated 65,000 tons of chemical weapons (including both shells or cylinders and chemical agents) were dumped in the Baltic Sea. Most prevalent were Clark I, Clark II, mustard gas, phosgene, Adamsite, Lewisite, and tabun.[78]

Throughout the 1940s and into the 1950s, two primary means of disposal were used. One practice was to simply throw wooden crates filled with chemical agents overboard. This was common, for example, in the Baltic Sea. Unfortunately, many of these crates would float for days and, if they didn't sink, would wash ashore. This posed the first major threat to marine environments as members of the general public began coming into contact with chemical agents washed ashore. Throughout the 1950s numerous crates of chemical weapons were reported along the Polish coastline; crates of chemical weapons washed ashore also throughout the southern Baltic region. Elsewhere, serious injuries were reported in Sweden, Germany, Poland,

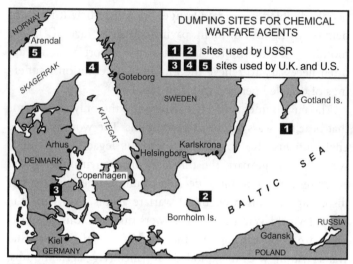

Figure 4.2
Map of Chemical Dump Sites in the Baltic Sea.

and Denmark as people encountered these legacies of a past war.[79] In July 1955, for example, children on summer holiday, playing along a beach of the southern Baltic Sea, found a barrel that had washed ashore. A group of children began to play with the barrel and, within 30 minutes, began to experience burning sensations on their skin. Ultimately over 100 children suffered skin burns and four suffered severe eye injuries. Although the agent was never formally identified, it most likely was a type of mustard gas.[80]

A second method of disposal was to load merchant ships and other vessels with stockpiled chemical weapons; these ships would then be scuttled. It is not entirely clear what happens to these materials. As discussed earlier, some chemical agents may break down into non-toxic compounds. Agents such as mustard gas, however, continue to pose a problem, especially for the fishermen who trawl these waters. It is not uncommon, for example, for lumps of viscous mustard gas to be brought to the surface through fishing activities. In 1997 a Polish fishing vessel was trawling for cod and flatfish 18 miles offshore. In one of the hauls the fishermen brought up a substance resembling clay. This was dumped in a trash container in the harbor and later disposed at the city scrap yard. The following day all fishermen experienced adverse skin reactions, burning sensations, and skin lesions. The substance was found and identified as mustard gas.[81]

It is not generally known how much of a risk these chemical agents pose. The behavior of chemical warfare agents in marine environments depends on both the physical-chemical properties of the agents themselves, as well as the characteristics of the environment in question (e.g., temperature, salinity, pH value, and turbulence).[82] It is believed that seawater contaminated with nerve agents, for example, will be naturally alleviated by degradation through hydrolysis.[83] Chemical agents are transformed to non-toxic, or less toxic, compounds. Some agents, however, are more persistent. Mustard gas, for example, transforms into an amber-colored, waxy solid mass and may remain stable (and dangerous) in this form for hundreds of years. In general, however, scientists warn of a significant threat to marine environments and especially because of the possibility of bio-accumulation in marine organisms once these contaminants enter the food chain.[84]

Now, into the twenty-first century, more and more sites contaminated by chemical weapons use or stockpiling are being (re)discovered. Indeed, it is becoming apparent that *no continent is immune from the legacy of chemical warfare*. Recent reports confirm that between 1930 and 1968 the United States maintained an active chemical weapons program in Panama. In part, the purpose of this installation was to test chemical munitions under tropical conditions. Members of the U.S.

Army Chemical Corps regularly conducted tests—more than 130 tests between 1944 and 1947—of mustard gas- and nerve agent–filled landmines, artillery shells, and rockets. Despite claims that all materials were either destroyed or dumped at sea, evidence suggests that many chemical munitions and contaminated sites remain in the jungles and marshes of Panama.[85]

China likewise continues to bear the legacy of Japan's occupation during the Second World War. In 1987, for example, over 200 people were injured when workers attempted to set fire to a discarded barrel to determine what it contained; the barrel, tragically, was filled with liquid mustard.[86] Since the 1990s, over 75 fact-finding missions and site investigations have identified the presence of 350,000 chemical weapons munitions—two million tons—strewn over 40 sites in 15 provinces. It is estimated that the total cost of removal and destruction of the weapons will exceed US$9 billion dollars. And Japan, ironically, also is not immune from its early chemical weapons program. In 2003 Japanese authorities identified that 114 sites were known to have stored chemical weapons, including phosgene and cyanide. Chemical munitions were also dumped in eight locations in the waters off Japan.[87]

Throughout the Cold War, the Soviet Union maintained seven chemical weapons factories in five cities: Berezniki, Chapaevsk, Dzerzhinsk, Volgograd, and Novocheboksarsk. The last four cities are located on the Volga River—Europe's largest river and the source of drinking water for millions of people. It is believed that more than 40,000 tons of chemical agents were stored at these sites.[88] The risks to Europe's population remain unclear.

From Mozambique to Myanmar, from South Korea to southern Vietnam, the dangers from a century of the mass production, stockpiling, and usage of chemical weapons has truly become a global reality. However, unlike the legacy of landmines, these dangers are not confined to former battlefields, but instead are found also in classified test sites and production facilities. This legacy is also found in the blood, tissue, and breast milk of the children and grandchildren of those exposed to these insidious weapons.

Furthermore, scientists now conclude that the hazards posed by stockpiled or discarded chemical weapons are more acute than those of weapons used in actual combat. Some chemical agents that have been sprayed or detonated dissipate rapidly, thus posing minimal long-term threats. However, chemical agents that are stored or abandoned in canisters or drums can survive for decades.[89]

In short, many of the lasting effects of chemical weapons are not well understood. Scientists are now trying to ascertain the possible legacies of these weapons, but much work remains to be done.[90] Owing to a lack of information on the characteristics of these weapons and the complexity of the natural environment, it is difficult to demarcate the interaction between chemical warfare agents and environments.

For many people throughout the world, therefore, the most frightening legacy of the military production, stockpiling, and use of chemical weapons is of simply not knowing what will happen. Such is the global reality of the military's unseen killers.

Five

For a population at war, it was, in Andrew Rotter's particularly apt phrase, a "disturbingly ordinary" morning.[1] Throughout the previous night people had been twice awakened by air-raid sirens; a third alert was announced around 7:10 am when a single plane was spotted flying overhead. And so, when a trio of American planes appeared approximately one hour later, the inhabitants of Hiroshima, Japan, while wary, continued their morning activities.

Eighteen-year-old Hiroka Fukada, for example, was beginning work at the Bureau of Post Communications. She had just sat down at her desk when the explosion hit. Twenty-eight-year-old Hiroshi Sawachika was likewise at work. An army doctor, Mr. Sawachika, had just finished saying "Good morning" to his colleagues when the sky lit up. And Akihiro Takahashi, a 14-year-old student at the Hiroshima Municipal Junior High School, had just lined up with his classmates when the blast came.

On August 6, 1945, Hiroshima was home to approximately 250,000 people—the exact total remains uncertain, given that thousands of people continually moved in and out of the city in response to repeated evacuation alerts.[2] The people of Hiroshima, prior to August 6, considered themselves somewhat lucky. Throughout the island nation of Japan, cities were subject to near-constant aerial bombardment and until this day, Hiroshima had largely been spared.

The three planes that flew over Hiroshima that morning were different, however, for one—the *Enola Gay*—carried a new and as yet unproven weapon. Nicknamed "Little Boy," the bomb measured 14 feet long, 5 feet in diameter, and weighed 10,000 pounds. Belying its name, "Little Boy" was equivalent to the explosive force of 20,000 tons of TNT.

At 8:15 am, the bomb was released. Approximately 45 seconds later, the bomb detonated in mid-air, about 1,800 feet above the city. There appeared a blinding flash of light, followed by a thunderous blast and blistering heat. Within seconds, an estimated 130,000 people died.[3]

Ms. Fukada was lucky. Although she was less than one mile from Ground Zero, she survived the initial blast. She describes seeing a flash of light, followed by a tremendous explosion. Everything turned yellow. Akihiro Takahashi, the student, also survived, although he was knocked 30 feet by the explosion. He had burns on the back of his head, as well as on his back, arms, and legs. He recounts: "We saw many victims. I saw a man whose skin was completely peeled off the upper half of his body and a woman whose eyeballs were sticking out. Her whole body was bleeding. A mother and her baby were lying with [their] skin completely peeled off."[4]

Incendiary fires, set in motion by the intense heat of the explosion, soon swept through the devastated city, killing many thousands more who had survived the initial blast. Even the dead were not spared the fires. Akiko Takahura, who worked at the Bank of Hiroshima, was 20 years old. She describes "a whirlpool of fire" that swept through the city and remembers that the "fingertips of . . . dead bodies caught fire and the fire gradually spread over their entire bodies from their fingers."[5]

Mr. Sawachicka remembers trying to help the injured. He came upon a pregnant woman, who pleaded with him. "I know that I am going to die," she said, "But I can feel that my baby is moving inside . . . [If] the baby is delivered now, it does not have to die with me. Please help my baby live." But the doctor had no way to help, and the mother and unborn child died later that afternoon.[6] Elsewhere, Akira Onogi, a 16-year-old student, found a small girl crying, asking for help. Her mother was trapped by a fallen beam. Akira tried, with the help of some neighbors, to move the heavy wooden beam, but was unable. Soon, the beam and other debris caught fire, and Akira had no choice but to leave the trapped mother and her crying daughter. Akira recalls, "She (the mother) was conscious and we deeply bowed to her with clasped hands to apologize to her and then we left."[7]

Three days later, a B-29 named *Bock's Car* dropped a second atomic bomb on the city of Nagasaki. The horrors of Hiroshima were repeated, as 40,000 people died in the initial blast.

The atomic bombing of Hiroshima was not simply an act perpetrated by the United States; rather, it was the product of years of scientific experimentation, ethical debate, and significant changes in the conduct of war—all undertaken globally.[8] Likewise, the legacy of nuclear weapons, and the corresponding militarized and lethal landscapes around the world, remains a global reality for millions of people. The legacy of the world's first use of nuclear weapons thus affects not only those who survived the bombings of Hiroshima and Nagasaki, but also untold hundreds of thousands of people far removed from those devastated cities.[9]

TO HIROSHIMA AND BEYOND

All matter is composed of infinitesimally small particles called atoms. They consist of a positively charged central nucleus around which negatively charged electrons orbit. The nucleus, moreover, is composed of two different types of particle of almost identical mass: the protons, which are positively charged, and neutrons, which carry no charge.[10]

The colossal energy contained in nuclear weapons is derived from the splitting of atoms. It was this discovery that ultimately led to the manufacture and use of the atomic bomb at the end of the Second World War.

The 1930s were fervid days in the development of nuclear physics, as significant and rapid advances in the fields of chemistry and physics were made in laboratories across Europe and North America.[11] Quite apart from the storm clouds that were gathering over Europe, and far removed from the economic hardships that confronted most of the world's population, scientists were unlocking the mysteries of the atomic universe. In France, Irène and Frédéric Joliot-Curie were able in 1934 to produce radioactive isotopes from ordinary stable elements by blasting them with alpha particles; the Italian Enrico Fermi was able to produce similar isotopes through the use of neutrons. In Germany, the Austrian physicist Lise Meitner and the German Otto Hahn, working with uranium, likewise replicated the discoveries, observing that substantial amounts of energy were released when the nucleus of an atom was split. In particular, Meitner and Hahn reasoned that when a neutron was projected into a uranium nucleus, the nucleus would split into two roughly equal parts. Otto Frisch would later term the process "nuclear fission," following the biological process of cell division and multiplication. By 1939, Fermi and the Hungarian-born physicist Leó Szilárd understood that the first split could cause a second split, and so on, in a series of chain reactions. It was at this moment that the scientific community realized that a weapon of unfathomable proportions could be produced.

Normal chemical reactions involve the forming or breaking

of bonds between the electrons of individual atoms; each reaction, subsequently, releases a few electron volts of energy. However, the fission of a single uranium nucleus results in an energy release of almost 200 million electron volts. Hence, the splitting of all 2.58 trillion trillion uranium atoms in one kilogram of uranium would yield an explosive force equal to 10,000 tons of dynamite.[12]

Uranium in its raw form cannot be used as an explosive. Rather, it must be processed, or "enriched." Uranium exists in several forms, or isotopes.[13] Most atoms in natural uranium are of isotope U-238; each atom has 92 protons and 146 neutrons for a total atomic weight of 238. When an atom of U-238 absorbs a neutron, it can undergo fission, but only about one-quarter of the time.[14] Hence, U-238 is not reliable when attempting to initiate a chain reaction. Other isotopes of uranium, however, are far more reliable. The isotope U-235 (92 protons and 143 neutrons), for example, will almost always split when hit by a neutron. The problem is that naturally occurring U-235 is extremely rare; in general, only one out of every 140 atoms in natural uranium is U-235. Consequently, U-235 must be separated out from U-238 to obtain sufficient fissile uranium to sustain a chain reaction. This process is called enrichment.[15] A second element, plutonium, was also discovered that could sustain a fast chain reaction.[16]

In the early 1940s the United States was the first among competing countries to develop a viable nuclear weapons industry—the Manhattan Project. That the Americans were able to do so was a combination of both global and local conditions. Globally, the gathering war clouds that spread across much of Europe had precipitated mass refugee flows. Beginning in the 1930s, the Nazi persecution of Europe's Jewish population set in motion a vast outflow of (among others) members of the scientific community. Both Jews and those who disapproved of the Nazis' discriminatory and (ultimately) murderous practices sought sanctuary in distant lands. For many scientists, the United States became home. It is important to understand that the United States never had a monopoly on nuclear energy and this was very apparent during the early twentieth century. If one were to consider the major scientific discoveries that contributed to the manufacture of the world's first nuclear bomb, for example, the top 70 nuclear discoveries and innovations between 1897 and 1948 came from scientists not only in the United States but also in the United Kingdom, Germany, Austria, Switzerland, France, Russia, the Netherlands, Denmark, Italy, and Japan.[17] And yet, because of the aforementioned persecution, the United States benefited from the exodus of many of Europe's top scientists.

America also capitalized on its massive industrial base.[18] A massive infrastructure was required to produce the necessary materials for an atomic weapon; this infrastructure would ultimately employ hundreds of thousands of workers dispersed over 30 sites throughout the United States and Canada. In the words of Andrew Rotter, the Manhattan Project involved not only Big Science but also Big Business.[19]

The actual design and construction of America's atomic bomb took place at Los Alamos, New Mexico. Other key sites included the Oak Ridge Laboratories, a 42-acre research and gaseous diffusion facility in Tennessee, and the Hanford nuclear plant, situated along the Columbia River. This latter facility, built by the DuPont Corporation which had been hired by the U.S. Army, would become the home of America's plutonium production reactors and reprocessing facilities.[20] Crucial research was also conducted at many of America's major academic institutions, notably the University of California at Berkeley and Columbia University in New York.

Substantial amounts of raw materials, especially uranium, were also required as part of the Manhattan Project. In part, this demand could be met by domestic supplies. However, the vast majority of America's uranium source was acquired from the Congo (present-day Democratic Republic of the Congo). Indeed, of the 6,000 tons of uranium acquired by the United States throughout the war, approximately 3,700 tons came from the African subcontinent.[21] Foreshadowing events to come, America's global quest for uranium would set in motion a process that would continue to the present day: the control of and access to the world's supply of nuclear weapons-related resources.

Throughout the lifetime of the Manhattan Project, the rate of progress was truly remarkable. Within three years the scientists associated with the project were able to test the world's first nuclear bomb at Alamogordo, New Mexico. At 5:30 am, on July 16, 1945, scientists detonated a plutonium-based bomb, known as "Trinity," that registered an explosive force of nearly 18,600 tons of TNT.[22] By way of comparison, prior to the Trinity test, the world's most powerful bomb, the British "Blockbuster," had an equivalency of just under five tons of TNT. The first actual use of atomic weapons followed less than a month later, with the attacks on Hiroshima and Nagasaki.

After the Second World War, attempts by American officials to control the proliferation of nuclear weapons technology were largely unsuccessful. Despite President Harry Truman's desire to retain a monopoly of nuclear power (and to prevent the future use of atomic weapons), the die had been cast. Both the United Kingdom and the Soviet Union, for example, quickly sought membership into the nuclear club. And indeed, by August 1949 the Soviet Union had conducted its first nuclear test (in Kazakhstan) and England followed in October 1952 (with a successful test in western Australia). Both France and Israel became nuclear powers in 1960 and China joined the ranks in 1964. A decade later India followed suit. Pakistan would later (1998) conduct a successful test of a nuclear device and most recently, in 2006 North Korea conducted a nuclear test.[23]

The decision to acquire nuclear weapons is, on the one hand, derived from the basic objectives of states and, on the other hand, from the demands of industrial capitalism. As summarized by Joseph Cirincione, states acquire nuclear weapons for five principal reasons: security, prestige, domestic politics, technology, and economics.[24] Just as security is the prime objective of states, national security considerations are privileged in justifications for the development of a nuclear weapons program. Such a *realist* understanding is premised on the belief that the international system of states is inherently anarchic and that each state will do whatever is necessary to guarantee and secure their sovereignty and territorial integrity. Nuclear weapons, therefore, are viewed as the ultimate arbiter in conflict.[25]

States seek to influence, if not dominate, other states in the realm of international relations. This involves a state's ability to alter the actions of other states, either through inducements or through the use (or threat) of force.[26] Political leaders, however, often operate with certain perceptions of what makes a powerful or influential state. Many leaders believe that nuclear weapons are necessary to meet their national destinies or to gain respect within the international community.[27] As explained by Jaswant Singh, India's former Finance Minister and Minister for External Affairs, "Nuclear weapons remain a key indicator of state power. . . . Since this currency is operational in large parts of the globe, India was left with no choice" but to develop a nuclear weapons program.[28]

The People's Republic of China well illustrates this facet

of nuclear weapons development. Since 1949 China's leaders have viewed the threat or use of force as a defense against threats to its own security and territorial integrity.[29] But equally important is that China's decision-makers have seen a modern military as crucial in their attempt to transform the country into a major world power. Consequently, China has invested large sums of money into the development of a self-sustaining defense research and development infrastructure and corresponding military-industrial complex.[30] Throughout the latter half of the twentieth century, nuclear weapons development was seen as a key component of this effort.

Along with national security and prestige concerns, domestic policy issues may also spur a nuclear weapons program. Three sets of actors are most important in this respect: scientists, soldiers, and state leaders.[31] Consequently, domestic policy considerations reaffirm the importance of militarist attitudes in the pursuit of state objectives. Nuclear scientists and the legions of public employees who work in national nuclear laboratories and civilian reactor facilities doing research often have a keen interest in the development of nuclear weapons because, at a rudimentary level, it is highly lucrative (resultant from government contracts) and academically prestigious.[32]

Members of the military establishment, likewise, support nuclear weapons programs because the development of such arms leads to requirements for more and better weapon systems and a larger role for their own branch of the military. Both the United States Air Force and the United States Navy, for example, often stand to benefit the most from nuclear weapons. The former is able to justify the procurement of ballistic missiles and nuclear-capable bombers, while the latter can point to the need for additional nuclear-propelled submarines and nuclear ballistic missile submarines.[33]

Political leaders may support nuclear weapons development because of their own close relations to defense contractors, the military, or some other corporation. These politicians may generate support for the development of nuclear weapons by emphasizing external security threats and/or by the employment-generating potential of nuclear weapons programs.[34]

A fourth driver of nuclear proliferation is technological: states develop nuclear weapons because they have the technological know-how to design and produce such weapons. This attitude was pervasive throughout the Manhattan Project, as scientists debated the morality of their own actions.[35] And similar to the development of landmines, chemical weapons, and other arsenals, there exists a pervasive belief that states must invest in the production of offensive weapons in order to develop counter-measures to such weapons. Consequently, any attempt to develop an "anti-nuclear" defense capability is dependent upon first producing the most frightening nuclear capability. As Cirincione explains, the decision of the United States to build the first hydrogen bomb provides a clear example of technological determinism. In the 1950s there was no urgent or objective security rationale for the development of such a powerful weapon. However, there was a widely held perception that it would be a political and security disaster if the Soviet Union developed such weapons first.[36] As explained by the researchers James Lindsay and Michael O'Hanlon, "a national security policy that deliberately leaves the American people vulnerable to attack when technology makes it possible to protect them is immoral and unacceptable. Not only does it fly in the face of common sense to leave the nation undefended, but it could hamstring America's role in the world."[37]

Economic considerations, lastly, are inseparable from foreign and domestic policy concerns. Proponents of nuclear weapons programs, for example, claim that these systems are more affordable than other, more conventional defenses. In the 1950s, for example, American military planners argued that nuclear weapons were cost-effective deterrents.[38] More accurate, though, is the recognition that nuclear weapons programs are *very* expensive. An elaborate infrastructure to design, manufacture, and stockpile the resultant arsenal is required; so too is the development of delivery systems (e.g., submarines and bombers) for a nuclear arsenal. Between 1940 and 2005, the United States spent approximately US$7.5 trillion developing, producing, deploying, and maintaining tens of thousands of nuclear weapons.[39]

The quest for nuclear power (and weapons) has left a deep imprint on the global landscape. From the United States to Russia, from China to India, the establishment of research facilities and testing grounds has adversely affected vast stretches of land, numerous waterways, and untold millions of people. And well into the twenty-first century, these sites continue to pose serious environmental and health risks (see below).

Of equal concern is the legacy derived from decades of nuclear testing. Since the American "Trinity" test at Alamogordo, the world has endured over 2,000 nuclear tests. And while some countries, such as China, largely conduct their nuclear tests within their own territory, other countries have "exported" their nuclear legacy to former colonies or possessions. Between 1960 and 1965, for example, France conducted four atmospheric tests and 13 underground tests in its (then) colony of Algeria. Ironically, Algeria at the time was waging an anti-colonial war against France. The French, in addition, also conducted 46 atmospheric and 147 underground tests throughout French Polynesia between 1966 and 1996; these occurred primarily at the Mururoa and Fangataufa atolls.

The legacy of nuclear weapons lies not so much with the

actual military use as it does with the proliferation of weapons development, testing, and storage. The legacy thus extends well beyond the bombings of Hiroshima and Nagasaki, to the extensive military-industrial complexes that continue to produce these weapons, and to the environments that have been and continue to be contaminated through the testing and stockpiling of weapons.

THE HUMAN COST OF NUCLEAR WEAPONS

Nuclear weapons produce both immediate (acute) and long-term (delayed or chronic) effects.[40] Upon detonation of a nuclear device, victims are immediately subjected to the effects of the explosive blast itself, thermal energy (intense heat), and radiation poisoning; injury and death occur in a matter of seconds (minutes at most) following the explosion.[41]

Most physical damage to areas subjected to a nuclear explosion is caused by the explosive blast. Blast effects are caused by the shock wave created by the nuclear explosion.[42] Upon detonation, a shock wave is generated; this wave travels faster than sound and causes an instantaneous jump in pressure (a pressure jump) at the shock front. The air immediately behind the shock front is accelerated to high velocities—many times faster than nature's most destructive tornadoes. These extreme winds (upwards of 900 mph) combine with the pressure jump to produce the damaging blast wave. Most injuries and deaths, however, are not necessarily the result of the shock wave. Indeed, the human body is able to withstand extreme differences in both pressure and winds. Most injuries and deaths result indirectly, i.e., from collapsing buildings, falling debris, or flying glass.[43]

The temperatures reached in a nuclear explosion are considerably greater than found in conventional weapons, with a large proportion of the energy in a nuclear explosion released as

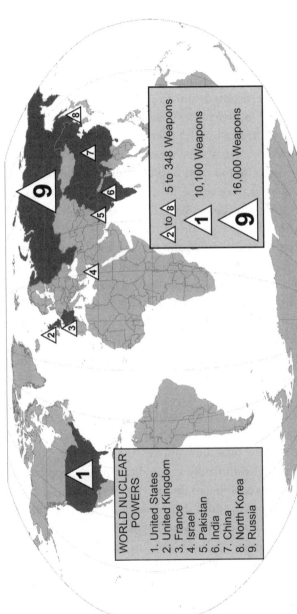

WORLD NUCLEAR
POWERS
1. United States
2. United Kingdom
3. France
4. Israel
5. Pakistan
6. India
7. China
8. North Korea
9. Russia

2 to 8 5 to 348 Weapons

1 10,100 Weapons

9 16,000 Weapons

Source: www.carnegieendowment.org/npp/numbers/default.cfm

Figure 5.1
Map of World Nuclear Powers.

thermal energy within the fireball. Indeed, temperatures are approximately 10,000 times hotter than the surface of the sun.[44]

Flash burns result from the absorption of radiant energy by the skin of the exposed individuals and may be especially lethal.[45] Burns, in general, are classified by their severity to humans, and range (typically) from first to third degree. First-degree burns are often not too serious. These are characterized by immediate pain, followed by a reddening of the skin. Pain and sensitivity may continue for minutes to hours. There is no tissue damage involved. Second-degree burns, conversely, do result in damage to the underlying dermal tissue of areas affected. Along with pain and redness, blistering also follows within a few hours, as fluids collect between the epidermis and the damaged tissue. Third-degree burns result in significant tissue death, including the stem cells required for tissue regeneration. Physicists estimate that a one-megaton nuclear device can cause first-degree burns at a distance of seven miles; second-degree burns may occur within six miles; and third-degree burns occur up to five miles from the point of detonation.[46]

Nuclear explosions may result in damage significantly greater than third-degree burns; these burns destroy tissues beneath the skin, including muscle and connective tissues. Studies of the Hiroshima event found that many people close to the hypocenter suffered burns that were 15 times the exposure required for third-degree burns. Indeed, the intense heating was "sufficient to cause exposed flesh to flash into steam, flaying exposed body areas to the bone." In other instances, victims simply vaporized.[47]

Eye injuries are also commonly associated with nuclear explosions. The brightness of the explosion may result in damage to the cornea and retina; temporary or permanent blindness may result. And, as observed in Hiroshima and Nagasaki, burn-related injuries and death also result from incendiary fires that accompany nuclear explosions.

Although proportionally the blast effects and thermal energy may account for the greatest number of deaths following a nuclear explosion, most people are worried about the effects of radiation. And for good reason. There are over 300 different fission products that may result from a nuclear reaction; these radioactive elements, moreover, have half-lives ranging from fractions of a second to centuries.[48] In short, the radioactive fallout of a nuclear explosion may continue to injure and kill people for many generations; entire areas may be contaminated and thus unsuitable for living or the cultivation of foodstuffs.

The release of radiation is unique to nuclear explosions and produces injuries primarily through damage to a body's chromosomes. Specifically, damage is caused when the radiation breaks up other molecules and forms chemically reactive free radicals or unstable compounds. These then cause damage to a person's DNA and/or disrupt their cellular chemistry. Deleterious effects are immediate, affecting the person's metabolic and replication processes. Tissues that are most sensitive (i.e., bone marrow, lymphatic tissues, hair follicles) to radiation injury are those that undergo rapid cell division. The gastrointestinal system is also particularly sensitive to radiation poisoning.[49]

Scientists measure radiation exposure in many different ways. Common measurements include *roentgens* and *rems*.[50] A roentgen is a unit of radiation exposure that measures ionization in the air; the term was eventually replaced in the late 1950s by the term *rem*. A rem measures the amount of radiation required to produce approximately the same biological effect as one roentgen.[51] Rems are often used to indicate the effects of radiation on human bodies. Within the nuclear community, certain guidelines have been established for "safe" occupational exposure to radiation. In general, people should not be exposed to more than 5 rem per year.[52]

Following a nuclear explosion, the severity and lethality of acute radiation poisoning is related to the size of the dose, the ability of radiation to harm human tissue, and which organs are affected. For people exposed to less than 100 rem, no obvious radiation sickness occurs. After exposure to 100 rem, however, serious consequences begin to emerge. In general, bodies exposed to between 100 and 200 rem will begin to exhibit symptoms (e.g., nausea and vomiting) of acute radiation sickness within three to six hours. These may last for several hours to a day. A latent period then sets in whereupon patients physically *seem* to get better. However, during this period, as blood cells naturally die off but are not replaced, mild symptoms gradually (within two weeks) begin to reappear. Victims often experience fatigue and a loss of appetite. Studies tracking survivors of the Hiroshima and Nagasaki explosions indicate that symptoms may continue for up to ten years; survivors may also have an increased risk of leukemia and lymphoma.[53]

Significant risk of mortality is found when a person is exposed to 200 to 400 rem. With this dosage, the initial onset of symptoms occurs within one to six hours and will last between one to two days. Again, following a latent period, symptoms reappear. However, the person will also experience hair loss, fatigue, chronic diarrhea, and hemorrhaging of the mouth, subcutaneous tissues, and the kidneys. The suppression of white blood cells is severe, resulting in a greater susceptibility to infection and illness. There is also a significant possibility of permanent sterility in women.[54]

At 400 to 600 rem, mortality rates increase rapidly. Initial symptoms appear within one-half to two hours and last for two days. A latent period of 7 to 14 days is followed by a more severe recurrence of sickness. Without proper treatment, death usually results within 2 to 12 weeks.[55]

For persons exposed to 600 to 1,000 rem, survival is only possible with immediate and extensive medical treatment. Onset of symptoms is less than 30 minutes, though many exposed persons may die immediately following heart failure. If the person survives the first few hours, the long-term prognosis is not good. The body's bone marrow is nearly or completely destroyed; the gastrointestinal system is damaged. A lingering death may result within a month of exposure; otherwise, recovery may require years of medical care and even then will never be complete.[56]

Finally, for those victims exposed to dosages over 1,000 rem, death is a near certainty. Debilitating symptoms may occur within seconds or minutes; these include nausea, convulsions, and diarrhea. The body may experience intestinal bleeding, brain seizures, or heart failure. Death resultant from circulatory collapse can occur within hours. For those who survive the first few hours, a latent period follows. This is known as the "walking ghost" phase. Symptoms reappear, whereupon the victim may become delirious or comatose prior to death.[57]

Exposure to radiation from a nuclear explosion (or from a nuclear accident) produces both acute (immediate) and latent (delayed) effects. Radiation is produced directly by nuclear reactions that generate the explosion and also by the decay of radioactive particles left over, appearing as "fallout." Acute effects (produced by the explosion) typically appear within minutes to hours (or possibly weeks) of exposure, while latent effects (produced from radioactive fallout) may not appear until months or even years later.

Initial nuclear radiation (also called "prompt" radiation) is defined as radiation that arrives during the first few seconds or minutes after an explosion; this is mostly gamma radiation and neutron radiation. The explosion causes very intense (and often extremely lethal) exposures for individuals closest to the point of detonation.[58] Most deaths following a nuclear explosion, however, would not be the result of lethal doses of radiation. At Hiroshima and Nagasaki, for example, most people—perhaps more than half of all deaths—were killed directly by the blast effect or by thermal heat.

Victims may also be exposed to radiation in the form of nuclear fallout. Depending on the yield of the nuclear device, the altitude at which detonation occurred, and other meteorological variables, nuclear fallout will begin to settle to the ground within an hour to a few hours. Exposure to radiation is cumulative and continues to accrue as long as individuals remain within the fallout zone.[59]

The delayed (long-term) effects of nuclear weapons are derived principally from radiation poisoning (primarily in the form of nuclear fallout) and may thus seriously debilitate or kill people over an extended period of time; indeed, people may fall ill (and die) from the effects of nuclear devices decades after the initial release of radiation. Continued exposure contributes to genetic mutations, microcephaly, and numerous types of cancers. Consequently, the true global legacy of nuclear devices stems from the delayed effects of radiation contamination.[60] Furthermore, these effects are often hidden. If the exposure rate is low enough, although accumulating over many years, the victim may never experience any symptoms. For example, areas in which the inhabitants are exposed to 0.25 rem per day over five years would receive a total exposure of 450 rems, the people living in the region may never exhibit any signs of overt sickness, but would as a whole experience very high mortality from radiation poisoning.[61]

Only two nuclear weapons have been used in warfare: the bombs dropped on Hiroshima and Nagasaki. However, the true cost, and ultimate legacy, of nuclear warfare is found in the lives of the hundreds of thousands of people who have been, and continue to be, exposed to radiation poisoning through the repeated production, testing, stockpiling, and dumping of nuclear weapons and radioactive wastes. As Sue Wareham explains, radioisotopes produced by nuclear tests, such as carbon-14, cesium-137, strontium-90, and plutonium-239, have half-lives of 5,730 years, 30 years, 28 years, and 24,400 years respectively, and thus pose sizeable risks to current and future generations.[62] When viewed from this perspective, the world itself becomes a militarized landscape of nuclear threats. Today, there are an estimated 400,000 to 700,000 sources of ionizing radiation; many of these local "hotspots" of radioactive contamination are considered to be highly hazardous.[63] Radiation poisoning thus becomes a global reality for large numbers of people far removed from any "traditional" battlefields.[64] And that reality is staggering. Since 1945, there have been more than 2,000 nuclear detonations.[65] These tests have contributed to the widespread dispersal of radioactive fallout, thus leading to serious health and environment problems on a global scale.

Atmospheric testing of nuclear devices generates substantial quantities of radioactive fallout. Radioactive fallout consists of microscopic particles that fall to earth as a result of nuclear explosion, not only from the blasts at Hiroshima and Nagasaki, but also from the approximately 500 above-ground nuclear tests that have been conducted since testing began in 1945 at Alamogordo, New Mexico. Fallout particles vary in size, ranging from thousandths of a millimeter to several millimeters. Depending on the atmospheric conditions at the

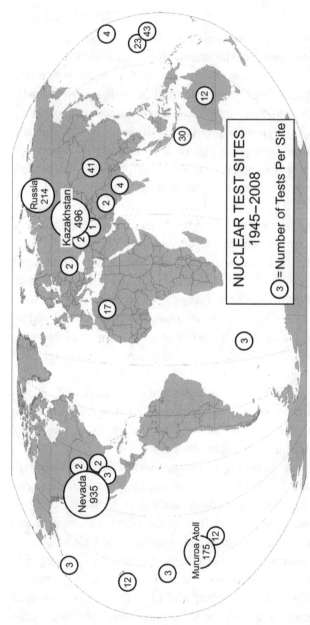

**NUCLEAR TEST SITES
1945–2008**

③ = Number of Tests Per Site

Source: National Resources Defense Council

Figure 5.2
Map of Nuclear Test Sites.

time of the explosion, most are deposited soon after explosion and, spatially, within relatively close proximity to the site of detonation. However, if conditions are right, the dispersal of radioactive fallout may be geographically extensive. For example, when these particles are exploded high into the atmosphere they may be dispersed over a period of hours, days, or even months and across an area many hundreds or thousands of miles beyond the test site.[66] A megaton-range nuclear explosion can contaminate an area of thousands of square miles, rendering those areas uninhabitable for years or even decades.

The health consequences of radioactive fallout generated from nuclear testing may last for generations and exert a devastating toll on the people affected. In the Marshall Islands, for example, the United States conducted 67 nuclear tests between 1946 and 1958. Today, residents of these islands suffer some of the highest rates of radiation sickness in the world. Cancer, leukemia, miscarriages, asthma, autism, and other medical conditions are prevalent. Most disturbing are the hundreds of malformed babies born throughout the islands. Known as "jellyfish" babies, these children are born with no bones; their weak hearts are visibly beating through translucent skin. Frequently, these unfortunate babies may live for a day or two until they die. Other babies are born with no arms, legs, or even heads.[67]

Residents in the United States continue to suffer from the legacy of American nuclear weapons production. In 1997 the National Cancer Institute announced that atmospheric tests conducted at the Nevada site resulted in a significant contamination of the nation's milk supply with iodine-131; the NCI estimated that upwards of 212,000 excess thyroid cancers were the direct result of the nuclear tests.[68] And in New Zealand, survivors of the British nuclear tests conducted in 1957 and 1958 (designated Operation Grapple) exhibit three times the normal level of chromosomal changes, thus foreshadowing the potential for intergenerational effects of genetic mutations.[69]

Compounding the problem of nuclear weapons development is that throughout the 1950s and 1960s, testing procedures, for many governments, were often haphazard, exhibiting scant regard for the safety of either local residents or the environment. Furthermore, nuclear devices were used in questionable ways to supplement other activities. In the Soviet Union, for example, approximately 100 underground nuclear explosions were conducted throughout the country in an attempt to improve oil and gas yields; Soviet officials likewise experimented with nuclear explosions to facilitate earth removal in the construction of irrigation canals. These usages led to the exposure of many thousands of Russians to dangerous levels of radiation.[70]

Future generations will also be confronted with the realization that throughout the Cold War, both the Soviet Union and the United States, in particular, gave relatively low priority to the problem of the storage and disposal of radioactive wastes. In the United States alone, nuclear waste has accumulated at 120 sites; this includes approximately 55,000 tons of high-level waste from civilian reactors and 15,000 tons from nuclear weapons production.[71]

In many ways, the nuclear waste legacy of the former Soviet Union epitomizes the magnitude of the problem. Throughout its existence, the Soviet Union's nuclear weapons industry was colossal in size. At its height, the former Soviet nuclear program was composed of over 700 military facilities involved in the use of radioactive materials. In addition, there were at least 16 large nuclear complexes designed solely or primarily for military purposes. The Kola Peninsula alone had 324 nuclear reactors.[72]

In the early 1990s, the extent of Russia's nuclear legacy

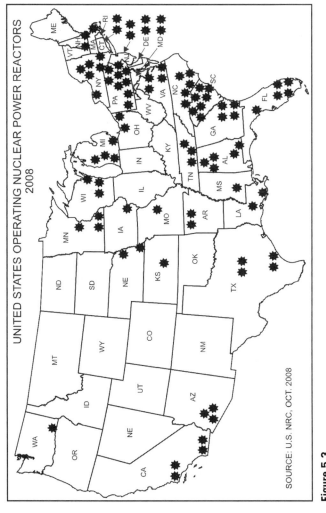

Figure 5.3
Map of US Nuclear Power Reactors.

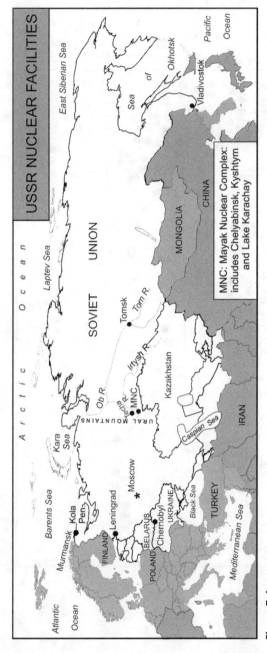

Figure 5.4
Map of USSR Nuclear Facilities.

gained widespread exposure. In 1991, for example, allegations surfaced that the Soviet Union had been for years illegally dumping nuclear wastes in the Arctic Sea; in 1993, the Russian Federation officially confirmed that high- and low-level waste had in fact been dumped between 1959 and 1991.[73] And, similar to the dumping of chemical weapons following the Second World War, Soviet officials simply discarded *tons* of radioactive materials into the northern waters of Europe. Consider that between 1964 and 1990 the former Soviet Union dumped 17,000 containers of nuclear waste and 16 nuclear reactors into the waters of the Barents and Kara seas. Moreover, most (if not all) of these reactors had previously experienced some type of accident and six of them still contained their nuclear fuel when they were dumped.[74]

The history of the Mayak facility is particularly informative. Built in less than two years by over 45,000 workers and an untold number of prisoners, the Mayak facility was located in the eastern Ural Mountains, situated between the larger industrial cities of Chelyabinsk and Kyshtym. This facility housed the first Soviet industrial reactor and was the largest of the former Soviet Union's three plutonium production centers.[75]

It is also the site of numerous nuclear accidents and questionable disposal practices. In 1957, for example, storage facilities at the site exploded. Radioactive pollutants were dispersed over a 20,000 square kilometer area, forcing an estimated 10,000 people to be evacuated. In total, over 270,000 were exposed to some level of radiation poisoning.[76]

In response to the accident in 1957, Soviet authorities constructed a new liquid storage facility at the Mayak site. Even this attempt proved inadequate, as radioactive liquid wastes contaminated local soils and groundwater supplies to a depth of 100 meters.[77]

Soviet authorities affiliated with the Mayak facility also gave little concern to the overall disposal of radioactive wastes. Between 1948 and 1956, for example, radioactive waste from the Mayak complex was dumped straight into the Techa River (a tributary of the larger Ob River). Years later, radioisotopes were detected in Arctic Ocean approximately 1,000 miles away. Incredulously, Soviet authorities also began to dispose radioactive wastes directly into Lake Karachay (also spelled as Karachai). Geologically, this inland lake lacks any natural outlets. Consequently, over the years, radioactive wastes (especially strontium-90 and cesium-137) steadily accumulated in the lake. In 1969, however, a severe drought resulted in a substantial drop in the lake's water level, causing mud flats to dry and become powdery. These heavily contaminated sediments were then wind-blown for thousands of kilometers, exposing upwards of 500,000 people to radioactive materials.[78] Even today, the waste discharge point at Lake Karachay remains so radioactive that a person standing there would receive a lethal dose of radiation within minutes.[79]

The Mayak facility is but one of the former Soviet Union's sites to pose environmental hazards. The Tomsk 7 nuclear plant, for example, came into operation in 1958. This site would become the Soviet Union's main nuclear fuel processing center and by 1970 was home to five nuclear reactors. Up to 1990, the Tomsk 7 plant produced about 33 million cubic meters of liquid waste and an estimated 127,000 metric tonnes of solid radioactive waste. Most of these wastes were ostensibly stored in underground containers approximately ten kilometers from the River Tom—a tributary of the Ob River. In 1991 it was acknowledged that the plant had for years discharged liquid wastes directly into the River Tom.[80]

Perhaps the most well-known symbol of Russia's nuclear legacy is the case of Chernobyl. On April 26, 1986, while

Figure 5.5
Located in Armenia, the Medzamor Nuclear Facility was part of the Soviet Union's large nuclear program. Kind permission of Dr. Shannon O'Lear.

operators were conducting low-power engineering tests, a succession of human and mechanical failures led to a series of explosions and the complete destruction of the Chernobyl nuclear reactor. This nuclear disaster is considered to be one of the most serious environmental catastrophes ever. Radioactive fallout covered a wide area throughout Europe, including the Ukraine, Belarus, Russia, Finland, Norway, Sweden, Austria, and Bulgaria; all told, tens of millions of people were exposed to some level of radiation. Studies have identified the existence of long-term health consequences for those people living in exposed areas, including an increased prevalence of brain cancer among children in Sweden and thyroid cancers in Russia and the Ukraine.[81] A post-disaster failure to prevent cattle from grazing on contaminated lands contributed to the health consequences, as radiation entered the region's milk supply.

And still, now, long after the acute effects of radiation have subsided, radiation damage continues to cause human and environmental damage.[82]

The other members of the world's nuclear club also suffer from the production, testing, and disposal of nuclear materials. In India, for example, villages in the vicinity of the Jadugoda mine exhibit increased rates of congenital deformities (in both people and domesticated animals), cancers, and sterility.[83] The mining of uranium is highly polluting and generates vast amounts of radioactive waste. On average, the mining and treatment of one metric ton of uranium results in nearly one-half cubic meter of liquid radioactive waste and upwards of 1.6 metric tonnes of solid waste.[84] Contaminated water associated with the mine has been discharged directly into the local river—which is used for irrigation, bathing, and drinking. Pollutants have also seeped into neighboring drinking wells and an estimated 80 percent of the surrounding farmlands have been polluted.[85] Many of these wastes will remain potentially hazardous for hundreds, or even thousands, of years.[86]

A WASTEFUL LEGACY

In George Orwell's *Nineteen Eighty-Four* wars were waged for the purpose of conducting future wars. The aim of warfare was not to win but to use the products of the war industry without raising the general standard of living. War had become a business in itself. Indeed, war was essential to facilitate the continued production, circulation, and consumption of war-related materials. Consider munitions. Once a bomb is expended, another one must be produced. And large stocks of weapons and munitions do not generate profits; rather, these goods must be sold and ultimately used. In the twenty-first century, munitions manufactured from depleted uranium epitomize the Orwellian logic of the military-industrial complex.[87]

The story of depleted uranium begins where the story of nuclear weapons production leaves off. Natural uranium must be altered before it becomes usable in nuclear reactors or weapons. The highly radioactive and unstable U-235 isotopes must be separated out to a reactor grade of approximately 3.6 percent. This enrichment process, however, results in a waste stream of "depleted" uranium, which is composed of 99 percent U-238 isotopes.[88]

As early as 1943 scientists recognized that depleted uranium posed a significant problem.[89] Although it is considered to be "weakly" radioactive—it is about 60 percent as radioactive as purified natural uranium—depleted uranium is potentially harmful. Strict guidelines have been in place since the mid-1940s as to the handling of depleted uranium.

Over the years, the storage of depleted uranium posed a seemingly insurmountable problem. In part, this problem was derived from the steady accumulation of the waste material. Worldwide, approximately 50,000 metric tonnes of depleted uranium are produced in the generation of nuclear power and weapons. In 2005 the world stock of depleted uranium was estimated at 1.2 million metric tonnes.[90]

Beginning in the 1970s, scientists sought to "kill two birds with one stone." Rather than viewing depleted uranium as a waste product that required costly (and potentially dangerous) storage, why not approach the material as a commodity? Consequently, scientists and military planners began to consider the actual uses of depleted uranium.

And indeed it was found that depleted uranium has some remarkable properties which were especially appealing. Compared to other metals, such as lead or tungsten, depleted uranium is exceptionally dense. This quality alone would

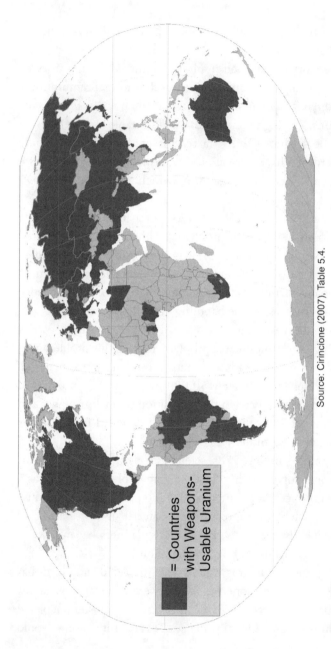

Figure 5.6
Map of Usable Uranium.

Source: Cirincione (2007), Table 5.4.

= Countries
with Weapons-
Usable Uranium

suggest that depleted uranium might be used as armor-plating on vehicles. And indeed, studies found that conventional weapons are unable to penetrate tanks protected by armor plates coated with, or made from, depleted uranium.

Depleted uranium was also found to be an effective source material for munitions. It is pyrophoric, meaning that it burns in the air; when a depleted uranium shell strikes a vehicle, it does not explode as conventional weapons will. Rather, the shell actually penetrates through armored plating much as a hot knife cuts through butter. The shell incinerates all occupants of the vehicle. It was thus viewed as a particularly effective weapon in the military's arsenal.

A second, and not inconsequential, consideration was economic. As a waste product derived from an already existing nuclear industry, there are no additional costs involved in the production of depleted uranium. And the producers of depleted uranium were all too happy to find a use for it. Now, depleted uranium is provided *free of charge* to defense companies for the manufacture of armored plating or munitions. In fact, artillery shells and other munitions produced with depleted uranium are ten times cheaper than those manufactured with other metals, such as tungsten. Furthermore, with respect to American weapons manufacturers, tungsten must be imported. Indeed, approximately 50 percent of America's tungsten is imported from China.[91]

The use of depleted uranium in the production of armored plates and munitions seemed to provide an ideal solution for all parties. The accumulating waste product could be addressed; defense contractors were able to utilize a low-cost source of materials; and the military added a new "super" weapon to its arsenal.[92] By the mid-1990s, the United States had manufactured nearly two million tank penetrator shells and 55 million small-caliber penetrators. And the United

149 **Beyond the Flash of War**

States was not alone in the production and/or acquisition of depleted uranium munitions. At the dawn of the twenty-first century, more than 15 countries or territories had acquired depleted uranium weapons, including Britain, France, Russia, Greece, Turkey, Israel, Saudi Arabia, Bahrain, Egypt, Kuwait, Pakistan, Thailand, Taiwan, and South Korea.[93]

The first military use of depleted uranium occurred during the 1991 Gulf War. Coalition forces, including the United States and the United Kingdom, expended numerous rounds of depleted uranium shells against the Iraqi Army. Throughout the campaign, over 860,000 rounds were used in Saudi Arabia, Kuwait, and Iraq.[94]

So successful were these weapons, they were widely used in the Balkans. In Bosnia (1994–1995) and Kosovo (1999), an estimated 11,000 and 31,000 rounds of depleted uranium shells were used by American forces, respectively.[95]

However, all was not well. Within two years of the Gulf War, veterans of the war in both the U.S. and the U.K. began to complain of "mysterious" illnesses, in time labeled "Gulf War Syndrome." These veterans exhibited weakness, fatigue, and respiratory and kidney problems. Doctors documented increased incidences of cancers and leukemia. Children conceived by returning vets were also found to exhibit higher rates of birth defects and other genetic deformities. By 1999 over one-third of the 600,000 U.S. troops deployed during the Gulf War had sought medical assistance and, as of 2004, more than 176,000 American veterans of the Gulf War were receiving some form of disability compensation. An additional 25,000 cases were still pending.[96] In Britain, likewise, 8,000 of the 29,000 troops deployed throughout the Gulf War complained of some illness. Within eight years, over 400 had already died.[97]

Within Iraq, Kuwait, and Saudi Arabia, doctors also reported a larger than normal number of cases of cancer. Doctors also noted unusually large numbers of horrible birth defects, of children being born without eyes, ears, brains, or limbs; infants born with their internal organs, such as bladders, outside of their bodies. Doctors compared these birth deformities to those survivors and descendants of the nuclear test sites of the Pacific—a population long known to be suffering from the legacy of nuclear contamination.[98] And in Bosnia, by 1997 doctors were reporting a threefold increase in cancers.[99]

Members of the medical communities in the affected regions, as well as the United States and the United Kingdom, began to suspect that depleted uranium weapons were the cause of these illnesses. It was known, for example, that when depleted uranium projectiles come into contact with a tank or other armored vehicle, millions of radioactive particles are instantaneously released into the air. In fact, upwards of 70 percent of the projectile will oxidize into dust, and between 50 and 96 percent of the particles will have a diameter of less than 10 millimeters. Consequently, the radioactive oxide aerosol is easily ingested, inhaled, or absorbed by all who come into contact. Particles might also become attached to dust and other particulate matter, and thus be carried by the wind.[100]

Military officials in both the United States and the United Kingdom continue to claim that the Gulf War sicknesses were most likely caused by the use of chemical weapons by Iraqi forces and/or reactions to the numerous vaccinations given to Coalition troops in anticipation of Iraqi chemical or biological weapons use.[101] And as recently as 2004, British officials even accused their soldiers of "faking" symptoms of Gulf War Syndrome.[102]

These same military officials also steadfastly deny any possibility that depleted uranium weapons might have contributed to the higher incidences of tumors, cancers, birth defects, kidney damage, respiratory problems, and other maladies. This, despite the fact that the medical establishment and scientific communities—since 1943—have established that exposure to depleted uranium can result in significant health problems. Laboratory studies on mice and rats have found that exposure results in increased incidences of tumors and cancers; kidney damage; and inhibitions in bone formation. Clinical studies of humans exposed to depleted uranium identify adverse effects on both the reproductive and nervous systems. Acute poisoning related to exposure to depleted uranium has also been linked to renal failure and death and has been posited to alter the genetic code, thus leading to birth deformities.[103] And significantly, while the Pentagon and other US officials continue to deny the negative health effects of exposure to depleted uranium, efforts are under way to "clean up" test sites within the United States. In both Nevada and Indiana, for example, billions of dollars are being spent to remove the waste from expended depleted uranium-based ammunition.[104]

Weapons manufactured from inexpensive depleted uranium stockpiles continue to be used. Coalition forces, and especially the United States, have widely used depleted uranium munitions in the Second Gulf (or Iraq) War that began in 2003. Indeed, within the first year of the conflict, U.S. and Coalition troops used more than five times as many depleted uranium bombs and shells than were used in the whole of the 1991 Gulf War.[105]

Beyond the flash of "Little Boy" exploding above the residents of Hiroshima, the legacy of nuclear weapons continues to highlight the legacy of twentieth-century warfare. And to that end, the recent proliferation and use of depleted uranium munitions further highlights the lethal legacies of an unfettered and globalizing military-industrial complex. As of 2004, the U.S. Department of Energy acknowledged that it had a stockpile of approximately 100 million tons of depleted uranium.[106] Vast amounts of this radioactive waste, subsequently, have been exported to other militaries around the world: an ominous portent of things to come. As Dr. Asaf Durakovic, a nuclear medicine expert who has conducted research on depleted uranium, explains, "Due to the current proliferation of DU weaponry, the battlefields of the future will be unlike any battlefields in history."[107] These weapons, and those still on the drawing board, will be more lethal, more lasting, more extensive, and more indiscriminate. And it will not simply be the battlefields that are deadly, but also the production facilities, the testing sites, and the storage locations associated with a globalized nuclear weapons industry.

> But the words of the vanquished come later, sometimes long after the war, when grown
> men and women unpack the suffering they endured as children: what it was like to see
> their mother or father killed or taken away, or what it was like to lose their homes, their
> community, their security, and to be discarded as human refuse. But by then few listen.
> The truth about war comes out, but usually too late. We are assured by the war-makers
> that these stories have no bearing on the glorious violent enterprise the nation is about to
> inaugurate. And, lapping up the myth of war and its sense of empowerment, we prefer
> not to look. [1]

Located in the northwest quarter of Cambodia, Battambang City, the provincial capital of Battambang Province, is the country's second largest city. Having endured 30 years of civil war, genocide, and military occupation, the city is recovering and is now growing rapidly. To accommodate this growth, efforts are underway to expand Highway 57, the main artery linking Battambang City and Pailin. Progress has been slowed, however, because of the presence of landmines. Despite the Herculean efforts of organizations such as the Mine Action Group, landmines—sown decades ago—continue to explode as heavy construction equipment eats into the tropical soils. Through late 2008 and early 2009, at least one construction worker was killed or injured every other week.

The ongoing deaths and injuries occurring along the roads of Cambodia are a continuation of previous wars. They are, in fact, a product of twentieth-century military violence which

Figure 6.1
Construction crews in Cambodia confront the dangers of landmines
and other unexploded ordinance. Kind permission of the author.

is distinctive in both its geographic scale and its historical
persistence. On the one hand, twentieth-century warfare
occurred on a scale previously unimaginable. From the horrific death tolls of the First World War and the incomprehensible carnage of the Second World War, through the
killings of Southeast Asia, Africa, and the Middle East during
the latter half of the century, modern warfare has taken a
phenomenal toll on humanity. According to Marc Pilisuk, war
has caused more than three times the number of casualties in
the last 90 years than in the previous 500; in the post-
Second World War era, upwards of 250 major wars have been
waged, claiming over 50 million lives and leaving tens of
millions homeless.[2]

As detailed throughout *Military Legacies*, people continue to be killed or injured long after wars have been concluded. They are casualties of the trauma of conflict as well as the material manifestation of war: landmines and cluster bombs, chemical and nuclear weapons. No continent has been spared the legacy of twentieth-century warfare; no body of water is immune from actual or potential pollution and contamination. These remnants are a product of a militarized globalization; the presence of this military legacy is our global reality.

Our military legacy is the product of a globalizing militarism that promotes economic profit over people's lives. The emergence of an industrial militarism throughout the twentieth century irrevocably altered the conduct of warfare and, by extension, made our world ever more dangerous. Over the past century, the tightening bonds between capital and the military radically changed the relationship between weapons production, circulation, and use. Modern conflicts and the demand for armaments and munitions are now driven more by profit motives than by security concerns. And these trends are both the catalyst and consequence of globalization.

Globalization is a much debated term.[3] For some writers, globalization signifies a unique moment in the expansion of capitalism; critics of globalization (as concept) contend that the term represents nothing more than the latest "fad" in academia. However, even the most cursory consideration of the inequalities among the peoples of the world, the proliferation of weapons of mass destruction, the callous disregard for the environment, and the acceptance of "collateral damage" during military campaigns suggests that something is wrong. Too many people are dying for "globalization" to be merely a fad.

"During most of history," Martin Van Creveld writes, "war had been a relatively simple activity as men discarded the refinements of civilization, took up the sword, and marched to slaughter one another."[4] This changed during the bloody twentieth century, as the *practice* of warfare became increasingly reliant upon the twin institutions of academics and economics. During the First World War, for example, the process of weapons research and development began to be institutionalized, as teams of scientists and engineers were assembled.[5] In part a response to the stagnant Western Front and the horrific casualties associated with trench warfare, governments increasingly fostered a state-private relationship that would become known as the military-industrial complex.

What counted to state governments initially was the capacity to maintain and supply their own (or their allies') armed forces. Prior to the First World War, most European countries had a mixed arms economy of state shipyards and arsenals alongside private firms. During the war, however, the driving force of arms manufacture was private profit, fueled and steered by state subsidies and contracts. Throughout Europe, as the conflict continued, factories were refitted to produce the massive arsenals needed for trench warfare, thus providing new-found business opportunities for the arms industry. In France (but similarly in other European countries), state plants and established arms firms concentrated on the manufacture of heavy artillery and machine guns, while simpler work, such as the filling of shell cases, went to firms that had converted from civilian production. In Britain, a Ministry of Munitions was formed in May 1915 to supply the required munitions that were being expended along the Western Front. Within one year, Britain increased its annual output of heavy guns from 90 to 3,200.[6] Many of these private factories garnered excessive profits, but when the government tried to force down prices, the industrialists threatened to withhold production.[7] Thus was set in a motion a trend that would continue to the present day: the production of munitions and weapons for profit, regardless of the consequences.

The belligerent states of the First World War also introduced new weapons technologies and applied existing ones more destructively. Chemical weapons, flame-throwers, land- and sea-mines were widely used and contributed to the dangers of twentieth-century battlefields and even home fronts. And the recipient governments of these weapons rarely resisted the temptation to violate the internationally agreed-upon restrictions on the conduct of battle, nor to ignore the restrictions against inflicting harm on civilian populations.[8]

These trends continued throughout the twentieth century, as more sophisticated weaponry and munitions were developed or existing technologies refined. From 1915 onward, airship and bomber raids on cities and countrysides brought about an awareness of the potential of air warfare as a strategic arm that could bring combat directly to enemy populations. During the Second World War, for example, Nazi Germany authorized the bombing of civilian targets. In response, Britain embarked on its own strategic bombing campaign. With the entry of the United States into the war, American forces likewise conducted intensive bombing campaigns over the skies of Europe and Japan—leading ultimately to the atomic bombs being dropped on Hiroshima and Nagasaki. In total, aerial bombardments during the Second World War claimed over one million civilian lives throughout Europe and Japan.[9] And to the destructiveness wrought by air campaigns can be added other indiscriminate weapons systems. By mid-century, numerous nations could point to massive stockpiles of chemical and nuclear weapons, cluster bombs and fragmentation grenades, and a cornucopia of anti-personnel and anti-vehicle landmines.

During the Cold War, the design, acceptance, transfer, and use of more indiscriminate and more lethal weapons was proliferating throughout the global community, dispersed by a rapacious arms trade that privileged profit over people. More importantly, the participants of this globalizing arms industry provided weapons and munitions not only to their own governments' security concerns, but also sought to feed the incessant hunger of the never-ending conflicts around the world.

The proliferation of weapons of mass destruction (including landmines and cluster bombs) has intensified to a degree unimagined a century ago. Currently, global military spending exceeds US$1 trillion annually—an amount that is approximately 15 times the expenditure on international aid.[10] As Richard Bitzinger concludes, the "globalization of arms production appears to be increasing not only in terms of the sheer number of collaborative arms activities but also in terms of depth, as armaments cooperation reaches down to the level of technology sharing and componentry; of sophistication, as defense firms around the world forge new, direct links with each other; and of geographic scope, as more countries in the developing world become players in international arms production as a result of increased collaborative arms programs."[11]

Globalization is uneven, marked by disparities and discontinuities, and the international arms trade is no exception. The global sale of weapons is dominated by only a few, mostly Western, states. The United States is the world's largest supplier of major conventional weapons, followed by Russia, France, the United Kingdom, and Germany. Combined, these states account for an estimated 82 percent of all major conventional arms transfers. However, other competitors are steadily increasing their share of the profits. Brazil, China, India, Pakistan, Singapore, South Korea, South Africa, Turkey; most of these countries' production is for export.[12]

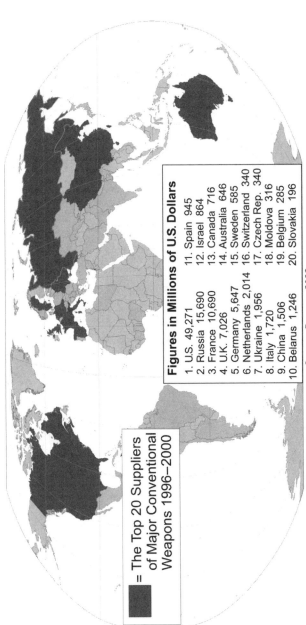

The Top 20 Suppliers of Major Conventional Weapons 1996–2000

Figures in Millions of U.S. Dollars

1. U.S. 49,271	11. Spain 945
2. Russia 15,690	12. Israel 864
3. France 10,690	13. Canada 716
4. U.K. 7,026	14. Australia 646
5. Germany 5,647	15. Sweden 585
6. Netherlands 2,014	16. Switzerland 340
7. Ukraine 1,956	17. Czech Rep. 340
8. Italy 1,720	18. Moldova 316
9. China 1,506	19. Belgium 285
10. Belarus 1,246	20. Slovakia 196

Source: Burrows 2002

Figure 6.2
Map of World's Weapon Suppliers.

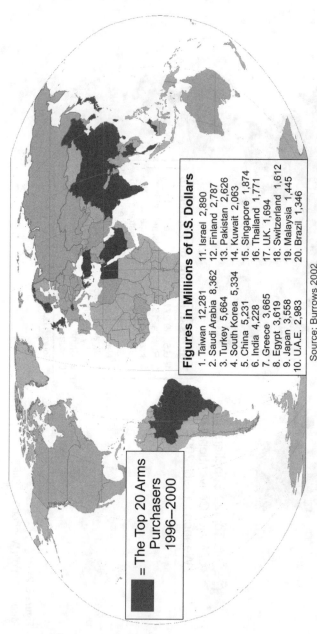

The Top 20 Arms Purchasers 1996–2000

Figures in Millions of U.S. Dollars

1. Taiwan 12,281	11. Israel 2,890
2. Saudi Arabia 8,362	12. Finland 2,787
3. Turkey 5,664	13. Pakistan 2,626
4. South Korea 5,334	14. Kuwait 2,063
5. China 5,231	15. Singapore 1,874
6. India 4,228	16. Thailand 1,771
7. Greece 3,665	17. U.K. 1,694
8. Egypt 3,619	18. Switzerland 1,612
9. Japan 3,558	19. Malaysia 1,445
10. U.A.E. 2,983	20. Brazil 1,346

Source: Burrows 2002

Figure 6.3
Map of World's Arms Purchasers.

Within the main exporting countries are found a handful of large transnational armament companies and hundreds of smaller components and specialist manufacturers.[13] These include behemoths such as Lockheed Martin, Boeing, Raytheon, Northrop Grumman, and General Dynamics. When viewed together, these transnational corporations constitute a significant part of a globalizing military-industrial complex. And the U.S. Department of Defense is the major funder of this industry. In 2002, for example, Lockheed Martin, Boeing, and Northrop Grumman ranked one, two, and three among the Pentagon's defense contractors, taking in US$17 billion, US$16.6 billion, and US$8.7 billion respectively.[14] And what of the product of these activities? These corporations have produced some of the most sophisticated and deadly arsenals, including the U-2 spy-plane (Lockheed), the B-52 Stratofortress (Boeing), and the B-2 Stealth Bomber (Northrop Grumman).[15]

Whereas these few countries are responsible for the production and export of the more sophisticated weaponry systems, there is an even greater globalization of small arms, light weapons, and munitions production. Currently, there are about 92 countries producing small arms and light weapons, while 76 countries manufacture ammunition for these weapons. And the output from these "minor" arms exporters can be truly remarkable. Beginning in 1998, for example, a factory in Kenya has been producing an estimated 20 million rounds of ammunition per year; it was able to do so after importing production equipment from Belgium in the late 1990s.[16]

The weapons of the twenty-first century are not always technologically sophisticated or expensive to produce and distribute. In the Iraq War, numerous American and other coalition force soldiers have succumbed to "improvised explosive devices" (IEDs). In 2007 alone, approximately 475 U.S. military personnel were killed by attacks involving IEDs.[17] Reports indicate that many of these weapons are produced in neighboring Iran.

And who imports these weapons? The purchasers of these weapons are mostly found in the conflict-prone regions of Asia and the Middle East, with key states and territories including Taiwan, Turkey, Saudi Arabia, South Korea, India, Pakistan, and Israel. According to Edmund Cairns, "some of the increased military spending is in countries least able to afford it. Some of the poorest countries in the world, including Botswana, the Democratic Republic of Congo, Nigeria, Rwanda, Sudan and Uganda, are among those that doubled their military spending between 1985 and 2000."[18] As Gideon Burrows summarizes, "developing nations purchase expensive systems they can't afford, diverting money away

Figure 6.4 Improvised Explosive Devices (IEDs) are a common feature of Iraq's battlefields. Kind permission of Lt. Col. Steve Oluic, Ph.D.

from health and education projects. . . . Democracy is under-mined, as lucrative 'consultancy' contracts are signed between weapons manufacturers and former ministers—or vice versa. And political parties gain unfair advantages by receiving huge sponsorship from arms producers on the unspoken promise of lucrative contracts after polling day."[19] The arms trade, in the end, contributes to the proliferation of conflicts, and also the indiscriminate killings associated with modern war-fare. In short, without the international arms trade, many governments—without their own arms industry—would be unable to equip their armed forces and pursue war as a polit-ical means.[20]

Well into the twenty-first century, the arms trade is not just larger, but is now more "globalized" than ever before; like products in most other industries, very few pieces of military equipment are manufactured in just one country; rather, components are sourced from across the globe, production facilities are set up in developing countries, technology is traded, new markets are sought.[21] Now, almost no modern weapon type is manufactured in just one place.[22]

And the intensity of the global arms trade is without prece-dent. During the Middle Ages, it took two centuries for cutting-edge arms technology (e.g., gunpowder) to be trans-ferred across the world, from China to Europe. Now, in the twenty-first century, the pace of diffusion is decidedly more rapid.[23] The U.S. government, for example, recently concluded an arrangement with the United Arab Emirates whereby the latter country would purchase 80 F-16 fighter jets equipped with a greater flying range and better radar and targeting accuracy than the aircraft currently used by the U.S. Air Force.[24]

Capitalist imperatives have become the defining feature of our contemporary global militarism. During the Cold War, for example, the United States government was largely opposed to the "free trade" of conventional weapons. U.S. arms exports were restricted in the name of national security. However, the demise of the Soviet Union and the collapse of the communist threat seemingly ushered in an era of peace and prosperity. Under such conditions, arms manufacturers sought a greater opportunity to buy and sell on the world market. As barriers and restrictions on arms exports were removed, financial gain and competition have become the dominant values governing arms exports in today's global marketplace.[25] As Tamar Gabelnick and Anna Rich write: "In today's global economy, the U.S. government (in particular the Pentagon) has become an advocate for U.S. companies in exporting arms. . . . The overarching goal has shifted from control for national security reasons to export promotion. . . . As a result of this new market orientation for decisions about arms transfers, the U.S. government has proved willing to export increasingly sophisticated weaponry to an ever-widening group of countries."[26]

The acceleration and intensification of a global militarism is also apparent in the changing character and moral foundation of warfare and military activities. In a trend established during the First World War, and exacerbated during the Second World War, the indiscriminate use of weapons against civilian populations has been routinely legitimated. The globalization of twentieth-century warfare, in short, has been accompanied by an intensified moral exclusion that continues to separate societies into "us" and "them." Consequently, whereas the globalization of weapons technology has brought more people into contact with the lethality of modern warfare, globalization has also distanced people in order to justify their continued slaughter.

Often eschewing the moral implications of their work, scientists continue to develop more and more sophisticated weapons of death and destruction. While the twentieth century saw the "improvement" of landmines, flame-throwers, bombers, tanks, and submarines, the twenty-first century is witnessing the "perfection" of drones, satellites, and robots used in war. The United States, for example, has invested tens of millions of dollars in the design, development, and production of the Area Denial Artillery Munitions (ADAM) mine. Classified as a "scatterable" mine, the ADAM is delivered by howitzer. Each 155mm shell contains 36 wedge-shaped mines which are dispersed over a wide area when the shell breaks open around 600 meters over the targeted area. Once deployed, each mine releases up to seven tripline sensors that can extend up to approximately 7 meters. The mine itself has a lethal blast radius of 4.5 meters. The minefield resultant from just a single shell is remarkable. Consider, also, that a battery of three howitzers would be able to lay a blanket of over 500 mines in less than a minute.[27]

Whereas the acceptance and global dispersal of weapons of mass destruction has proliferated rapidly throughout the world, a concomitant anathema to their use has lagged behind. In the First World War, for example, military leaders and planners were initially horrified at the thought of using indiscriminate weapons, such as chemical gases and aerial bombing. However, as the war progressed, and the belligerents of both sides sought victory, the abhorrence of their use waned. By the war's end, all the participants had come to accept the realities of "modern" combat. The distinctions between combatants and non-combatants became increasingly blurred, as a pervasive anti-civilian ideology permeated the conduct of war. By the Second World War, numerous governments maintained an essentially tolerant view of the ambiguity of civilian identity.[28] Such a callous attitude—embodied in such phrases as "collateral damage"—has directly contributed to the incomprehensible death toll of the twentieth and twenty-first centuries.[29]

The willingness of states to sacrifice civilian populations—including their own—is well illustrated by the technological development of nuclear weapons. As Michael Adas writes, by the middle decades of the Cold War, "American scientists and technicians had proved to be the supreme architects of the sophisticated weapons systems whose overkill potential and global reach defied any logic imaginable." He continues that, "consistent with the illogic of the continuing proliferation of ever more lethal nuclear weaponry, U.S. military planners gave little serious thought to shielding the civilian population that had become the primary target of late twentieth-century warfare." Adas concludes that "despite a great deal of hype about civil defense early in the cold war, the overwhelming majority of civilians, as well as the complex technological systems on which they depended, were simply written off because there was no effective way to protect them."[30] As Gabelnick and Rich conclude, the "rush to globalize arms production and sales ignores the grave humanitarian and strategic consequences of global weapons proliferation. Already, profit motives in the military industry have resulted in arms export decisions that contravene such U.S. foreign policy goals as preserving stability and promoting human rights and democracy."[31]

The proliferation-for-profit of weaponry and munitions poses a global risk. As weapons of mass destruction are "improved," these new technologies pose unforeseen risks to future battlefields and future generations. Furthermore, the dangers posed, for example, by the production, storage, and disposal of chemical and nuclear weapons do not respect national borders. Consequently, we need not actually *go* to a battlefield to be at risk, for increasingly the battlefield is coming to us. One need only consider the polluting of the Arctic Sea by radioactive wastes dumped in the former Soviet Union.

The global proliferation of weapons, the technological sophistication of indiscriminate weapons of mass destruction, an intensification of arms development and manufacture, a pervasive militarism that accepts war as political arbiter: combined, these trends are sowing the seeds of future calamities. And the system is out of control. As Andrew Bacevich writes, "Since the beginning of the industrial age, war has time and again proven itself to be all but ungovernable. The shattered reputations of generals and statesmen who presumed to bring it under their control litter the twentieth century."[32]

The legacy of a global industrial militarism is not, however, an abstract process of academic study; it is, rather, intimately personal. As Howard Zinn writes, "we have to show, in the most graphic way . . . the effect of war on human beings. And how wars, even when they are over, leave a legacy of death . . ."[33] We must heed the words of those who endure the brunt of war, rather than those who celebrate a sanitized and censored war. "The vanquished know war," Chris Hedges writes. "They see through the empty jingoism of those who use the abstract words of 'glory,' 'honor,' and 'patriotism' to mask the cries of the wounded, the brutal killing, war profiteering, and chest-pounding grief. They know the lies the victors often do not acknowledge, the lies covered up in stately war memorials and mythic war narratives, filled with stories of courage and comradeship. They know the lies that permeate the thick, self-important memoirs by amoral statesmen who make wars but do not know war."[34]

Globalization is both *lived* and *died*. It is inscribed on the body of Chisola Pezo, the Angolan woman whose life was literally torn apart when she stepped on a landmine while gathering cassava roots. It is burned into the skin of Hiroka

Fukada, Akihiro Takahashi and the other survivors of the Hiroshima blast. It is seen in the disfigured bodies of children born of veterans of both the Vietnam and Gulf Wars. It is relived every day and every night in the memories of those who have experienced war and conflict. These are real people, who day by day, hour by hour, live with the legacy of rampant militarism, of a global proliferation of indiscriminate weapons, and of a moral acceptance of these weapons. In their voices, across the globe, we hear the echoes of twentieth-century militarism. Will we hear the echoes in their children's voices as well?

Endnotes

ONE

1. Although commonly called Laos, especially in Western societies, the country is termed Lao People's Democratic Republic, or Lao PDR.

2. Since the "discovery" of the jars, there have emerged many hypotheses as to their origin and purpose. Some archaeologists, for example, speculate that objects are funerary jars, while others suggest that they were used for fermentation.

3. Nay Htun, "Landmines Prolong Conflicts and Impede Socioeconmic Development," in *Landmines and Human Security: International Politics and War's Hidden Legacy*, edited by Richard A. Matthew, Bryan McDonald, and Kenneth R. Rutherford (Albany: State University of New York Press, 2004), 169–177; at 173. See also Marilyn B. Young, *The Vietnam Wars, 1945–1990* (New York: HarperCollins, 1990), 235.

4. H.D.S. Greenway, "Laos," *Atlantic Monthly* 228(1971): 6, 10–12, 16; at 10.

5. Quoted in Young, *The Vietnam Wars*, 235.

6. Masahiro Morikawa, Sebastian Taylor, and Marjie Persons, "Deaths and Injuries Due to Unexploded Ordnance (UXO) in Northern Lao PDR (Laos)," *Injury* 29(1998): 301–304.

7. The Battle of Flodden was fought on September 9, 1513; it resulted in a staggering defeat for the Scots. To my knowledge, no civilian—either contemporaneous with the battle, or after—was killed as a result of the battle.

8. Chris McNab and Hunter Keeter, *Tools of Violence: Guns, Tanks and Dirty Bombs* (New York: Osprey Publishing, 2008), 28–29.

9. Donovan Webster, *Aftermath: The Remnants of War* (New York: Vintage Books, 1998), 9; Philip C. Winslow, *Sowing the Dragon's*

Teeth: Land Mines and the Global Legacy of War (Boston: Beacon Press, 1997); Carolyn Nordstrom, *Shadows of War: Violence, Power, and International Profiteering in the Twenty-First Century* (Berkeley: University of California Press, 2004).

10. In recent years, more attention has focused on the role of "non-state" actors in the pursuit and conduct of war. This is especially pertinent when considering the actions of "terrorist" groups such as Al-Qaeda and Jemaah Islamiya.

11. Chalmers Johnson, *The Sorrows of Empire: Militarism, Secrecy, and the End of the Republic* (New York: Metropolitan Books, 2004), 23.

12. Kathleen E. Braden and Fred M. Shelley, *Engaging Geopolitics* (New York: Prentice Hall, 2000), 7.

13. Gearóid Ó Tuathail, *Critical Geopolitics: The Politics of Writing Global Space* (Minneapolis: University of Minnesota Press, 1996), 11.

14. James M. Danzinger, *Understanding the Political World: A Comparative Introduction to Political Science*, 2nd ed. (New York: Longman, 1994), 121.

15. Danzinger, *Understanding the Political World*, 309.

16. Danzinger, *Understanding the Political World*, 310.

17. Rachel Woodward, "From Military Geography to Militarism's Geographies: Disciplinary Engagements with the Geographies of Militarism and Military Activities," *Progress in Human Geography* 29 (2005): 718–740; at 721. Woodward's definition of militarism is useful in that it highlights the intersection of military and civilian spheres of life. However, it tends to be one-sided, with military objectives positioned as the determining agent. Alternatively, we should not lose sight that economic ideologies have greatly impacted the role and function of the military. Indeed, as discussed throughout *Military Legacies* civilians and civilian institutions have often expanded the scale and scope of the military far beyond the boundaries desired or recommended by the military itself.

18. Johnson, *Sorrows of Empire*, 24. See also Clyde Prestowitz, *Rogue Nation: American Unilateralism and the Failure of Good Intentions* (New York: Basic Books, 2003), Andrew J. Bacevich, *The New American Militarism: How Americans are Seduced by War* (Oxford: Oxford University Press, 2005) and Iain Boal, T.J. Clark, Joseph Matthews, and Michael Watts, *Afflicted Powers: Capital and Spectacle in a New Age of War* (New York: Verso, 2005). Clyde Prestowitz (pp. 144, 161), for example, suggests that the United States "relies very heavily on one card in the international poker game, the military card." According to Prestowitz, recent events (e.g., the United States-

led invasion and occupation of Iraq) show that the U.S. is becoming more and more dependent on the military for its conduct of foreign policy as well as for the economy. He notes, first, that in recent years America has rejected or weakened several landmark treaties, including the ban on the use of landmines, the ban on trade in small arms, the biological warfare treaty, the nuclear nonproliferation treaty, and the International Criminal Court. All of this suggests to Prestowitz that the U.S. government has no use for the United Nations or other multilateral institutions and, instead, places complete faith in American military power. Bacevich (pp. 1–2) likewise emphasizes the impact of militarism on American society, and the tendency among many civilians (but especially politicians) to see military power as the ultimate arbiter. Bacevich argues, for example, that Americans have fallen prey to militarism, manifesting itself in a romanticized view of soldiers, and a tendency to view military power as the truest measure of national greatness. In short, Americans have come to define the nation's strength and well-being in terms of military preparedness, military action, and the forwarding of military ideals.

19. Barry S. Levy and Victor W. Sidel, "War and Public Health: An Overview," in *War and Public Health*, 2nd ed., edited by Barry S. Levy and Victor W. Sidel (Oxford: Oxford University Press, 2008), 3–20; at 10.

20. Quoted in Bacevich, *New American Militarism*, 7.

21. Ismael Hossein-Zadeh, *The Political Economy of U.S. Militarism* (New York: Palgrave Macmillan, 2006), 11–12.

22. Congress of the United States of America, 1784, as quoted in Hossein-Zadeh, *Political Economy of U.S. Militarism*, 12.

23. Paul Knox, John Agnew, and Linda McCarthy, *The Geography of the World Economy*, 4th ed. (New York: Arnold, 2003), 143.

24. Throughout much of Europe, during the sixteenth century, feudalism was replaced by an economic system known as merchant capitalism. As an economic system, merchant capitalism was a self-propelling growth system in which the continued expansion of trade was paramount. It remained the dominant economic system of Europe until the eighteenth century. See Knox et al., *Geography of the World Economy*, 127–129; Richard Peet, *Global Capitalism: Theories of Societal Development* (New York: Routledge, 1991), chapter 8.

25. Knox et al., *Geography of the World Economy*, 144.

26. John Horne, "Civilian Populations and Wartime Violence:

Towards an Historical Analysis," *International Social Science Journal* 54 (2002): 483–490; at 484.

27. Hossein-Zadeh, *Political Economy of U.S. Militarism*, 6.

28. Max Boot, *War Made New: Weapons, Warriors, and the Making of the Modern World* (New York: Gotham Books, 2006), 150.

29. Boot, *War Made New*, 150–151.

30. Hubert C. Johnson, *Breakthrough! Tactics, Technology, and the Search for Victory on the Western Front in World War I* (Novato, CA: Presidio, 1994), 117.

31. Boot, *War Made New*, 152.

32. Paul Bartrop, "The Relationship Between War and Genocide in the Twentieth Century: A Consideration," *Journal of Genocide Research* 4(2002): 519–532; at 520.

33. Johnson, *Breakthrough!*, 118.

34. Johnson, *Breakthrough!*, 118. For further discussions of European military-industrial developments, both pre- and post-First World War, see B.M. Downing, *The Military Revolution and Political Change in Early Modern Europe* (Princeton, NJ: Princeton, 1992); Michael Epkenhans, "Military-Industrial Relations in Imperial Germany, 1870–1914," *War in History* 10 (2003): 1–26; and Talbot Imlay, "Preparing for Total War: the *Conseil Supérieur de la Défense Nationale* and France's Industrial and Economic Preparations for War after 1918," *War in History* 15 (2008): 43–71.

35. Michael Adas, *Dominance by Design: Technological Imperatives and America's Civilizing Mission* (Cambridge, MA: Belknap Press, 2006), 199.

36. Terrence J. Gough, "Origins of the Army Industrial College: Military-Business Tensions After World War I," *Armed Forces & Society* 17 (1991): 259–275; at 269.

37. Hossein-Zadeh, *Political Economy of U.S. Militarism*, 25. See also Paul A.C. Koistinen, *The Military-Industrial Complex: A Historical Perspective* (New York: Praeger Publishers, 1980); Joe R. Feagin and Kelly Riddell, "The State, Capitalism, and World War II: The U.S. Case," *Armed Forces & Society* 17 (1990): 53–79; Ira Chernus, "Eisenhower's Ideology in World War II," *Armed Forces & Society* 23 (1997): 595–613; Carlos Aguiar de Medeiros, "The Post-War American Technological Development as a Military Enterprise," *Contributions to Political Economy* 22 (2003): 41–62; Kerry E. Irish, "Apt Pupil: Dwight Eisenhower and the 1930 Industrial Mobilization Plan," *The Journal of Military History* 70 (2006): 31–61.

38. Alfred Vagts, *A History of Militarism: Civilian and Military* (New York: Meridian Books, 1959), 463.

39. Mark Kurlansky, *Nonviolence: Twenty-Five Lessons from the History of a Dangerous Idea* (New York: Modern Library, 2006), 118.

40. Hossein-Zadeh, *Political Economy of U.S. Militarism*, 19.

41. H. Jack Geiger, "The Impact of War on Human Rights," in *War and Public Health*, edited by Barry S. Levy and Victor W. Sidel (New York: Oxford University Press, 1997), 39–50; at 40.

42. Chris Hedges, *War is a Force That Gives Us Meaning* (New York: Anchor Books, 2002), 28.

43. Steve Carlton-Ford, Ann Hamill, and Paula Houston, "War and Children's Mortality," *Childhood* 7(2000): 401–419; at 401.

44. Carlton-Ford et al., "War and Children's Mortality," 401; Geiger, "Impact of War," 40.

45. Hugo Slim, *Killing Civilians: Method, Madness, and Morality in War* (New York: Columbia University Press, 2008), 3.

46. Derek Gregory, *The Colonial Present* (Malden, MA: Blackwell Publishing, 2004), 212.

47. The following is taken from Geiger, "Impact of War," 40–47.

48. Geiger, "Impact of War," 40–41.

49. Geiger, "Impact of War," 44.

50. Geiger, "Impact of War," 45–46.

51. Geiger, "Impact of War," 46.

52. Geiger, "Impact of War," 43.

53. Hedges, *War is a Force*, 13.

54. Slim, *Killing Civilians*, 12–13.

55. Slim, *Killing Civilians*, 29; Kurlansky, *Nonviolence*, 27, 31. Kurlanksy (p. 33) explains also that by the eleventh century many Christian leaders were of the opinion that not only was violence acceptable, but that killing pleased God when done in the cause of the Church. In fact, a term was invented for the killing of non-Christians: *malicide*, Latin for the killing of a bad person. This term was used to differentiate accepted killing from unacceptable killing (i.e., homicide).

56. Michael Walzer, *Just and Unjust Wars: A Moral Argument with Historical Illustrations*, 3rd ed. (New York: Basic Books, 2000), 21.

57. Although both *jus ad bello* and *jus in bello* figure in my subsequent discussions of militarism and warfare, it is with the latter concept that I am most concerned. Simply put, the way that modern wars are now fought accounts for the continued death and destruction of both people and the environment long after the fighting has stopped. Moreover, in anticipation of my later arguments, the dying of women, men, and children, for example, from landmines in Cambodia and other parts of the world today

is the result of previous decisions to actually use landmines in the first place. Were consideration of future deaths and injuries considered, and considered to be morally wrong, these weapons would not have been used, and those people enduring the legacy of these weapons would not still be suffering.

58. Walzer, *Just and Unjust Wars*, 153.
59. Slim, *Killing Civilians*, 151.
60. Kurlansky, *Nonviolence*, 62.
61. Quoted in Slim, *Killing Civilians*, 14.
62. Quoted in Slim, *Killing Civilians*, 15.
63. Slim, *Killing Civilians*, 17.
64. Slim, *Killing Civilians*, 19–20. Prior to the advent of "civilian," terms such as "unarmed inhabitants," "non-combatants," or "occupied populations" were used.
65. Slim, *Killing Civilians*, 23.
66. Slim, *Killing Civilians*, 33.
67. Susan Opotow, "Reconciliation in Times of Impunity: Challenges for Social Justice," *Social Justice Research* 14(2001): 149–170; at 156.
68. Horne, "Civilian Populations," 484.
69. Horne, "Civilian Populations," 485.
70. Sergey N. Tikhomirov, "1939–1945: Environmental Aspects of the War in Europe," *Review of Central and East European Law* 31 (2006): 111–125; at 112.
71. Tikhomirov, "1939–1945," at 113 and 115.
72. Hedges, *War is a Force*, 83.
73. Kurlansky, *Nonviolence*, 141.
74. Slim, *Killing Civilians*, 39.

TWO

1. Michael Clodfelter, *Mad Minutes and Vietnam Months: A Soldier's Story* (Jefferson, NC: McFarland & Co., 1988), 105, 121, 149.
2. Sey's name is a pseudonym; her story is detailed in Devon E. Hinton, Vuth Pich, Dara Chhean, and Mark H. Pollack, " 'The Ghost Pushes You Down': Sleep Paralysis-Type Panic Attacks in a Khmer Refugee Population," *Transcultural Psychiatry* 42 (2005): 46–77; see especially pp. 61–62.
3. Menachem Z. Rosensaft, "I Was Born in Bergen-Belsen," in *Second Generation Voices: Reflections of Holocaust Survivors and Perpetrators*, edited by Alan L. Berger and Naomi Berger (Syracuse: Syracuse University Press, 2001), 188–207; at 188.

4. Liesel Appel, "Honor Thy Mother: Reflections on Being the Daughter of Nazis," in *Second Generation Voices: Reflections of Holocaust Survivors and Perpetrators*, edited by Alan L. Berger and Naomi Berger (Syracuse: Syracuse University Press, 2001), 303–309; at 303–304.

5. Daniel J. Flannery, *Violence and Mental Health in Everyday Life: Prevention and Intervention Strategies for Children and Adolescents* (Lanham, MD: Altamira Press, 2006), 39.

6. Flannery, *Violence and Mental Health*, 141.

7. Ernst Jünger, *Storm of Steel*, translated by Michael Hofmann (New York: Penguin, 2004 [1920]), 198, 201.

8. Ilona Meagher, *Moving a Nation to Care: Post-Traumatic Stress Disorder and America's Returning Troops* (New York: Ig Publishing, 2007), 13.

9. Meagher, *Moving a Nation to Care*, 14.

10. Ronald J. Glasser, *Wounded: Vietnam to Iraq* (New York: George Braziller, 2006), 85.

11. Glasser, *Wounded*, 85.

12. Glasser, *Wounded*, 93.

13. Glasser, *Wounded*, 86.

14. Glasser, *Wounded*, 87.

15. There were some early attempts to provide a non-physical explanation of war-trauma; see, for example, Abram Kardiner, *War Stress and Neurotic Illness* (New York: Hoeber, 1947).

16. Glasser, *Wounded*, 88–91.

17. Philip A. Saigh, Bonnie L. Green, and Mindy Korol, "The History and Prevalence of Posttraumatic Stress Disorder with Special Reference to Children and Adolescents," *Journal of School Psychology* 34 (1996): 107–131; at 109–110.

18. Robert E. Strange and Dudley E. Brown, Jr., "Home From the War: A Study of Psychiatric Problems in Viet Nam Returnees," *American Journal of Psychiatry* 127 (1970): 488–492; Jonathan F. Borus, "Reentry: II. 'Making It' Back in the States," *American Journal of Psychiatry* 139 (1973): 850–854; Charles R. Figley, "Symptoms of Delayed Combat Stress Among a College Sample of Vietnam Veterans," *Military Medicine* 143 (1978): 107–110; Kathy A. Pearce, Andrew H. Schauer, Nancy J. Garfield, Carroll O. Ohlde, and Tom W. Patterson, "A Study of Post Traumatic Stress Disorder in Vietnam Veterans," *Journal of Clinical Psychology* 41 (1985): 9–14; Robert H. Stretch, "Posttraumatic Stress Disorder Among U.S. Army Reserve Vietnam and Vietnam-Era Veterans," *Journal of Consulting and Clinical Psychology* 53 (1985): 935–936.

19. M.D. Horowitz and G.F. Solomon, "A Prediction of Delayed

Stress Response Syndrome in Vietnam Veterans," *Journal of Social Issues* 4 (1975): 67–79.

20. The definitional classification of PTSD has been modified in subsequent editions, notably in 1983, 1987, and 1994.

21. Symptoms, furthermore, are manifest in one of three ways: re-experience; avoidance; and increased arousal. First, the traumatic event(s) may be re-experienced in any number of ways, including recurrent and intrusive recollections; recurrent dreams of the event(s); feelings that the event is re-occurring, which may include a sense of reliving the experience; intense psychological distress when exposed to internal or external cues that resemble an aspect of the traumatic event; or a physiological reactivity when exposed to internal or external cues. Second, the person may exhibit avoidance behaviors, including efforts to avoid thoughts, feelings, or conversations associated with the trauma; efforts to avoid activities, places, or people that trigger recollections of the trauma; an inability to recall important aspects of the traumatic event; markedly diminished interest or participation in significant activities; a restricted range of affect; and/or a sense of a foreshortened future (e.g., the individual does not expect to get married, have children, or live a normal lifespan). Third, the person may exhibit persistent symptoms of increased arousal, such as difficulty in falling or staying asleep; irritability or anger outbursts; difficulty in concentration; hyper-vigilance; or an exaggerated startle response; see Saigh et al., "History and Prevalence," 113.

22. Patrick Bracken, Joan E. Giller, and Derek Summerfield, "Psychological Responses to War and Atrocity: The Limitations of Current Concepts," *Social Science & Medicine* 40 (1995): 1073–1082; Charles Watters, "Emerging Paradigms in the Mental Health Care of Refugees," *Social Science & Medicine* 52 (2001): 1709–1718; Howard Johnson and Andrew Thompson, "The Development and Maintenance of Post-Traumatic Stress Disorder (PTSD) in Civilian Adult Survivors of War Trauma and Torture: A Review," *Clinical Psychology Review* 28 (2008): 36–47.

23. Bracken et al., "Psychological Responses," 1081.

24. Quoted in Luc Capdevila and Danièle Voldman, *War Dead: Western Societies and the Casualties of War*, translated by Richard Veasey (Edinburgh: Edinburgh University Press, 2006), xii.

25. Carolyn Nordstrom, *Shadows of War: Violence, Power, and International Profiteering in the Twenty-First Century* (Berkeley: University of California Press, 2004), 58–59.

26. Chris McNab and Hunter Keeter, *Tools of Violence: Guns, Tanks and Dirty Bombs* (New York: Oxprey, 2008), 15.
27. Quoted in Glasser, *Wounded*, 102.
28. Marc Pilisuk with Jennifer Achord Rountree, *Who Benefits from Global Violence and War: Uncovering a Destructive System* (Westport, CT: Praeger Security International, 2008), 3.
29. F. Bodman, "War Conditions and the Mental Health of the Child," *British Medical Journal* 11 (1941): 486–488; T. Bradner, "Psychiatric Observations Among Finnish Children During the Russo-Finnish War of 1939–1940," *Nervous Child* 2 (1943): 313–319; M.H. Mercer and J.M. Despert, "Psychological Effects of the War on French Children," *Psychosomatic Medicine* 5 (1943): 266–272.
30. Joshua Barenbaum, Vladislav Ruchkin, and Mary Schwab-Stone, "The Psychosocial Aspects of Children Exposed to War: Practice and Policy Initiatives," *Journal of Child Psychology and Psychiatry* 45 (2004): 41–62; at 42.
31. Some researchers have suggested the youngest children experience some protection from severity of trauma because they do not understand the full measure of its negative consequences; in the context of continuous war, for example, some events and circumstances may be perceived as normal, everyday reality to which the child may become adjusted. If this is the case, then it is truly tragic that the horrors of war, the killing and maiming and separation, should become "normal." Rather, we should heed Helene Berman's assertion that "When children are repeatedly forced to confront violence, the trauma becomes a central condition of their lives; there is no 'post' trauma period." She continues: "Even if they are fortunate enough to escape from immediate harm, the task goes beyond getting over a horrible experience." She explains that, for the children, "the challenge is to find ways to *make sense of a world in which terrifying experiences are part of everyday reality.*" See Barenbaum et al., "Psychosocial Aspects of Children," 44; see also Helene Berman, "Children and War: Current Understandings and Future Directions," *Public Health Nursing* 18 (2001): 243–252; at 248.
32. Meagher, *Moving a Nation to Care*, 86–87.
33. This does not include those children who "serve" as child-soldiers.
34. Chris Hedges and Laila Al-Arian, *Collateral Damage: America's War Against Iraqi Civilians* (New York: Nation Books, 2008), 42–43.
35. Hedges and Al-Arian, *Collateral Damage*, 44–45.

36. Quoted in Hedges and Al-Arian, *Collateral Damage*, 63–64.

37. Meagher, *Moving a Nation to Care*, p. xx.

38. Hugo Slim, *Killing Civilians: Method, Madness, and Morality in War* (New York: Columbia University Press, 2008), 115. See, for example, Derek Summerfield and Leslie Toser, " 'Low Intensity' War and Mental Trauma in Nicaragua: A Study in a Rural Community," *Medicine and War* 7 (1991): 84–99; A. Abdulboughi, "Symptoms of Posttraumatic Stress Disorders Among Displaced Kurdish Children in Iraq," *Nordic Journal of Psychiatry* 46 (1992): 315–319; K.O. Nader and L.A. Fairbanks, "The Supervision of Reexperiencing: Impulse Control and Somatic Symptoms in Children Following Traumatic Exposure," *Anxiety, Stress and Coping: An International Journal* 7 (1994): 229–239; Abeer M. Awadh, Booney Vance, Viola El-Beblawi, and Andres J. Pumariega, "Effects of Trauma of the Gulf War on Kuwaiti Children," *Journal of Child and Family Studies* 7 (1998): 493–498; Denise Michultka, Edward B. Blanchard, and Tom Kalous, "Responses to Civilian War Experiences: Predictors of Psychological Functioning and Coping," *Journal of Traumatic Stress* 11 (1998): 571–577.

39. McNab and Keeter, *Tools of Violence*, 7.

40. Paula Braveman, Alan Meyers, Thomas Schlenker, and Curt Wands, "Public Health and War in Central America," in *War and Public Health*, edited by Barry S. Levy and Victor W. Sidel (New York: Oxford University Press, 1997), 238–253; at 240–241.

41. Summerfield and Toser, " 'Low Intensity' War," 84.

42. Pilisuk, *Who Benefits*, 2.

43. Quoted in Patricia D. Rozée and Gretchen Van Boemel, "The Psychological Effects of War Trauma and Abuse on Older Cambodian Refugee Women," *Women & Therapy* 8 (1989): 23–50; at 37.

44. There exists a substantial body of literature detailing the Cambodian genocide. Excellent starting points include David Chandler, *The Tragedy of Cambodian History: Politics, War, and Revolution Since 1945* (New Haven, CT: Yale University Press, 1991); Ben Kiernan, *The Pol Pot Regime: Policies, Race and Genocide in Cambodia Under the Khmer Rouge, 1975–1979* (New Haven, CT: Yale University Press, 1996); Alexander L. Hinton, *Why Did They Kill? Cambodia in the Shadow of Genocide* (Berkeley: University of California Press, 2005); Craig Etcheson, *After the Killing Fields: Lessons from the Cambodian Genocide* (Lubbock: Texas Tech University Press, 2005); and James A. Tyner, *The Killing of Cambodia: Geography, Genocide and the Unmaking of Space* (Aldershot, UK: Ashgate, 2008).

45. Haing Ngor (with R. Warner), *Survival in the Killing Fields* (New York: Carroll and Graf Publishers, 1987), 247.
46. There is a sizeable literature on the mental health aspects of the Cambodian genocide and, especially, among the Cambodian refugee population. See J. David Kinzie, R.H. Fredrickson, Rath Ben, Jenelle Fleck, and William Karls, "Posttraumatic Stress Disorder Among Survivors of Cambodian Concentration Camps," *American Journal of Psychiatry* 141 (1984): 645–650; Richard F. Mollica, Grace Wyshak, and James Lavelle, "The Psychosocial Impact of War Trauma and Torture on Southeast Asian Refugees," *American Journal of Psychiatry* 144 (1987): 1567–1572; J. David Kinzie and James J. Boehnlein, "Post-traumatic Psychosis Among Cambodian Refugees," *Journal of Traumatic Stress* 2 (1989): 185–198; Eve Bernstein Carlson and Rhonda Rosser-Hogan, "Mental Health Status of Cambodian Refugees Ten Years After Leaving Their Homes," *American Journal of Orthopsychiatry* 63 (1993): 223–231; Robert G. Blair, "Risk Factors Associated with PTSD and Major Depression Among Cambodian Refugees in Utah," *Health & Social Work* 25 (2000): 23–30.
47. Ngor, *Survival in the Killing Fields*, 311.
48. Sreytouch Svay-Ryser, "New Year's Surprise," in *Children of Cambodia's Killing Fields: Memoirs by Survivors*, compiled by Dith Pran and edited by Kim DePaul (New Haven, CT: Yale University Press, 1997), 35–41; at 38.
49. Rouen Sam, "Living in Darkness," in *Children of Cambodia's Killing Fields: Memoirs by Survivors*, compiled by Dith Pran and edited by Kim DePaul (New Haven, CT: Yale University Press, 1997), 73–81; at 78.
50. Henri Locard, *Pol Pot's Little Red Book: The Sayings of Angkar* (Chiang Mai, Thailand: Silkworm Books, 2004), 91.
51. Locard, *Pol Pot's Little Red Book*, 91.
52. Sam, "Living in Darkness," 76.
53. Sam, "Living in Darkness," 77. Sam continues that later, she felt angry and sorrowful; she was disturbed that she was unable to help the prisoner.
54. See, for example, Maurice Eisenbruch, "From Post-Traumatic Stress Disorder to Cultural Bereavement: Diagnosis of Southeast Asian Refugees," *Social Science & Medicine* 33 (1991): 673–680.
55. Hinton et al., " 'The Ghost Pushes You Down,' " 47.
56. Hinton et al., " 'The Ghost Pushes You Down,' " 56–57.
57. A particular type of spirit, an *ap* appears during the day as a normal human; at night, however, the head floats from the body

with the intestines and liver dangling down; according to Khmer culture, the head leaves the body in search of blood for nourishment. See Hinton et al., " 'The Ghost Pushes You Down,' " 61.

58. Hinton et al., " 'The Ghost Pushes You Down,' " 60–61.
59. James K. Boehnlein, "Clinical Relevance of Grief and Mourning Among Cambodian Refugees," *Social Science & Medicine* 25 (1987): 765–772; at 766–767.
60. Boehnlein, "Clinical Relevance of Grief," 768.
61. Boehnlein, "Clinical Relevance of Grief," 767–768.
62. Hinton et al., " 'The Ghost Pushes You Down,' " 62–63.
63. Boehnlein, "Clinical Relevance of Grief," 769.
64. Berman, "Children and War," 243; Rozée and Van Boemel, "Psychological Effects of War Trauma," 34.
65. Kinzie and Boehnlein, "Post-Traumatic Psychosis," 188–189.
66. Kinzie and Boehnlein, "Post-Traumatic Psychosis," 189–190.
67. Kinzie and Boehnlein, "Post-Traumatic Psychosis," 194.
68. More has been written on the Holocaust than any other episode of genocide or mass violence. Useful introductions to the Holocaust include Michael Burleigh and Wolfgang Wippermann, *The Racial State: Germany, 1933–1945* (Cambridge: Cambridge University Press, 1991); Henry Friedlander, *The Origins of Nazi Genocide: From Euthanasia to the Final Solution* (Chapel Hill: The University of North Carolina Press, 1995); Christopher R. Browning, *Nazi Policy, Jewish Workers, German Killers* (Cambridge: Cambridge University Press, 2000); Benjamin A. Valentino, *Final Solutions: Mass Killing and Genocide in the 20th Century* (Ithaca: Cornell University Press, 2004); Laurence Rees, *Auschwitz: A New History* (New York: Public Affairs, 2005); Heather Pringle, *The Master Plan: Himmler's Scholars and the Holocaust* (New York: Hyperion, 2006).
69. Donald M. McKale, *Hitler's Shadow War: The Holocaust and World War II* (New York: Taylor Trade, 2006), 454. McKale provides additional numbers by country: Greece (59,185 Jews killed, or 85 percent), the Netherlands (102,000; 73 percent), Germany (165,000; 70 percent), Romania (211,214; 48 percent), the Soviet Union (2,100,000; 45 percent).
70. Quoted in Rees, *Auschwitz*, 12.
71. Browning, *Nazi Policy*, 25.
72. Quoted in Rees, *Auschwitz*, 52.
73. Rees, *Auschwitz*, 54. The cyanide used by the Germans was called Zyklon B. The name is derived from the brand name under

which the cyanide was marketed (Zyklon, for cyclone) and Blausäure (for prussic acid).

74. McKale, *Hitler's Shadow War*, 255, 259.

75. Rachel Lev-Wiesel, "Intergenerational Transmission of Trauma Across Three Generations," *Qualitative Social Work* 6 (2007): 75–94; at 79–80.

76. Quoted in Rees, *Auschwitz*, 76. Chełmno, according to Rees, was the first center for the extermination of Jews established within the Nazi state. Constructed in 1941, the large-scale gassing of (mostly) Polish Jews commenced in early December 1941 and continued through April 1943; it briefly reopened in 1944 and early 1945. Approximately 215,000 Jews were killed at the site. See McKale, *Hitler's Shadow War*, 255, 261.

77. Lev-Wiesel, "Intergenerational Transmission," 76.

78. John Parsons, Thomas J. Kehle, and Steve V. Owen, "Incidence of Behavior Problems Among Children of Vietnam War Veterans," *School Psychology International* 11 (1990): 253–259; Robert Rosenheck and Alan Fontana, "Transgenerational Effects of Abusive Violence on the Children of Vietnam Combat Veterans," *Journal of Traumatic Stress* 11 (1998): 731–742; Jan Westerink and Leah Giarratano, "The Impact of Posttraumatic Stress Disorder on Partners and Children of Australian Vietnam Veterans," *Australian and New Zealand Journal of Psychiatry* 33 (1999): 841–847.

79. Westerink and Giarratano, "Impact of Posttraumatic Stress," 842.

80. D. Bar-On, J. Eland, R.J. Kleber, R. Krell, Y. Moore, A. Sagi, E. Soriano, P. Suedfeld, P.G. Van Der Velden, and M.H. Van Izendoorn, "Multigenerational Perspectives on Coping with the Holocaust Experience: An Attachment Perspective for Understanding the Development Sequel of Trauma Across Generations," *International Journal of Behavioral Development* 22 (1998): 315–338; D. Rowland-Klein and R. Dunlop, "The Transmission of Trauma Across Generations: Identification with Parental Trauma in Children of Holocaust Survivors," *Australian and New Zealand Journal of Psychiatry* 32 (1998): 358–369.

81. Lev-Wiesel, "Intergenerational Transmission."

82. Eva Hoffman, *After Such Knowledge: Memory, History, and the Legacy of the Holocaust* (New York: Public Affairs, 2004).

83. Hoffman, *After Such Knowledge*, 5.

84. Hoffman, *After Such Knowledge*, 5.

85. Hoffman, *After Such Knowledge*, 25.

86. Nordstrom, *Shadows of War*, 59–60.

87. Berman, "Children and War," 248.

THREE

1. Frantz Fanon, *The Wretched of the Earth*, translated by Constance Farrington (New York: Grove Press, 1963), 249.

2. The following account is taken from Philip C. Winslow, *Sowing the Dragon's Teeth: Land Mines and the Global Legacy of War* (Boston: Beacon Press, 1997); see pp. 21–29.

3. Wilson, *Sowing the Dragon's Teeth*, 26–27.

4. International Campaign to Ban Landmines (ICBL), *Landmine Monitor Report 2007, Country Report: Angola*, available at http://www.icbl.org/lm/2007/angola.html.

5. Chris McNab and Hunter Keeter, *Tools of Violence: Guns, Tanks and Dirty Bombs* (New York: Osprey, 2008), 76; Stacy Bernard Davis and Donald F. Patierno, "Tackling the Global Landmine Problem: The United States Perspective," in *Landmines and Human Security: International Politics and War's Hidden Legacy*, edited by Richard A. Matthew, Bryan McDonald, and Kenneth R. Rutherford (Albany: State University of New York Press, 2004), 125–137; at 127. See also International Campaign to Ban Landmines (ICBL), *Landmine Monitor Report 2007: Toward a Mine-Free World*, available at http://www.icbl.org/lm.

6. A.A. Berhe, "The Contributions of Landmines to Land Degradation," *Land Degradation and Development* 18 (2007): 1–15; at 2. See also Joseph R. Oppong and Ezekiel Kalipeni, "The Geography of Landmines and Implications for Health and Disease in Africa: A Political Ecology Approach," *Africa Today* 52 (2005): 3–25.

7. ICBL, *Landmine Monitor Report 2007*.

8. ICBL, *Landmine Monitor Report 2007*.

9. Shawn Roberts and Jody Williams, *After the Guns Fall Silent: The Enduring Legacy of Landmines* (Washington, D.C.: Vietnam Veterans of America Foundation, 1995), 34–35.

10. Donovan Webster, *Aftermath: The Remnants of War* (New York: Vintage Books, 1996).

11. Webster, *Aftermath*, 232. See also Paul Davies, *War of the Mines: Cambodia, Landmines and the Impoverishment of a Nation* (London: Pluto Press, 1994).

12. Ted Gaulin, "A Necessary Evil? Reexamining the Military Utility of Antipersonnel Landmines," in *Landmines and Human Security: International Politics and War's Hidden Legacy*, edited by Richard A. Matthew, Bryan McDonald, and Kenneth R. Rutherford (Albany: State University of New York Press, 2004), 209–223.

13. Roberts and Williams, *After the Guns Fall Silent*, 4.

14. Earl Conteh-Morgan, *Collective Political Violence: An Introduction to the Theories and Cases of Violent Conflicts* (New York: Routledge, 2004), 43–45.

15. Michael Flynn, "Political Minefield," in *Landmines and Human Security: International Politics and War's Hidden Legacy*, edited by Richard A. Matthew, Bryan McDonald, and Kenneth R. Rutherford (Albany: State University of New York Press, 2004), 117–124; at 120.

16. Ibrahim Elbadawi and Nicholas Sambanis, "Why Are There So Many Civil Wars in Africa? Understanding and Preventing Violent Conflict," *Journal of African Economies* 9 (2000): 244–269; at 244.

17. Gerard Prunier, *Africa's World War: Congo, the Rwandan Genocide, and the Making of a Continental Catastrophe* (Oxford: Oxford University Press, 2008).

18. R. Albertyn, S.W. Bickler, A.B. van As, A.J.W. Millar, and H. Rode, "The Effects of War on Children in Africa," *Pediatric Surgeon International* 19 (2003): 227–232; at 227.

19. In the United States of America, there are approximately 30 companies that continue to produce anti-personnel mine components. However, in the U.S. no company produces mines from beginning to end, thus ensuring plausible deniability. The U.S. industry consists of component suppliers and final assembly of mines is undertaken at government-owned and contractor-operator Army Ammunition plants. Human Rights Watch report, "The Recalcitrant Producers," http://www.hrw.org/campaigns/mines/IV.2.recalcitrant.html (accessed August 29, 2008).

20. Webster, *Aftermath*, 235. See also Donna McIvor Joss, "Anti-Personnel Landmine Injuries: A Global Epidemic," *Work: A Journal of Prevention, Assessment & Rehabilitation* 8 (1997): 299–304.

21. The latter may also be referred to as anti-tank mines.

22. Landmines may either be "victim-activated" or "controller-activated." Victim-activated mines are usually detonated by pressure plates, exposed prongs, tripwires, tiltrods, breakwires, or infrared beams. Other mines may also be detonated by acoustic-, seismic-, or magnetic-activated mechanisms. Controller-activated landmines are frequently used to coordinate attacks.

23. McNab and Keeter, *Tools of Violence*, 80.

24. McNab and Keeter, *Tools of Violence*, 80.

25. McNab and Keeter, *Tools of Violence*, 81.

26. McNab and Keeter, *Tools of Violence*, 81.

27. ICBL, *Landmine Monitor Report 2007*.

28. ICBL, *Landmine Monitor Report 2007*.

29. ICBL, *Landmine Monitor Report 2007*. See also Mohamed Taghioullah Ould Nema, "The Rise of ERW as a Threat to Civilians," *Journal of Mine Action* 10 (2006), available at http:maic.jmu.edu/journal/ 10.2/editorials/nema/nema.htm (accessed July 29, 2009).

30. Rob Nixon, "Of Landmines and Cluster Bombs," *Cultural Critique* 67 (2007): 160–174.

31. Eric Prokosch, "Technology and its Control: Antipersonnel Weapons," *International Social Science Journal* 28 (1976): 341–358; at 345; Michael Krepon, "Weapons Potentially Inhumane: The Case of Cluster Bombs," *Foreign Affairs* 52 (1974): 595–611; at 597.

32. There are scores of different types of cluster bombs in use. These differ in the areal coverage of the blast, as well as the type of fragments expelled. Some cluster bombs, for example, are filled with napalm, landmines, sarin nerve gas, or nail-like flechettes. Fiberglass fragments have also been employed. Unlike their metallic counterparts, these fiberglass flechettes are invisible to x-rays and thus more difficult and painful to remove. See Jonathan Neale, *A People's History of the Vietnam War* (New York: The New Press, 2003), 78).

33. Oleg O. Bilukha, Muireann Brennan, and Bradley A. Woodruff, "Death and Injury from Landmines and Unexploded Ordnance in Afghanistan," *Journal of the American Medical Association* 290 (2003): 650–653; at 651.

34. Andrew Wells-Dang, "A Regional Approach: Mine and UXO Risk Reduction in Vietnam, Laos and Cambodia," *Journal of Mine Action* 9 (2005): n.p., available at http:maic.jmu.edu/ journal/9.2/focus/wells-dang/wells-dang.htm (accessed July 29, 2009). Wells-Dang notes that throughout Vietnam, Laos, and even Cambodia, UXO casualties often exceed anti-personnel landmine casualties.

35. Masahiro Morikawa, Sebastian Taylor, and Marjie Persons, "Deaths and Injuries Due to Unexploded Ordnance (UXO) in Northern Lao PDR (Laos)," *Injury* 29 (1998): 301–304.

36. Bounpheng Sisavath, "UXO Laos' Fight Against Unexploded Ordnance," *Journal of Mine Action* 9 (2005): n.p., available at http: //maic.jmu.edu/journal/9.2/focus/sisavath/sisavath.htm (accessed July 29, 2009).

37. Katie FitzGerald, "The Aftermath of War," *Journal of Mine Action* 10 (2006): n.p., available at http:maic.jmu.edu/journal/10.2/ focus/fitzgerald/fitzgerald.htm (accessed July 29, 2009).

38. Nixon, "Of Landmines and Cluster Bombs," 168.

39. Ian Brown, *Cambodia* (Oxford: Oxfam, 2000), 49.

40. Peter Meade, "Additional Comment Added in Press," *The Journal of Trauma: Injury, Infection, and Critical Care* 48 (2000): 739.

41. Roberts and Williams, *After the Guns Fall Silent*.

42. Hameed Reza Jahunlu, Hans Husum, and Torben Wisborg, "Mortality in Land-Mine Accidents in Iran," *Prehospital Disaster Medicine* 17 (2002): 107–109; Peter Meade and James Mirocha, "Civilian Landmine Injuries in Sri Lanka," *The Journal of Trauma: Injury, Infection, and Critical Care* 48 (2000): 735–739.

43. Ronald J. Glasser, *Wounded: Vietnam to Iraq* (New York: George Braziller, 2006), 70–71.

44. Survivors of fragmentation blasts may suffer from the effects for decades to come. Indeed, in 2002 a 70-year-old man complained of an inflammatory nodule that had developed on the left side of his chin; a similar nodule had developed three months earlier. Upon inspection, it was discovered that the nodules were grenade fragments. As a boy during the Second World War, the patient was injured by a grenade. Sixty years later, fragments of the grenade were still being extruded from his flesh. See Pierre-Dominique Ghislain, "Spontaneous Extrusion of Hand Grenade Fragments From the Face 60 Years After Injury," *Journal of the American Medical Association* 290 (2003): 1317–1318.

45. Prokosch, "Technology and its Control," 349.

46. Davies, *War of the Mines*, 27.

47. Oppong and Kalipeni, "Geography of Landmines," 18.

48. Alberto Ascherio, Robin Biellik, Andy Epstein, Gail Snetro, Steve Gloyd, Barbara Ayotte, and Paul R. Epstein, "Deaths and Injuries Caused by Land Mines in Mozambique," *The Lancet* 346 (1995): 721–724.

49. Roberts and Williams, *After the Guns Fall Silent*, 9.

50. Fiona King, "Landmine Injury in Cambodia: A Case Study", M.Sc Thesis (London School of Hygiene and Tropical Medicine, 1992), quoted in Davies, *War of the Mines*, 30.

51. Roberts and Williams, *After the Guns Fall Silent*, 9.

52. Davies, *War of the Mines*, 30.

53. Ascherio et al., "Deaths and Injuries," 723; Oleg O. Bilukha, Zaur Tsitsaev, Ramzan Ibragimov, Mark Anderson, and Eliza Murtazaeva, "Epidemiology of Injuries and Deaths from Landmines and Unexploded Ordnance in Chechnya, 1994 Through 2005," *Journal of American Medical Association* 296 (2006): 516–518.

54. Shannon K. Mitchell, "Death, Disability, Displaced Persons and Development: The Case of Landmines in Bosnia and Herzegovina," *World Development* 32 (2004): 2105–2120; at 2113.

55. Hans Husum, Kirsten Resell, Gyri Vorren, Yang Van Heng, Mudhafar Murad, Mads Gilbert, and Torben Wisborg, "Chronic Pain in Land Mine Accident Survivors in Cambodia and Kurdistan," *Social Science & Medicine* 55 (2002): 1813–1816.

56. Davies, *War of the Mines*, 27.

57. Jahunlu et al., "Mortality in Land-Mine Accidents," 107.

58. Joss, "Anti-Personnel Landmine Injuries," 302.

59. ICBL, *Landmine Monitor Report 2007*.

60. Berhe, "Contributions of Landmines," 11.

61. Nay Htun, "Landmines Prolong Conflicts and Impede Socioeconomic Development," in *Landmines and Human Security: International Politics and War's Hidden Legacy*, edited by Richard A. Matthew, Bryan McDonald, and Kenneth R. Rutherford (Albany: State University of New York Press, 2004), 169–177.

62. Mitchell, "Death, Disability," 2113.

63. Oppong and Kalipeni, "Geography of Landmines," 5.

64. Davies, *War of the Mines*, 28.

65. Htun, "Landmines Prolong Conflicts," 172.

66. Berhe, "Contributions of Landmines," 10.

67. Berhe, "Contributions of Landmines," 10.

68. Oppong and Kalipeni, "Geography of Landmines," 4.

69. Berhe, "Contributions of Landmines," 7.

70. Claudio Torres Nachón, "The Environmental Impacts of Landmines," in *Landmines and Human Security: International Politics and War's Hidden Legacy*, edited by Richard A. Matthew, Bryan McDonald, and Kenneth R. Rutherford (Albany: State University of New York Press, 2004), 191–207.

71. Berhe, "Contributions of Landmines," 3.

72. Berhe, "Contributions of Landmines," 8.

73. Judith C. Pennington and James M. Brannon, "Environmental Fate of Explosives," *Thermochimica Acta* 384 (2002): 163–172.

74. Berhe, "Contributions of Landmines," 9.

75. M. Van Meirvenne, T. Meklit, S. Verstraete, M. De Boever, and F. Tack, "Could Shelling in the First World War Have Increased Copper Concentrations in the Soil Around Ypres?" *European Journal of Soil Science* 59 (2008): 373–379.

76. P. Souvent and S. Pirc, "Pollution Caused by Metallic Fragments Introduced into Soils Because of World War I Activities," *Environmental Geology* 49 (2001): 317–323. See also S. Pirc and T.

Budkovič, "Remains of World War I Geochemical Pollution in the Landscape," in *Environmental Xenobiotics*, edited by M. Richardson (Hertfordshire, UK: Taylor & Francis, 1996), 375–418.

77. Pennington and Brannon, "Environmental Fate," 164.
78. Colin King, "As Mines Grow Old," *Journal of Mine Action* 11 (2007): n.p., available at http://maic.jmu.edu/journal/11.2/editorials/king/king.htm (accessed July 29, 2009).
79. Pennington and Brannon, "Environmental Fate," 170.
80. Raafat Misak and S. Omar, "Environmental Damage from Minefields," *Journal of Mine Action* 11(2007): n.p., available at http://maic.jmu.edu/journal/11.2/feature/misak/misak.htm (accessed July 29, 2009). See also J.M. Al-Awadhi, S.A. Omar, and R.F. Misak, "Land Degradation Indicators in Kuwait," *Land Degradation & Development* 16 (2005): 163–176.
81. Berhe, "Contributions of Landmines," 7.
82. N. Andersson, C.P. da Sousa, and S. Pareds, "Social Cost of Land Mines in Four Countries: Afghanistan, Bosnia, Cambodia, and Mozambique," *British Medical Journal* 311 (1995): 718–721.
83. Nachón, "Environmental Impacts," 197–200.
84. Oppong and Kalipeni, "Geography of Landmines," 17.
85. Allan R. Vosburgh, "The War Goes On," *Journal of Mine Action* 9 (2005): n.p., available at http://maic.jmu.edu/journal/9.2/focus/vosburgh/vosburgh.htm (accessed July 29, 2009).
86. Ascherio et al., "Deaths and Injuries," 723.
87. Richard Brown, Eddie Chaloner, Steve Mannion, and Tim Cheatle, "10-Year Experience of Injuries Sustained During Clearance of Anti-Personnel Mines," *Lancet* 358 (2001): 2048–2049. During this period, de-miners disposed of 81,243 mines, 637,487 other types of unexploded ordnance, and cleared 30,192,000 square meters of land.
88. ICBL, *Landmine Monitor Report 2007*.
89. ICBL, *Landmine Monitor Report 2007*.
90. Joss, "Anti-Personnel Landmine Injuries," 302–303.
91. Editorial, "Landmines and Cluster Bombs—Picking Up the Pieces," *Lancet* 359 (2002): 273.
92. Nixon, "Of Landmines and Cluster Bombs," 169.

FOUR

1. Comment posted July 7, 2007 at *Agent Orange Birth Defects Blogspot*, http://agentorangebirthdefects.blogspot.com (accessed May 19, 2009).

2. Comment posted July 10, 2007 at *Agent Orange Birth Defects Blogspot*, http://agentorangebirthdefects.blogspot.com (accessed May 19, 2009).

3. Comment posted July 12, 2007 at *Agent Orange Birth Defects Blogspot*, http://agentorangebirthdefects.blogspot.com (accessed May 19, 2009).

4. See Matthew Benns and Frank Walker, "Agent Orange Town," *Sydney Morning Herald*, May 18, 2008, http://www.smh.com.au/news/national/agent-orange-town/2008/05/18/1210765 247617.html (accessed May 19, 2009); Barbara McMahon, "Australia Cancer Deaths Linked to Agent Orange," *Guardian*, May 19, 2008, http://www.guardian.co.uk/world/2008/may/19/australia (accessed May 19, 2009). In a follow-up to the reports, authorities in Queensland denied the allegation that Innisfail's cancer rates were significantly higher than other locations.

5. For more extensive discussions on the specific histories and properties of chemical weapons, see Robert Harris and Jeremy Paxman, *A Higher Form of Killing: The Secret History of Chemical and Biological Warfare* (New York: Random House, 2002); Rohit Shenoi, "Chemical Warfare Agents," *Clin. Ped. Emerg. Med.* 3 (2002): 239–247; Ladislaus Szinicz, "History of Chemical and Biological Warfare Agents," *Toxicology* 214 (2005): 167–181; and Arnold Schecter, Linda Birnbaum, John J. Ryan, and John D. Constable, "Dioxins: An Overview," *Environmental Research* 101 (2006): 419–428.

6. Ernest C. Lee and Stefanos N. Kales, "Chemical Weapons," in *War and Public Health*, 2nd ed., edited by Barry S. Levy and Victor W. Sidel (Oxford: Oxford University Press, 2008), 117–134; at 119.

7. Chris McNab and Hunter Keeter, *Tools of Violence: Guns, Tanks and Dirty Bombs* (New York: Osprey Publishing, 2008), 256–7.

8. McNab and Keeter, *Tools of Violence*, 257.

9. Lee and Kales, "Chemical Weapons," 123; see also William G. Eckert, "Mass Deaths by Gas or Chemical Poisoning," *American Journal of Forensic Medicine and Pathology* 12 (1991): 119–125; at 119.

10. Lee and Kales, "Chemical Weapons," 119.

11. Lee and Kales, "Chemical Weapons," 124.

12. Shenoi, "Chemical Warfare Agents," 242.

13. McNab and Keeter, *Tools of Violence*, 258.

14. Shenoi, "Chemical Warfare Agents," 241.

15. Shenoi, "Chemical Warfare Agents," 239.

16. Shenoi, "Chemical Warfare Agents," 240.

17. Shenoi, "Chemical Warfare Agents," 240.
18. Harris and Paxman, *A Higher Form of Killing*, 29.
19. Eckert, "Mass Deaths by Gas," 120.
20. Szinicz, "History of Chemical and Biological Warfare Agents," 167.
21. Harris and Paxman, *A Higher Form of Killing*, 11.
22. Harris and Paxman, *A Higher Form of Killing*, 23.
23. Eckert, "Mass Deaths by Gas," 120.
24. J.B. Neilands, "Vietnam: Progress of the Chemical War," *Asian Survey* 10 (1970): 209–229; at 211.
25. Eckert, "Mass Deaths by Gas," 120.
26. For more complete discussions on the Holocaust, see: Robert Jay Lifton, *The Nazi Doctors: Medical Killing and the Psychology of Genocide* (New York: Basic Books, 1986); Robert N. Proctor, *Racial Hygiene: Medicine Under the Nazis* (Cambridge, MA: Harvard University Press, 1988); Michael Burleigh and Wolfgang Wippermann, *The Racial State: Germany, 1933–1945* (Cambridge: Cambridge University Press, 1991); Michael Burleigh, *Death and Deliverance: Euthanasia in Germany, 1900–1945* (Cambridge: Cambridge University Press, 1994); Stefan Kühl, *The Nazi Connection: Eugenics, American Racism, and German National Socialism* (Oxford: Oxford University Press, 1994); Henry Friedlander, *The Origins of Nazi Genocide: From Euthanasia to the Final Solution* (Chapel Hill: University of North Carolina Press, 1995); Laurence Rees, *Auschwitz: A New History* (New York: Public Affairs, 2005); Donald McKale, *Hitler's Shadow War: The Holocaust and World War II* (New York: Taylor Trade Publishing, 2006); Heather Pringle, *The Master Plan: Himmler's Scholars and the Holocaust* (New York: Hyperion, 2006).
27. Proctor, *Racial Hygiene*, 6–7.
28. Ervin Staub, *The Roots of Evil: The Origins of Genocide and Other Group Violence* (Cambridge: Cambridge University Press, 1989), 137.
29. Known as Zyklon Blausaure (or, more commonly, Zyklon B), this poison was initially used to remove infestations around concentration camps.
30. William A. Buckingham, *Operation Ranch Hand: The Air Force and Herbicides in Southeast Asia, 1961–1971* (Washington, D.C.: Office of the Air Force History, 1982), 5.
31. Paul F. Cecil, *Herbicidal Warfare: The RANCH HAND Project in Vietnam* (Westport, CT: Praeger, 1986), 17.
32. See, for example, Susan M. Booker, "Dioxin in Vietnam: Fighting a Legacy of War," *Environmental Health Perspectives* 109 (2001): 116–117. L. Wayne Dwernychuck, Hoang Dinh Cau, Christopher

T. Hatfield, Thomas G. Boivin, Tran Manh Hung, Phung Tri Dung, and Nguyen Dinh Thai, "Dioxin Reservoirs in Southern Viet Nam—A Legacy of Agent Orange," *Chemosphere* 47 (2002): 117–137; Arnold Schecter, Marian Pavuk, Rainer Malisch, and John Jake Ryan, "Dioxin, Dibenzofuran, and Polychlorinated Biphyenyl (PCB) Levels in Food from Agent Orange-Sprayed and Nonsprayed Areas of Laos," *Journal of Toxicology and Environmental Health, Part A* 66 (2003): 2165–2186; Michael G. Palmer, "The Legacy of Agent Orange: Empirical Evidence from Central Vietnam," *Social Science & Medicine* 60 (2005): 1061–1070; Anh D. Ngo, Richard Taylor, Christine L. Roberts, and Tuan V. Nguyen, "Association Between Agent Orange and Birth Defects: Systematic Review and Meta-Analysis," *International Journal of Epidemiology* 35 (2006): 1220–1230; Michael G. Palmer, "The Case of Agent Orange," *Contemporary Southeast Asia* 29 (2007): 172–195.

33. Buckingham, *Operation Ranch Hand*, 15.

34. Richard Stone, "Agent Orange's Bitter Harvest," *Science* 315 (2007): 176–179; at 177. See also Jeanne Mager Stellman, Steven D. Stellman, Richard Christian, Tracy Weber, and Carrie Tomasallo, "The Extent and Patterns of Usage of Agent Orange and Other Herbicides in Vietnam," *Nature* 422 (2003): 681–687; at 681.

35. Stone, "Agent Orange," 177.

36. Buckingham, *Operation Ranch Hand*, 15.

37. During the Korean War, the United States was accused by North Korea of using biological weapons. Although most studies have concluded that the U.S. is innocent of charges, there does remain some doubt and controversy.

38. Quoted in Cathy Scott-Clark and Adrian Levy, "Spectre Orange," *Guardian*, March 29, 2003, http://www.guardian.co.uk/world/2003/mar/29/usa.adrianlevy (accessed May 17, 2009).

39. For additional information on Operation Sherwood Forest, see Buckingham, *Operation Ranch Hand*; and Cecil, *Herbicidal Warfare*.

40. There is also some evidence indicating that Iran used chemical weapons (but not nerve gases) against Iraqi forces. See "Iran–Iraq War," http://www.globalsecurity.org/military/world/war/iran-iraq.htm (accessed May 19, 2009); Julian Perry Robinson and Jozef Goldblat, "Chemical Warfare in the Iran–Iraq war, 1980–1988," May 1984, http://www.iranchamber.com/history/articles/chemical_warfare_iran_iraq_war.php (accessed May 19, 2009); Alexander H. Joffe, "The Environmental Legacy of Saddam Husayn: The Archaeology of Totalitariansim in

Modern Iraq," *Crime, Law & Social Change*, 33 (2000): 313–328; and Richard L. Russell, "Iraq's Chemical Weapons Legacy: What Others Might Learn from Saddam," *Middle East Journal* 59(2005): 187–208.

41. Russell, "Iraq's Chemical Weapons Legacy," 194.

42. Frank Barnaby, "Iran–Iraq War: The Use of Chemical Weapons Against the Kurds," *Ambio* 17 (1988): 407–408; Ian Black, "The Legacy of Chemical Warfare," *Guardian*, November 26, 2008, http://www.guardian.co.uk/world/2008/nov/26/iran-iraq-war (accessed May 17, 2009).

43. Steven Rose and Abraham Baravi, "The Meaning of Halabja: Chemical Warfare in Kurdistan," *Race & Class* 30 (1988): 74–77; Dlawer A.A. Ala'Aldeen, "Long Term Hazards of Chemical Weapon Agents: Analysis of Soil Samples from Kurdistan Years After Exposure to Sulphur Mustard and Nerve Agents," *Zanín: Journal of Kurdish Scientific and Medical Association* 1 (2005): 1–10.

44. Robert E. McCreight and Stephen L. Weigert, "Up in Smoke: Political Realities and Chemical Weapons Use Allegations during Mozambique's Civil War," *International Politics* 38 (2001): 253–272.

45. Tuan Anh Mai, Thanh Vu Doan, Joseph Tarradellas, Luiz Felippe de Alencastro, and Dominique Grandjean, "Dioxin Contamination in Soils of Southern Vietnam," *Chemosphere* 67 (2007): 1802–1807; at 1802.

46. Philip M. Boffey, "Herbicides in Vietnam: AAAS Study Finds Widespread Devastation," *Science* 171 (1971): 43–47; at 44.

47. Boffey, "Herbicides," 44.

48. The damaging effects of herbicidal warfare throughout Vietnam were augmented through repeated sprayings. Based on years of first-hand empirical research in Vietnam, for example, Westing found that a single herbicidal attack on dense upland forests resulted in a fairly complete leaf abscission within two to three weeks; however, only about 10 percent of trees (depending on type) were killed outright by a single spraying. With repeated sprayings, however, the extent of the devastation increased dramatically. Westing estimated that two herbicidal attacks resulted in a mortality rate of about 25 percent, while three sprayings increased the rate to approximately 50 percent. A fourth spraying resulted in 85 to 100 percent mortality for all trees. See Arthur Westing, "Environmental Consequences of the Second Indochina War: A Case Study," *Ambio* 4 (1975): 216–222; at 219.

49. Arthur H. Westing, "Ecological Effects of Military Deforestation on the Forests of South Vietnam," *BioScience* 21 (1971): 893–898.

50. Neilands, "Vietnam," 223.

51. Boffey, "Herbicides," 45.

52. Neilands, "Vietnam," 220.

53. Colin Norman, "Vietnam's Herbicide Legacy," *Science* 219 (1983): 1196–1197; at 1197.

54. Arthur H. Westing, "The Impact of War on the Environment," in *War and Public Health*, 2nd ed., edited by Barry S. Levy and Victor W. Sidel (Oxford: Oxford University Press, 2008), 69–84; at 73.

55. Neil S. Oatsvall, "War on Nature, War on Bodies: The United States' Chemical Defoliant Use During the Vietnam War and Its Consequences," Master's Thesis (North Carolina State University, 2008), 49–52.

56. Stellman et al., "Extent and Patterns," 685.

57. Palmer, "Case of Agent Orange," 175.

58. Palmer, "Legacy of Agent Orange," 1062.

59. According to Michael Palmer, recent evidence suggests that the concentration of TCDD in Agent Orange was far greater than initially claimed. He cites a level of 13 parts per million compared with earlier estimates of three parts per million. See Palmer, "Case of Agent Orange," 173.

60. Tuyet Le Thi Nham and Annika Johansson, "Impact of Chemical Warfare with Agent Orange on Women's Reproductive Lives in Vietnam: A Pilot Study," *Reproductive Health Matters* 9 (2001): 156–164; at 157.

61. Palmer, "Legacy of Agent Orange," 1062.

62. Schecter et al., "Dioxins," 422.

63. Booker, "Dioxin in Vietnam," 116.

64. Dwernychuk, et al., "Dioxin Reservoirs," 127.

65. Bea Duffield, "The Science of Chemical Warfare has Left a Deadly Legacy in Vietnam," *On Line Opinion: Australia's e-Journal of Social and Political Debate*, July 21, 2003, http://www.onlineopinion.com.au/view.asp?article=562 (accessed May 17, 2009).

66. Schecter et al., "Dioxin, Dibenzofuran," 2166.

67. Dwernychuk et al., "Dioxin Reservoirs," 120, 126; see also Tuyet and Johansson, "Impact of Chemical Warfare," 157.

68. Palmer, "Legacy of Agent Orange," 1061.

69. Stone, "Agent Orange," 176.

70. Stone, "Agent Orange," 176.

71. Stellman et al., "Extent and Patterns," 686.

72. Palmer, "Legacy of Agent Orange," 1062.

73. Palmer, "Case of Agent Orange," 174–5.

74. Scott-Clark and Levy, "Spectre Orange."

75. Ngo et al., "Association Between Agent Orange and Birth Defects," 1227.

76. Scott-Clark and Levy, "Spectre Orange."

77. Ngo et al., "Association Between Agent Orange and Birth Defects," 1227.

78. Eugeniusz Andrulewicz, "Chemical Weapons Dumped in the Baltic Sea," in *Assessment of the Fate and Effects of Toxic Agents on Water Resources*, edited by I.E. Gonenc et al. (London: Springer, 2007), 299–319; at 307.

79. Andrulewicz, "Chemical Weapons Dumped," 309.

80. Andrulewicz, "Chemical Weapons Dumped," 311.

81. Andrulewicz, "Chemical Weapons Dumped," 311.

82. Andrulewicz, "Chemical Weapons Dumped," 304.

83. Hosny Khordagui, "Potential Fate of G-Nerve Chemical Warfare Agents in the Coastal Waters of the Arabian Gulf," *Marine Environmental Research* 41(1996): 133–143; at 141.

84. Galina Garnaga, Eric Wyse, Sabine Azemard, Algirdas Stankevičius, and Stephen de Mora, "Arsenic in Sediments from the Southeastern Baltic Sea," *Environmental Pollution* 144 (2006): 855–861; at 856.

85. John Lindsay, "US Chemical Weapons in Panama: A Dangerous Legacy," *Revista Envío*, September 1998, http://www.envio.org.ni/articulo/1386 (accessed May 19, 2009).

86. Lindsay, "US Chemical Weapons in Panama."

87. John Hart, "Looking Back: The Continuing Legacy of Old and Abandoned Chemical Weapons," *Arms Control Association*, 2008, http://armscontrol.org/act/2008_03/Lookingback (accessed May 17, 2009).

88. Ruben Mnatsakanian, "A Poisoned Legacy," *Our Planet* 8.6, March 1997, http://www.unep.org/ourplanet/imgversn/86/sakan.html (accessed May 17, 2009).

89. Lindsay, "US Chemical Weapons in Panama."

90. See, for example Hans Sanderson, Patrik Fauser, Marianne Thomsen, and Peter B. Sørensen, "PBT Screening Profile of Chemical Warfare Agents (CWAs)," *Journal of Hazardous Materials* 148 (2007): 210–215.

FIVE

1. Andrew J. Rotter, *Hiroshima: The World's Bomb* (Oxford: Oxford University Press, 2008), 194. See also "Eyewitness Accounts of Hiroshima/Nagasaki Survivors," compiled at the Nuclear Weapon Archive, http://nuclearweaponarchive.org/Japan/Eyewit.html (accessed May 24, 2009); Miyoko Matsubara, "The Spirit of Hiroshima," 1999, http://www.wagingpeace.org/articles/1999/00/00_matsubara_spirit-hiroshima.htm (accessed May 24, 2009); and David Krieger, "Remembering Hiroshima and Nagasaki," August 1, 2003, http://www.wagingpeace.org/articles/2003/08/01_krieger_remembering.htm (accessed May 24, 2009).

2. Some estimates place Hiroshima's population closer to 350,000.

3. John D. Chappell, *Before the Bomb: How America Approached the End of the Pacific War* (Lexington: The University Press of Kentucky, 1997), 142.

4. "Eyewitness Accounts."

5. "Eyewitness Accounts."

6. "Eyewitness Accounts."

7. "Eyewitness Accounts."

8. Rotter, *Hiroshima*, 3. See also Thomas C. Reed and Danny B. Stillman, *The Nuclear Express: A Political History of the Bomb and its Proliferation* (Minneapolis, MN: Zenith Press, 2009).

9. See also Stephen I. Schwartz (editor), *Atomic Audit: The Costs and Consequences of US Nuclear Weapons Since 1940* (Washington, D.C.: Brookings Institution Press, 1998).

10. I.D. White, D.N. Mottershead, and S.J. Harrison, *Environmental Systems: An Introductory Text* (London: Allen & Unwin, 1984), 17. See also John Siracusa, *Nuclear Weapons: A Very Short Introduction* (Oxford: Oxford University Press, 2008), 2–3; Rotter, *Hiroshima*, 7–11; Joseph Cirincione, *Bomb Scare: The History and Future of Nuclear Weapons* (New York: Columbia University Press, 2008), 5–6.

11. The following account is derived from Rotter, *Hiroshima*, 54–55; Siracusa, *Nuclear Weapons*, 14–15;

12. Cirincione, *Bomb Scare*, 6. The "yield" of a nuclear weapon is a measure of the amount of explosive energy it can produce. Yield is typically given in terms of the quantity of TNT that would generate an identical explosion. Thus, a one kiloton nuclear device is equivalent to 1,000 tons of TNT; a one megaton device would yield the equivalent energy produced by one million tons of TNT. See Atomic Archive, "The Effects of Nuclear

Weapons," http://www.atomicarchive.com/Effects/index.shtml (accessed July 31, 2009).

13. Atoms are classified by their atomic number and mass. An atom's atomic number is defined as the number of protons present; this defines the chemical properties of the atom. Atoms may have identical numbers of protons (thus maintaining identical electrical charges) but differ in the number of neutrons—thus exhibiting a different atomic mass. Atoms with the same atomic number but different masses are known as isotopes. Chemically identical isotopes may have significantly different nuclear properties. See Siracusa, *Nuclear Weapons*, 3–4.

14. Cirincione, *Bomb Scare*, 7.

15. Cirincione, *Bomb Scare*, 7.

16. When some U-238 atoms absorb an additional neutron, a new element (known as neptunium) is formed; this has 93 protons and an atomic weight of 239. In 1941 scientists discovered how to separate a new element itself from neptunium, which they named plutonium. Less plutonium is required to sustain a chain reaction. See Cirincione, *Bomb Scare*, 8–9.

17. Reed and Stillman, *Nuclear Express*, 14–15.

18. Reed and Stillman, *Nuclear Express*, 15.

19. Rotter, *Hiroshima*, 115.

20. Reed and Stillman, *Nuclear Express*, 16; see also Cirincione, *Bomb Scare*, 9.

21. Rotter, *Hiroshima*, 112.

22. Cirincione, *Bomb Scare*, 19.

23. See Reed and Stillman, *Nuclear Express*.

24. Cirincione, *Bomb Scare*, 47.

25. Cirincione, *Bomb Scare*, 51.

26. James N. Danziger, *Understanding the Political World: A Comparative Introduction to Political Science*, 2nd ed. (New York: Longman, 1994), 309.

27. Cirincione, *Bomb Scare*, 59.

28. Quoted in Cirincione, *Bomb Scare*, 61.

29. Michael D. Swaine, "Chinese Crisis Management: Framework for Analysis, Tentative Observations, and Questions for the Future," in *Chinese National Security Decisionmaking Under Stress*, edited by Andrew Scobell and Larry M. Wortzel (Carlisle, PA: U.S. Army War College, Strategic Studies Institute, 2005), 5–53; at 16.

30. Paul H.B. Godwin, "China as a Major Asian Power: the Implications of its Military Modernization (A View from the United States)," in Andrew Scobell and Larry M. Wortzel, *Shaping China's*

Security Environment: The Role of the People's Liberation Army (Carlisle, PA: U.S. Army War College, Strategic Studies Institute, 2006), 105–135; at 106.

31. Cirincione, Bomb Scare, 64.
32. Cirincione, Bomb Scare, 64.
33. Cirincione, Bomb Scare, 65.
34. Cirincione, Bomb Scare, 66.
35. Cirincione, Bomb Scare, 71.
36. Cirincione, Bomb Scare, 72–73.
37. Quoted in Siracusa, Nuclear Weapons, 85.
38. Cirincione, Bomb Scare, 77. Cirincione notes that these arguments are in fact misleading; nuclear weapons are exceptionally expensive and more often than not, nuclear weapons systems are developed in conjunction with conventional weapons, not as substitutes.
39. Cirincione, Bomb Scare, 77.
40. This section is based on Carey Sublette, "Nuclear Weapons Frequently Asked Questions," May 15, 1997, http://nuclear-weaponarchive.org/Nwfaq/Nfaq5.html (accessed May 21, 2009). See also Atomic Archive, "Effects of Nuclear Weapons."
41. The proportion of immediate deaths attributable to blast, thermal radiation, or radiation poisoning is in part dependent on the yield of the nuclear explosion. In Hiroshima, for example, with a yield of approximately 15 kilotons, casualties were reported from all three causes; however, most victims—two-thirds of those recorded—died from burn-related injuries.
42. The magnitude of the blast effect is related to the height of the burst above ground. See Atomic Archive, "Effects of Nuclear Weapons."
43. Sublette, "Nuclear Weapons."
44. Sublette, "Nuclear Weapons;" Atomic Archive, "Effects of Nuclear Weapons."
45. Atomic Archive, "Effects of Nuclear Weapons."
46. Atomic Archive, "Effects of Nuclear Weapons."
47. Sublette, "Nuclear Weapons."
48. Atomic Archive, "Effects of Nuclear Weapons."
49. Sublette, "Nuclear Weapons."
50. Other units of measurement include the rad, gray, and sievert. The rad, also commonly seen in the literature, refers to the amount of energy absorbed per gram of body tissue.
51. Jonathan M. Weisgall, Operation Crossroads: The Atomic Tests at Bikini Atoll (Annapolis, MD: Naval Institute Press, 1994), 213.

52. It should be noted that humans are naturally exposed to radiation. The Sun, as well as the Earth itself, emits radiation. Depending on location, humans are subjected to approximately 0.18 rem per year of naturally occurring radiation. See Sublette, "Nuclear Weapons."
53. Sublette, "Nuclear Weapons;" Atomic Archive, "Effects of Nuclear Weapons."
54. Sublette, "Nuclear Weapons."
55. Sublette, "Nuclear Weapons."
56. Sublette, "Nuclear Weapons;" Atomic Archive, "Effects of Nuclear Weapons."
57. Sublette, "Nuclear Weapons."
58. Sublette, "Nuclear Weapons" Atomic Archive, "Effects of Nuclear Weapons."
59. Sublette, "Nuclear Weapons."
60. See Sublette, "Nuclear Weapons."
61. Sublette, "Nuclear Weapons."
62. Sue Wareham, "Nuclear Weapons, Nature and Society," paper presented to the Nature and Society Forum, November 2008, available at www.mapw.org.au/files/downloads/2008–11_Nuclear-weapons-nature-society_SW.pdf (accessed May 24, 2009).
63. O. Bridges and J.W. Bridges, "Radioactive Waste Problems in Russia," *Journal of Radiological Protection* 15 (1995): 223–234; at 230.
64. See, for example, Andree Kirchner, "The Destructive Legacy of the Cold War: The Dumping of Radioactive Wastes in the Arctic," *European Environmental Law Review* February (2000): 47–55; John D. Boice, Jr., "Thyroid Disease 60 Years After Hiroshima and 20 Years After Chernobyl," *Journal of the American Medical Association* 295 (2006): 1060–1062; A.P. Møller and T.A. Mousseau, "Species Richness and Abundance of Forest Birds in Relation to Radiation at Chernobyl," *Biology Letters* 3 (2007): 483–486.
65. Wareham, "Nuclear Weapons." Approximately 500 of these nuclear devices were tested in the atmosphere, underwater, or in space; the remaining 1,400 tests were conducted underground.
66. Atomic Archive, "Effects of Nuclear Weapons."
67. Darlene Keju-Johnson, "Nuclear Testing in the Pacific," *Eve Online* Fall (1990), available at http://eve.enviroweb.org/perspectives/issues/nuclear.html (accessed May 20, 2009); Nuke-Free World, "We Are Killing Our Own," available at http://nuke-freeworld.com/human.html (accessed May 20, 2009); Zohl de

Ishtar, "A Survivor's Warning on Nuclear Contamination," *Pacific Ecologist* Summer (2006/2007): 50–53.

68. Wareham, "Nuclear Weapons."
69. Wareham, "Nuclear Weapons;" M.A. Wahab et al., "Elevated Chromosome Translocation Frequencies in New Zealand Nuclear Test Veterans," *Cytogenetic and Genome Research* 121(2008): 79–87; Gerry Wright, "Operation Grapple—50 Years On and the Veterans' Still Wait," *RSA Review* March (2009), available at http://www.rsa.org.nz/review/art2009march/article_4.html (accessed May 28, 2009).
70. W. Burkart, "Radioepidemiology in the Aftermath of the Nuclear Program of the Former Soviet Union: Unique Lessons to be Learnt," *Radiat Environ Biophys* 35 (1996): 65–73; at 65.
71. Wareham, "Nuclear Weapons."
72. Bridges and Bridges, "Radioactive Waste Problems," 226.
73. Kirchner, "Destructive Legacy," 48.
74. Bridges and Bridges, "Radioactive Waste Problems," 230; see also Steven G. Sawhill, "Cleaning-up the Arctic's Cold War Legacy: Nuclear Waste and Arctic Military Environmental Cooperation," *Cooperation and Conflict* 35 (2000): 5–36; at 5–6.
75. Cirincione, *Bomb Scare*, 23; Reed and Stillman, *Nuclear Express*, 32.
76. Burkart, "Radioepidemiology," 67.
77. Bridges and Bridges, "Radioactive Waste Problems," 228.
78. Bridges and Bridges, "Radioactive Waste Problems," 228.
79. Wareham, "Nuclear Weapons."
80. Bridges and Bridges, "Radioactive Waste Problems," 226.
81. Kirsten B. Moysich, Ravi J. Menezes, and Arthur M. Michalek, "Chernobyl-related Ionizing Radiation Exposure and Cancer Risk: An Epidemiological Review," *Lancet Oncology* 3 (2002): 269–279.
82. Atomic Archive, "Effects of Nuclear Weapons."
83. Wareham, "Nuclear Weapons."
84. Bridges and Bridges, "Radioactive Waste Problems," 226.
85. P.P. Karan, Wilford A. Bladen, and James R. Wilson, "Technological Hazards in the Third World," *Geographical Review* 76 (1986): 195–208; at 198.
86. Bridges and Bridges, "Radioactive Waste Problems," 224.
87. Felicity Arbuthnot, "Poisoned Legacy," *New Internationalist* 316 (1999), http://www.newint.org/issue316/poisoned.htm (accessed May 24, 2009); John Pilger, "Iraq: The Great Cover-Up," *New Statesman*, January 22, 2001, http://www.newstatesman.com/print/200101220006 (accessed May 24,

2009); Gert Harigel, "Depleted Uranium Weapons—A Threat to Human Health?" *Nuclear Age Peace Foundation*, November 2001, http://www.wagingpeace.org/articles/2001/11/00_harigel_du.htm (accessed May 24, 2009); Aqel W. Abu-Qare and Mohamed B. Abou-Donia, "Depleted Uranium—The Growing Concern," *Journal of Applied Toxicology* 22 (2002): 149–152; Christopher Bollyn, "The Real Dirty Bombs: Depleted Uranium," August 6, 2004, http://www.wagingpeace.org/articles/2004/08/06_bollyn_real-dirty-bombs.htm (accessed May 24,2009); Christopher Bollyn, "Depleted Uranium Blamed for Cancer Clusters Among Iraq War Vets," August 5, 2004, http://www.wagingpeace.org/articles/2004/08/15_bollyn_depleted-uranium-blamed-cancer.htm (accessed May 24, 2009); Forrest Wilder, "In the Battlefields of Depleted Uranium," *Nuclear Age Peace Foundation*, August 2004, http://www.wagingpeace.org/articles/2004/08/00_wilder_battlefields-depleted-uranium.htm (accessed May 24, 2009); and Rob White, "Depleted Uranium, State Crime and the Politics of Knowing," *Theoretical Criminology* 12 (2008): 31–54.

88. Wilder, "Battlefields of Depleted Uranium."
89. Pilger, "Iraq."
90. White, "Depleted Uranium," 33.
91. Harigel, "Depleted Uranium Weapons."
92. Wilder, "Battlefields of Depleted Uranium."
93. Harigel, "Depleted Uranium Weapons."
94. Arbuthnot, "Poisoned Legacy."
95. Harigel, "Depleted Uranium Weapons."
96. Bollyn, "Real Dirty Bombs."
97. Arbuthnot, "Poisoned Legacy."
98. Arbuthnot, "Poisoned Legacy."
99. Arbuthnot, "Poisoned Legacy."
100. Harigel, "Depleted Uranium Weapons."
101. For a good starting point on Gulf War Syndrome, see Patrick G. Eddington, *Gassed in the Gulf: The Inside Story of the Pentagon-CIA Cover-up of Gulf War Syndrome* (Washington, D.C.: Insignia Publishing, 1997).
102. Wilder, "Battlefields of Depleted Uranium."
103. Abu-Qare and Abou-Donia, "Depleted Uranium," 150–151.
104. Wilder, "Battlefields of Depleted Uranium." Wilder also reports that the U.S. Navy opted to use shells manufactured from tungsten rather than depleted uranium.

105. Bollyn, "Real Dirty Bombs."
106. Bollyn, "Real Dirty Bombs."
107. Quoted in Bollyn, "Depleted Uranium Blamed."

SIX

1. Chris Hedges, "Introduction," in Chris Hedges and Laila Al-Arian, *Collateral Damage: America's War Against Iraqi Civilians* (New York: Nation Books, 2008), xxix.
2. Marc Pilisuk with Jennifer Achord Rountree, *Who Benefits from Global Violence and War: Uncovering a Destructive System* (Westport, CT: Praeger Security International, 2008), 2.
3. Manfred B. Steger, *Globalization: A Very Short Introduction* (Oxford: Oxford University Press, 2003), 9.
4. Martin Van Creveld, *The Changing Face of War: Combat from the Marne to Iraq* (New York: Presidio Books, 2008), 148.
5. Van Creveld, *Changing Face of War*, 149.
6. Robin Prior and Trevor Wilson, *The First World War* (London: Cassell & Co., 2001), 117.
7. David Stevenson, *Cataclysm: The First World War as Political Tragedy* (New York: Basic Books, 2005), 188.
8. Stevenson, *Cataclysm*, 84.
9. John Horne, "Civilian Populations and Wartime Violence: Towards an Historical Analysis," *International Social Science Journal* 54 (2002): 483–490; at 483.
10. Edmund Cairns, *Arms Without Borders: Why a Globalised Trade Needs Global Controls* (Control Arms Campaign, 2006), p. 6, available at www.controlarms.org (accessed June 28, 2009).
11. Richard A. Bitzinger, "The Globalization of the Arms Industry: The Next Proliferation Challenge," *International Security* 19 (1994): 170–198; at 195. See also Gideon Burrows, *The No-Nonsense Guide to the Arms Trade* (Oxford: Verso, 2002).
12. Cairns, *Arms Without Borders*, 9.
13. Burrows, *Guide to the Arms Trade*, 15. Between 2000 and 2004, the top 100 companies reportedly increased their domestic and international sales of conventional weapons from US$157 billion to US$268 billion. Eighty-five of the world's top 100 arms companies in 2003 were headquartered in the industrialized world. See Cairns, *Arms Without Borders*, 6.
14. Nick Turse, *The Complex: How the Military Invades our Everyday Lives* (New York: Metropolitan Books, 2008), 23.
15. Turse, *The Complex*, 24.

16. Cairns, *Arms Without Borders*, 10.
17. Landmine Monitor (2008), http://lm.icbl.org/index.php/publications/display?url=lm/2008/countries/usa.html (accessed June 28, 2009).
18. Cairns, *Arms Without Borders*, 6.
19. Burrows, *Guide to the Arms Trade*, 111.
20. Cairns, *Arms Without Borders*, 25.
21. Cairns, *Arms Without Borders*, 7.
22. Cairns, *Arms Without Borders*, 12.
23. Cairns, *Arms Without Borders*, 7.
24. Tamar Gabelnick and Anna Rich, "Globalized Weaponry," *Foreign Policy in Focus* (2002), http://www.fpif.org/briefs/vol5/v5n16arms_body.html (accessed June 28, 2009).
25. Gabelnick and Rich, "Globalized Weaponry."
26. Gabelnick and Rich, "Globalized Weaponry."
27. Chris McNab and Hunter Keeter, *Tools of Violence: Guns, Tanks and Dirty Bombs* (New York: Osprey Publishing, 2008), 82; see also "M67/M72 Area Denial Anti-Personnel Mine (ADAM), *GlobalSecurity.Org*, http://www.globalsecurity.org/military/systems/munitions/adam.htm (accessed June 28, 2009).
28. Hugo Slim, *Killing Civilians: Method, Madness, and Morality in War* (New York: Columbia University Press, 2008), 123.
29. James A. Tyner, *War, Violence, and Population: Making the Body Count* (New York: The Guilford Press, 2009).
30. Michael Adas, *Dominance by Design: Technological Imperatives and America's Civilizing Mission* (Cambridge, MA: Belknap Press, 2006), 392.
31. Gabelnick and Rich, "Globalized Weaponry."
32. Andrew J. Bacevich, *The New American Militarism: How Americans are Seduced by War* (Oxford: Oxford University Press, 2005), 147.
33. Howard Zinn, *Just War* (Milan: Edizioni Charta, 2005), 55.
34. Hedges, "Introduction," xxviii–xxix.

Bibliography

Abdulboughi, A. "Symptoms of Posttraumatic Stress Disorders Among Displaced Kurdish Children in Iraq," *Nordic Journal of Psychiatry* 46 (1992): 315–319.

Abu-Qare, Aqel W. and Mohamed B. Abou-Donia. "Depleted Uranium—The Growing Concern," *Journal of Applied Toxicology* 22 (2002): 149–152.

Adas, Michael. *Dominance by Design: Technological Imperatives and America's Civilizing Mission* (Cambridge, MA: Belknap Press, 2006).

Ala'Aldeen, Dlawar A.A. "Long Term Hazards of Chemical Weapons Agents: Analysis of Soil Samples from Kurdistan Years After Exposure to Sulphur Mustard and Nerve Agents," *Zanín: Journal of Kurdish Scientific and Medical Association* 1 (2005): 1–10.

Al-Awadhi, J.M., S.A. Omar, and R.F. Misak. "Land Degradation Indicators in Kuwait," *Land Degradation & Development* 16 (2005): 163–176.

Albertyn, R., S.W. Bickler, A.B. van As, A.J.W. Millar, and H. Rode. "The Effects of War on Children in Africa," *Pediatric Surgeon International* 19 (2003): 227–232.

Andersson, N., C.P. da Sousa, and S. Pareds. "Social Cost of Land Mines in Four Countries: Afghanistan, Bosnia, Cambodia, and Mozambique," *British Medical Journal* 311 (1995): 718–721.

Andrulewicz, Eugeniusz. "Chemical Weapons Dumped in the Baltic Sea," in *Assessment of the Fate and Effects of Toxic Agents on Water Resources*, edited by I.E. Gonenc et al. (London: Springer, 2007), 299–319.

Appel, Liesel. "Honor Thy Mother: Reflections on Being the Daughter of Nazis," in *Second Generation Voices: Reflections of Holocaust Survivors and Perpetrators*, edited by Alan L. Berger and Naomi Berger (Syracuse: Syracuse University Press, 2001), 303–309.

Ascherio, Alberto, Robin Biellik, Andy Epstein, Gail Snetro, Steve Gloyd, Barbara Ayotte, and Paul R. Epstein. "Deaths and Injuries

Caused by Land Mines in Mozambique," *Lancet* 346 (1995): 721–724.

Awadh, Abeer M., Booney Vance, Viola El-Beblawi, and Andres J. Pumariega. "Effects of Trauma of the Gulf War on Kuwaiti Children," *Journal of Child and Family Studies* 7 (1998): 493–498.

Bacevich, Andrew J. *The New American Militarism: How Americans are Seduced by War* (Oxford: Oxford University Press, 2005).

Barenbaum, Joshua, Vladislav Ruchkin, and Mary Schwab-Stone. "The Psychosocial Aspects of Children Exposed to War: Practice and Policy Initiatives," *Journal of Child Psychology and Psychiatry* 45 (2004): 41–62.

Barnaby, Frank. "Iran–Iraq War: The Use of Chemical Weapons Against the Kurds," *Ambio* 17 (1988): 407–408.

Bar-On, D., J. Eland, R.J. Kleber, R. Krell, Y. Moore, A. Sagi, E. Soriano, P. Suedfeld, P.G. Van Der Velden, and M.H. Van Izendoorn. "Multigenerational Perspectives on Coping with the Holocaust Experience: An Attachment Perspective for Understanding the Development Sequel of Trauma Across Generations," *International Journal of Behavioral Development* 22 (1998): 315–338.

Bartrop, Paul. "The Relationship Between War and Genocide in the Twentieth Century: A Consideration," *Journal of Genocide Research* 4 (2002): 519–532.

Berhe, A.A. "The Contributions of Landmines to Land Degradation," *Land Degradation and Development* 18 (2007): 1–15.

Berman, Helene. "Children and War: Current Understandings and Future Directions," *Public Health Nursing* 18 (2001): 243–252.

Bilukha, Oleg O., Muireann Brennan, and Bradley A. Woodruff. "Death and Injury from Landmines and Unexploded Ordnance in Afghanistan," *Journal of the American Medical Association* 290 (2003): 650–653.

Bilukha, Oleg O., Zaur Tsitsaev, Ramzan Ibragimov, Mark Anderson, and Eliza Murtazaeva. "Epidemiology of Injuries and Deaths from Landmines and Unexploded Ordnance in Chechnya, 1994 Through 2005," *Journal of the American Medical Association* 296 (2006): 516–518.

Bitzinger, Richard A. "The Globalization of the Arms Industry: The Next Proliferation Challenge," *International Security* 19 (1994): 170–198.

Blair, Robert G. "Risk Factors Associated with PTSD and Major Depression Among Cambodian Refugees in Utah," *Health & Social Work* 25 (2000): 23–30.

Boal, Ian, T.J. Clark, Joseph Matthews, and Michael Watts. *Afflicted*

Powers: Capital and Spectacle in a New Age of War (New York: Verso, 2005).

Bodman, F. "War Conditions and the Mental Health of the Child," British Medical Journal 11 (1941): 486–488.

Boehnlein, James K. "Clinical Relevance of Grief and Mourning Among Cambodian Refugees," Social Science & Medicine 25 (1987): 765–772.

Boffey, Philip M. "Herbicides in Vietnam: AAAS Study Finds Widespread Devastation," Science 171 (1971): 43–47.

Boice, John D., Jr. "Thyroid Disease 60 Years After Hiroshima and 20 Years After Chernobyl," Journal of the American Medical Association 295 (2006): 1060–1062.

Booker, Susan M. "Dioxin in Vietnam: Fighting a Legacy of War," Environmental Health Perspectives 109 (2001): 116–117.

Boot, Max. War Made New: Weapons, Warriors, and the Making of the Modern World (New York: Gotham Books, 2006).

Borus, Jonathan F. "Reentry: II. 'Making It' Back in the States," American Journal of Psychiatry 139 (1973): 850–854.

Bracken, Patrick, Joan E. Giller, and Derek Summerfield. "Psychological Responses to War and Atrocity: The Limitations of Current Concepts," Social Science & Medicine 40 (1995): 1073–1082.

Braden, Kathleen and Fred M. Shelley. Engaging Geopolitics (New York: Prentice Hall, 2000).

Bradner, T. "Psychiatric Observations Among Finnish Children During the Russo-Finnish War of 1939–1940," Nervous Child 2 (1943): 313–319.

Braveman, Paula, Alan Meyers, Thomas Schlenker, and Curt Wands. "Public Health and War in Central America," in War and Public Health, edited by Barry S. Levy and Victor W. Sidel (New York: Oxford University Press, 1997), 238–253.

Bridges, O. and J.W. Bridges. "Radioactive Waste Problems in Russia," Journal of Radiological Protection 15 (1995): 223–234.

Brown, Ian. Cambodia (Oxford: Oxfam, 2000).

Brown, Richard, Eddie Chaloner, Steve Mannion, and Tim Cheatle. "10-Year Experience of Injuries Sustained During Clearance of Anti-Personnel Mines," Lancet 358 (2001): 2048–2049.

Browning, Christopher R. Nazi Policy, Jewish Workers, German Killers (Cambridge: Cambridge University Press, 2000).

Buckingham, William A. Operation Ranch Hand: The Air Force and Herbicides in Southeast Asia, 1961–1971 (Washington, D.C.: Office of the Air Force History, 1982).

Burkart, W. "Radioepidemiology in the Aftermath of the Nuclear

Program of the Former Soviet Union: Unique Lessons to be Learnt," *Radiat Environ Biophys* 35 (1996): 65–73.

Burleigh, Michael. *Death and Deliverance: Euthanasia in Germany, 1900–1945* (Cambridge: Cambridge University Press, 1994).

Burleigh, Michael and Wolfgang Wippermann. *The Racial State: Germany, 1933–1945* (Cambridge: Cambridge University Press, 1991).

Burrows, Gideon. *The No-Nonsense Guide to the Arms Trade* (Oxford: Verso, 2002).

Capdevila, Luc and Danièle Voldman. *War Dead: Western Societies and the Casualties of War*, translated by Richard Veasey (Edinburgh: Edinburgh University Press, 2006).

Carlson, Eve Bernstein and Rhonda Rosser-Hogan. "Mental Health Status of Cambodian Refugees Ten Years After Leaving Their Homes," *American Journal of Orthopsychiatry* 63 (1993): 223–231.

Carlton-Ford, Steve, Ann Hamill, and Paula Houston. "War and Children's Mortality," *Childhood* 7 (2000): 401–419.

Cecil, Paul F. *Herbicidal Warfare: The RANCH HAND Project in Vietnam* (Westport, CT: Praeger, 1986).

Chandler, David. *The Tragedy of Cambodian History: Politics, War, and Revolution Since 1945* (New Haven, CT: Yale University Press, 1991).

Chappell, John D. *Before the Bomb: How America Approached the End of the Pacific War* (Lexington: The University Press of Kentucky, 1997).

Chernus, Ira. "Eisenhower's Ideology in World War II," *Armed Forces & Society* 23 (1997): 595–613.

Cirincione, Joseph. *Bomb Scare: The History and Future of Nuclear Weapons* (New York: Columbia University Press, 2008).

Clodfelter, Michael. *Mad Minutes and Vietnam Months: A Soldier's Story* (Jefferson, NC: McFarland & Co., 1988).

Conteh-Morgan, Earl. *Collective Political Violence: An Introduction to the Theories and Cases of Violent Conflicts* (New York: Routledge, 2004).

Danziger, James M. *Understanding the Political World: A Comparative Introduction to Political Science*, 2nd edition (New York: Longman, 1994).

Davies, Paul. *War of the Mines: Cambodia, Landmines and the Impoverishment of a Nation* (London: Pluto Press, 1994).

Davis, Stacy Bernard and Donald F. Patierno. "Tackling the Global Landmine Problem: The United States Perspective," in *Landmines and Human Security: International Politics and War's Hidden Legacy*, edited by Richard A. Matthew, Bryan McDonald, and Kenneth R. Rutherford (Albany: State University of New York Press, 2004), 125–137.

De Ishtar, Zohl. "A Survivor's Warning on Nuclear Contamination," *Pacific Ecologist* Summer (2006/2007): 50–53.

De Medeiros, Carlos Aguiar. "The Post-War American Technological Development as a Military Enterprise," *Contributions to Political Economy* 22 (2003): 41–62.

Downing, B.M. *The Military Revolution and Political Change in Early Modern Europe* (Princeton, NJ: Princeton University Press, 1992).

Dwernychuck, L. Wayne, Christopher T. Hatfield, Thomas G. Boivin, Tran Manh Hung, Phung Tri Dung, and Nguyen Dinh Thai. "Dioxin Reservoirs in Southern Viet Nam—A Legacy of Agent Orange," *Chemosphere* 47 (2002): 117–137.

Eckert, William G. "Mass Deaths by Gas or Chemical Poisoning," *American Journal of Forensic Medicine and Pathology* 12 (1991): 119–125.

Eddington, Patrick G. *Gassed in the Gulf: The Inside Story of the Pentagon-CIA Cover-Up of Gulf War Syndrome* (Washington, D.C.: Insignia Publishing, 1997).

Eisenbruch, Maurice. "From Post-Traumatic Stress Disorder to Cultural Bereavement: Diagnosis of Southeast Asian Refugees," *Social Science & Medicine* 33 (1991): 673–680.

Elbadawi, Ibrahim and Nicholas Sambanis. "Why Are There So Many Civil Wars in Africa? Understanding and Preventing Violent Conflict," *Journal of African Economies* 9 (2000): 244–269.

Epkenhans, Michael. "Military-Industrial Relations in Imperial Germany, 1870–1914," *War in History* 10 (2003): 1–26.

Etcheson, Craig. *After the Killing Fields: Lessons from the Cambodian Genocide* (Lubbock: Texas Tech University Press, 2005).

Fanon, Frantz. *The Wretched of the Earth*, translated by Constance Farrington (New York: Grove Press, 1963).

Feagin, Joe R. and Kelly Riddell. "The State, Capitalism, and World War II: The U.S. Case," *Armed Forces & Society* 17 (1990): 53–79.

Figley, Charles R. "Symptoms of Delayed Combat Stress Among a College Sample of Vietnam Veterans," *Military Medicine* 143 (1978): 107–110.

Flannery, Daniel J. *Violence and Mental Health in Everyday Life: Prevention and Intervention Strategies for Children and Adolescents* (Lanham, MD: Altamira Press, 2006).

Flynn, Michael. "Political Minefield," in *Landmines and Human Security: International Politics and War's Hidden Legacy*, edited by Richard A. Matthew, Bryan McDonald, and Kenneth R. Rutherford (Albany: State University of New York Press, 2004), 117–124.

Friedlander, Henry. *The Origins of Nazi Genocide: From Euthanasia to the Final Solution* (Chapel Hill: The University of North Carolina Press, 1995).

Garnaga, Galina, Eric Wyse, Sabine Azemard, Algirdas Stankevičius, and Stephen de Mora. "Arsenic in Sediments from the Southeastern Baltic Sea," *Environmental Pollution* 144 (2006): 855–861.

Gaulin, Ted. "A Necessary Evil? Reexamining the Military Utility of Antipersonnel Landmines," in *Landmines and Human Security: International Politics and War's Hidden Legacy*, edited by Richard A. Matthew, Bryan McDonald, and Kenneth R. Rutherford (Albany: State University of New York Press, 2004), 209–223.

Geiger, H. Jack. "The Impact of War on Human Rights," in *War and Public Health*, edited by Barry S. Levy and Victor W. Sidel (New York: Oxford University Press, 1997), 39–50.

Ghislain, Pierre-Dominique. "Spontaneous Extrusion of Hand Grenade Fragments From the Face 60 Years After Injury," *Journal of the American Medical Association* 290 (2003): 1317–1318.

Glasser, Ronald J. *Wounded: Vietnam to Iraq* (New York: George Braziller, 2006).

Godwin, Paul H.B. "China as a Major Asian Power: The Implications of Its Military Modernization (A View From the United States)," in *Shaping China's Security Environment: The Role of the People's Liberation Army*, edited by Andrew Scobell and Larry M. Wortzel (Carlisle, PA: U.S. Army War College, Strategic Studies Institute, 2006).

Gough, Terrence J. "Origins of the Army Industrial College: Military-Business Tensions After World War I," *Armed Forces & Society* 17 (1991): 259–275.

Greenway, H.D.S. "Laos," *Atlantic Monthly* 228 (1971): 6, 10–12, 16.

Gregory, Derek. *The Colonial Present* (Malden, MA: Blackwell Publishing, 2004).

Harris, Robert and Jeremy Paxman. *A Higher Form of Killing: The Secret History of Chemical and Biological Warfare* (New York: Random House, 2002).

Hedges, Chris. *War is a Force that Gives Us Meaning* (New York: Anchor Books, 2002).

Hedges, Chris and Laila Al-Arian. *Collateral Damage: America's War Against Iraqi Civilians* (New York: Nation Books, 2008).

Hinton, Alexander L. *Why Did They Kill? Cambodia in the Shadow of Genocide* (Berkeley: University of California Press, 2005).

Hinton, Devon E., Vuth Pich, Dara Chhean, and Mark H. Pollack, " 'The Ghost Pushes You Down': Sleep Paralysis-Type Panic Attacks in Khmer Refugee Population," *Transcultural Psychiatry* 42 (2005): 46–77.

Hoffman, Eva. *After Such Knowledge: Memory, History, and the Legacy of the Holocaust* (New York: Public Affairs, 2004).

Horne, John. "Civilian Populations and Wartime Violence: Towards an Historical Analysis," *International Social Science Journal* 54 (2002): 483–490.

Horowitz, M.D. and G.F. Solomon. "A Prediction of Delayed Stress Response Syndrome in Vietnam Veterans," *Journal of Social Issues* 4 (1975): 67–79.

Hossein-Zadeh, Ismael. *The Political Economy of U.S. Militarism* (New York: Palgrave Macmillan, 2006).

Htun, Nay. "Landmines Prolong Conflicts and Impede Socio-economic Development," in *Landmines and Human Security: International Politics and War's Hidden Legacy*, edited by Richard A. Matthew, Bryan McDonald, and Kenneth R. Rutherford (Albany: State University of New York Press, 2004), 169–177.

Husum, Hans, Kirsten Resell, Gyri Vorren, Yang Van Heng, Mudhafar Murad, Mads Gilbert, and Torben Wisborg. "Chronic Pain in Land Mine Accident Survivors in Cambodia and Kurdistan," *Social Science & Medicine* 55 (2002): 1813–1816.

Imlay, Talbot. "Preparing for Total War: The *Conseil Supérieur de la Défense Nationale* and France's Industrial and Economic Preparations for War after 1918," *War in History* 15 (2008): 43–71.

Irish, Kerry E. "Apt Pupil: Dwight Eisenhower and the 1930 Industrial Mobilization Plan," *Journal of Military History* 70 (2006): 31–61.

Jahunlu, Hameed Reza, Hans Husum, and Torben Wisborg. "Mortality in Land-Mine Accidents in Iran," *Prehospital Disaster Medicine* 17 (2002): 107–109.

Joffe, Alexander H. "The Environmental Legacy of Saddam Husayn: The Archaeology of Totalitarianism in Modern Iraq," *Crime, Law & Social Change* 33 (2000): 313–328.

Johnson, Chalmers. *The Sorrows of Empire: Militarism, Secrecy, and the End of the Republic* (New York: Metropolitan Books, 2004).

Johnson, Howard and Andrew Thompson. "The Development and Maintenance of Post-Traumatic Stress Disorder (PTSD) in Civilian Adult Survivors of War Trauma and Torture: A Review," *Clinical Psychology Review* 28 (2008): 36–47.

Johnson, Hubert C. *Breakthrough! Tactics, Technology, and the Search for Victory on the Western Front in World War I* (Novato, CA: Presidio, 1994).

Joss, Donna McIvor. "Anti-Personnel Landmine Injuries: A Global Epidemic," *Work: A Journal of Prevention, Assessment & Rehabilitation* 8 (1997): 299–304.

Jünger, Ernst. *Storm of Steel*, translated by Michael Hofmann (New York: Penguin, 2004 [1920]).

Karan, P.P., Wilford A. Bladen, and James R. Wilson. "Technological

Hazards in the Third World," *Geographical Review* 76 (1986): 195–208.

Kardiner, Abram. *War Stress and Neurotic Illness* (New York: Hoeber, 1947).

Khordagui, Hosny. "Potential Fate of G-Nerve Chemical Warfare Agents in the Coastal Waters of the Arabian Gulf," *Marine Environmental Research* 41 (1996): 133–143.

Kiernan, Ben. *The Pol Pot Regime: Policies, Race and Genocide in Cambodia Under the Khmer Rouge, 1975–1979* (New Haven, CT: Yale University Press, 1996).

Kinzie, J. David and James J. Boehnlein. "Post-Traumatic Psychosis Among Cambodian Refugees," *Journal of Traumatic Stress* 2 (1989): 185–198.

Kinzie, J. David, R.H. Fredrickson, Rath Ben, Jenelle Fleck, and William Karls. "Posttraumatic Stress Disorder Among Survivors of Cambodian Concentration Camps," *American Journal of Psychiatry* 141 (1984): 645–650.

Kirchner, Andree. "The Destructive Legacy of the Cold War: The Dumping of Radioactive Wastes in the Arctic," *European Law Review* February (2000): 47–55.

Knox, Paul, John Agnew, and Linda McCarthy. *The Geography of the World Economy*, 4th ed. (New York: Arnold, 2003).

Koistinen, Paul A.C. *The Military-Industrial Complex: A Historical Perspective* (New York: Praeger Publishers, 1980).

Krepon, Michael. "Weapons Potentially Inhumane: The Case of Cluster Bombs," *Foreign Affairs* 52 (1974): 595–611.

Kühl, Stefan. *The Nazi Connection: Eugenics, American Racism, and German National Socialism* (Oxford: Oxford University Press, 1994).

Kurlansky, Mark. *Nonviolence: Twenty-Five Lessons from the History of a Dangerous Idea* (New York: Modern Library, 2006).

Lee, Ernest C. and Stefanos N. Kales. "Chemical Weapons," in *War and Public Health*, 2nd ed., edited by Barry S. Levy and Victor W. Sidel (Oxford: Oxford University Press, 2008), 117–134.

Lev-Wiesel, Rachel. "Intergenerational Transmission of Trauma Across Three Generations," *Qualitative Social Work* 6 (2007): 75–94.

Levy, Barry S. and Victor W. Sidel. "War and Public Health: An Overview," in *War and Public Health*, 2nd ed., edited by Barry S. Levy and Victor W. Sidel (Oxford: Oxford University Press, 2008), 3–20.

Lifton, Robert Jay. *The Nazi Doctors: Medical Killing and the Psychology of Genocide* (New York: Basic Books, 1986).

Locard, Henri. *Pol Pot's Little Red Book: The Sayings of Angkar* (Chiang Mai, Thailand: Silkworm Books, 2004).

Mai, Tuan Anh, Thanh Vu Doan, Joseph Tarradellas, Luiz Felippe de Alencastro, and Dominique Grandjean. "Dioxin Contamination in Soils of Southern Vietnam," *Chemosphere* 67 (2007): 1802–1807.

McCreight, Robert E. and Stephen L. Weigert. "Up in Smoke: Political Realities and Chemical Weapons Use Allegations During Mozambique's Civil War," *International Politics* 38 (2001): 253–272.

McKale, Donald M. *Hitler's Shadow War: The Holocaust and World War II* (New York: Taylor Trade Publishing, 2006).

McNab, Chris and Hunter Keeter. *Tools of Violence: Guns, Tanks and Dirty Bombs* (New York: Osprey Publishing, 2008).

Meade, Peter. "Additional Comment Added in Press," *The Journal of Trauma: Injury, Infection, and Critical Care* 48 (2000): 739.

Meade, Peter and James Mirocha. "Civilian Landmine Injuries in Sri Lanka," *Journal of Trauma: Injury, Infection, and Critical Care* 48 (2000): 735–739.

Meagher, Ilona. *Moving a Nation to Care: Post-Traumatic Stress Disorder and America's Returning Troops* (New York: Ig Publishing, 2007).

Mercer, M.H. and J.M. Despert. "Psychological Effects of the War on French Children," *Psychosomatic Medicine* 5 (1943): 266–272.

Michultka, Denise, Edward B. Blanchard, and Tom Kalous. "Responses to Civilian War Experiences: Predictors of Psychological Functioning and Coping," *Journal of Traumatic Stress* 11 (1998): 571–577.

Mitchell, Shannon K. "Death, Disability, Displaced Persons and Development: The Case of Landmines in Bosnia and Herzegovina," *World Development* 32 (2004): 2105–2120.

Møller, A.P. and T.A. Mousseau. "Species Richness and Abundance of Forest Birds in Relation to Radiation at Chernobyl," *Biology Letters* 3 (2007): 483–486.

Mollica, Richard F., Grace Wyshak, and James Lavelle. "The Psychosocial Impact of War Trauma and Torture on Southeast Asian Refugees," *American Journal of Psychiatry* 144 (1987): 1567–1572.

Morikawa, Masahiro, Sebastian Taylor, and Marjie Persons. "Deaths and Injuries Due to Unexploded Ordnance (UXO) in Northern Lao PDR (Laos)," *Injury* 29 (1998): 301–304.

Moysich, Kirsten B., Ravi J. Menezes, and Arthur M. Michalek. "Chernobyl-Related Ionizing Radiation Exposure and Cancer Risk: An Epidemiological Review," *Lancet Oncology* 3 (2002): 269–279.

Nachón, Claudio Torres. "The Environmental Impacts of Landmines," in *Landmines and Human Security: International Politics and War's Hidden Legacy*, edited by Richard A. Matthew, Bryan McDonald, and

Kenneth R. Rutherford (Albany: State University of New York Press, 2004), 191–207.

Nader, K.O. and L.A. Fairbanks. "The Supervision of Reexperiencing: Impulse Control and Somatic Symptoms in Children Following Traumatic Exposure," *Anxiety, Stress and Coping: An International Journal* 7 (1994): 229–239.

Neale, Jonathan. *A People's History of the Vietnam War* (New York: The New Press, 2003).

Neilands, J.B. "Vietnam: Progress of the Chemical War," *Asian Survey* 10 (1970): 209–229.

Ngo, Anh D., Richard Taylor, Christine L. Roberts, and Tuan V. Nguyen. "Association Between Agent Orange and Birth Defects: Systematic Review and Meta-Analysis," *International Journal of Epidemiology* 35 (2006): 1220–1230.

Ngor, Haing, with R. Warner. *Survival in the Killing Fields* (New York: Carroll and Graf Publishers, 1987).

Nixon, Rob. "Of Landmines and Cluster Bombs," *Cultural Critique* 67 (2007): 160–174.

Nordstrom, Carolyn. *Shadows of War: Violence, Power, and International Profiteering in the Twenty-First Century* (Berkeley: University of California Press, 2004).

Norman, Colin. "Vietnam's Herbicide Legacy," *Science* 219 (1983): 1196–1197.

Oatsvall, Neil S. "War on Nature, War on Bodies: The United States' Chemical Defoliant Use During the Vietnam War and Its Consequences" Master's Thesis (North Carolina State University).

Opotow, Susan. "Reconciliation in Times of Impunity: Challenges for Social Justice," *Social Justice Research* 14 (2001): 149–170.

Oppong, Joseph R. and Ezekiel Kalipeni. "The Geography of Landmines and Implications for Health and Disease in Africa: A Political Ecology Approach," *Africa Today* 52 (2005): 3–25.

Ó Tuathail, Gearóid. *Critical Geopolitics: The Politics of Writing Global Space* (Minneapolis: University of Minnesota Press, 1996).

Palmer, Michael G. "The Legacy of Agent Orange: Empirical Evidence from Central Vietnam," *Social Science & Medicine* 60 (2005): 1061–1070.

Palmer, Michael G. "The Case of Agent Orange," *Contemporary Southeast Asia* 29 (2007): 172–195.

Parsons, John, Thomas J. Kehle, and Steve V. Owen. "Incidence of Behavior Problems Among Children of Vietnam War Veterans," *School Psychology International* 11 (1990): 253–259.

Pearce, Kathy A., Andrew H. Schauer, Nancy J. Garfield, Carroll O.

Ohlde, and Tom W. Patterson. "A Study of Post Traumatic Stress Disorder in Vietnam Veterans," *Journal of Clinical Psychology* 41 (1985): 9–14.

Peet, Richard. *Global Capitalism: Theories of Societal Development* (New York: Routledge, 1991).

Pennington, Judith C. and James M. Brannon. "Environmental Fate of Explosives," *Thermochimica Acta* 384 (2002): 163–172.

Pilisuk, Marc, with Jennifer Achord Rountree. *Who Benefits from Global Violence and War: Uncovering a Destructive System* (Westport, CT: Praeger Security International, 2008).

Pirc, S. and T. Budkovič. "Remains of World War I Geochemical Pollution in the Landscape," in *Environmental Xenobiotics*, edited by M. Richardson (Hertfordshire, UK: Taylor & Francis, 1996), 375–418.

Prestowitz, Clyde. *Rogue Nation: American Unilateralism and the Failure of Good Intentions* (New York: Basic Books, 2003).

Pringle, Heather. *The Master Plan: Himmler's Scholars and the Holocaust* (New York: Hyperion, 2006).

Prior, Robin and Trevor Wilson. *The First World War* (London: Cassell & Co., 2001).

Proctor, Robert N. *Racial Hygiene: Medicine Under the Nazis* (Cambridge, MA: Harvard University Press, 1988).

Prokosch, Eric. "Technology and its Control: Antipersonnel Weapons," *International Social Science Journal* 28 (1976): 341–358.

Prunier, Gerard. *Africa's World War: Congo, the Rwandan Genocide, and the Making of a Continental Catastrophe* (Oxford: Oxford University Press, 2008).

Reed, Thomas C. and Danny B. Stillman. *The Nuclear Express: A Political History of the Bomb and its Proliferation* (Minneapolis, MN: Zenith Press, 2009).

Rees, Laurence. *Auschwitz: A New History* (New York: Public Affairs, 2005).

Roberts, Shawn and Jody Williams. *After the Guns Fall Silent: The Enduring Legacy of Landmines* (Washington, D.C.: Vietnam Veterans of America Foundation, 1995).

Rose, Steven and Abraham Baravi. "The Meaning of Halabja: Chemical Warfare in Kurdistan," *Race & Class* 30 (1988): 74–77.

Rosenheck, Robert and Alan Fontana. "Transgenerational Effects of Abusive Violence on the Children of Vietnam Combat Veterans," *Journal of Traumatic Stress* 11 (1998): 731–742.

Rosensaft, Menachem. "I Was Born in Bergen-Belsen," in *Second Generation Voices: Reflections of Holocaust Survivors and Perpetrators*, edited by

Alan L. Berger and Naomi Berger (Syracuse: Syracuse University Press, 2001), 188–207.

Rotter, Andrew J. *Hiroshima: The World's Bomb* (Oxford: Oxford University Press, 2008).

Rowland-Klein, D. and R. Dunlop. "The Transmission of Trauma Across Generations: Identification with Parental Trauma in Children of Holocaust Survivors," *Australian and New Zealand Journal of Psychiatry* 32 (1998): 358–369.

Rozée, Patricia and Gretchen Van Boemel. "The Psychological Effects of War Trauma and Abuse on Older Cambodian Refugee Women," *Women & Therapy* 8 (1989): 23–50.

Russell, Richard L. "Iraq's Chemical Weapons Legacy: What Others Might Learn from Saddam," *Middle East Journal* 59 (2005): 187–208.

Saigh, Philip A., Bonnie L. Green, and Mindy Korol. "The History and Prevalence of Posttraumatic Stress Disorder with Special Reference to Children and Adolescents," *Journal of School Psychology* 34 (1996): 107–131.

Sam, Rouen. "Living in Darkness," in *Children of Cambodia's Killing Fields: Memoirs by Survivors*, compiled by Dith Pran and edited by Kim DePaul (New Haven, CT: Yale University Press, 1997), 73–81.

Sanderson, Hans, Patrik Fauser, Marianne Thomsen, and Peter B. Sørensen. "PBT Screening Profile of Chemical Warfare Agents (CWAs)," *Journal of Hazardous Materials* 148 (2007): 210–215.

Sawhill, Steven G. "Cleaning-up the Arctic's Cold War Legacy: Nuclear Waste and Arctic Military Environmental Cooperation," *Cooperation and Conflict* 35 (2000): 5–36.

Schecter, Arnold, Linda Birnbaum, John J. Ryan, and John D. Constable. "Dioxins: An Overview," *Environmental Research* 101 (2006): 419–428.

Schecter, Arnold, Marian Pavuk, Rainer Malisch, and John Jake Ryan. "Dioxin, Dibenzofuran, and Polychlorinated Biphyenyl (PCB) Levels in Food from Agent Orange-sprayed and Nonsprayed Areas of Laos," *Journal of Toxicology and Environmental Health, Part A* 66 (2003): 2165–2186.

Schwartz, Stephen I. (editor). *Atomic Audit: The Costs and Consequences of US Nuclear Weapons Since 1940* (Washington, D.C.: Brookings Institution Press, 1998).

Shenoi, Rohit. "Chemical Warfare Agents," *Clin. Ped. Emerg. Med.* 3 (2002): 239–247.

Siracusa, John. *Nuclear Weapons: A Very Short Introduction* (Oxford: Oxford University Press, 2008).

Slim, Hugo. *Killing Civilians: Method, Madness, and Morality in War* (New York: Columbia University Press, 2008).

Souvent, P. and S. Pirc. "Pollution Caused by Metallic Fragments Introduced into Soils Because of World War I Activities," *Environmental Geology* 49 (2001): 317–323.

Staub, Ervin. *The Roots of Evil: The Origins of Genocide and Other Group Violence* (Cambridge: Cambridge University Press, 1989).

Steger, Manfred B. *Globalization: A Very Short Introduction* (Oxford: Oxford University Press, 2003).

Stellman, Jeanne Mager, Steven D. Stellman, Richard Christian, Tracy Weber, and Carrie Tomasallo. "The Extent and Patterns of Usage of Agent Orange and Other Herbicides in Vietnam," *Nature* 422 (2003): 681–687.

Stevenson, David. *Cataclysm: The First World War as Political Tragedy* (New York: Basic Books, 2005).

Stone, Richard. "Agent Orange's Bitter Harvest," *Science* 315 (2007): 176–179.

Strange, Robert E. and Dudley E. Brown, Jr. "Home From the War: A Study of Psychiatric Problems in Viet Nam Returnees," *American Journal of Psychiatry* 127 (1970): 488–492.

Stretch, Robert H. "Posttraumatic Stress Disorder Among U.S. Army Reserve Vietnam and Vietnam-Era Veterans," *Journal of Consulting and Clinical Psychology* 53 (1985): 935–936.

Summerfield, Derek and Leslie Toser. " 'Low Intensity' War and Mental Trauma in Nicaragua: A Study in a Rural Community," *Medicine and War* 7 (1991): 84–99.

Svay-Ryser, Sreytouch. "New Year's Surprise," in *Children of Cambodia's Killing Fields: Memoirs by Survivors*, compiled by Dith Pran and edited by Kim DePaul (New Haven, CT: Yale University Press, 1997), 35–41.

Swaine, Michael D. "Chinese Crisis Management: Framework for Analysis, Tentative Observations, and Questions for the Future," in *Chinese National Security: Decisionmaking Under Stress*, edited by Andrew Scobell and Larry M. Wortzel (Carlisle, PA: U.S. Army War College, Strategic Studies Institute, 2005), 5–53.

Szinicz, Ladislaus. "History of Chemical and Biological Warfare Agents," *Toxicology* 214 (2005): 167–181.

Tikhomirov, Sergey N. "1939–1945: Environmental Aspects of the War in Europe," *Review of Central and East European Law* 31 (2006): 111–125.

Turse, Nick. *The Complex: How the Military Invades Our Everyday Lives* (New York: Metropolitan Books, 2008).

Tuyet Le Thi Nham and Annika Johansson. "Impact of Chemical Warfare with Agent Orange on Women's Reproductive Lives in Vietnam: A Pilot Study," *Reproductive Health Matters* 9 (2001): 156–164.

Tyner, James A. *The Killing of Cambodia: Geography, Genocide and the Unmaking of Space* (Aldershot, UK: Ashgate, 2008).

Tyner, James A. *War, Violence, and Population: Making the Body Count* (New York: The Guilford Press, 2009).

Vagts, Alfred. *A History of Militarism: Civilian and Military* (New York: Meridian Books, 1959).

Valentino, Benjamin A. *Final Solutions: Mass Killing and Genocide in the 20th Century* (Ithaca: Cornell University Press, 2004).

Van Creveld, Martin. *The Changing Face of War: Combat from the Marne to Iraq* (New York: Presidio Books, 2008).

Van Meirvenne, M., T. Meklit, S. Verstraete, M. De Boever, and F. Tack. "Could Shelling in the First World War Have Increased Copper Concentrations in the Soil Around Ypres?" *European Journal of Soil Science* 59 (2008): 373–379.

Wahab, M.A. et al. "Elevated Chromosome Translocation Frequencies in New Zealand Nuclear Test Veterans," *Cytogenetic and Genome Research* 121 (2008): 79–87.

Walzer, Michael. *Just and Unjust Wars: A Moral Argument with Historical Illustrations*, 3rd ed. (New York: Basic Books, 2000).

Watters, Charles. "Emerging Paradigms in the Mental Health Care of Refugees," *Social Science & Medicine* 52 (2001): 1709–1718.

Webster, Donovan. *Aftermath: The Remnants of War* (New York: Vintage Books, 1998).

Weisgall, Jonathan M. *Operation Crossroads: The Atomic Tests at Bikini Atoll* (Annapolis, MD: Naval Institute Press, 1994).

Westerink, Jan and Leah Giarratano. "The Impact of Posttraumatic Stress Disorder on Partners and Children of Australian Vietnam Veterans," *Australian and New Zealand Journal of Psychiatry* 33 (1999): 841–847.

Westing, Arthur H. "Ecological Effects of Military Deforestation on the Forests of South Vietnam," *BioScience* 21 (1971): 893–898.

Westing, Arthur H. "Environmental Consequences of the Second Indochina War: A Case Study," *Ambio* 4 (1975): 216–222.

Westing, Arthur H. "The Impact of War on the Environment," in *War and Public Health*, 2nd edition, edited by Barry S. Levy and Victor W. Sidel (Oxford: Oxford University Press, 2008), 69–84.

White, I.D., D.N. Mottershead, and S.J. Harrison. *Environmental Systems: An Introductory Text* (London: Allen & Unwin, 1984).

White, Rob. "Depleted Uranium, State Crime and the Politics of Knowing," *Theoretical Criminology* 12 (2008): 31–54.

Winslow, Philip C. *Sowing the Dragon's Teeth: Land Mines and the Global Legacy of War* (Boston: Beacon Press, 1997).

Woodward, Rachel. "From Military Geography to Militarism's Geographies: Disciplinary Engagements with the Geographies of Militarism and Military Activities," *Progress in Human Geography* 29 (2005): 718–740.

Young, Marilyn B. *The Vietnam Wars, 1945–1990* (New York: HarperCollins, 1990).

Zinn, Howard. *Just War* (Milan: Edizioni Charta, 2005).

Index

DATE DUE

GAYLORD			PRINTED IN U.S.A.